UNDERSTANDING THE BOOK OF REVELATION SERIES

THE VICTORIOUS KINGDOM

UNDERSTANDING THE BOOK OF REVELATION SERIES

THE VICTORIOUS KINGDOM

UNDERSTANDING THE BOOK OF REVELATION BOOK 3

Dr. Richard Booker

DESTINY IMAGE₌ PUBLISHERS, INC.
P.O. Box 310, Shippensburg, PA 17257-0310
"Promoting Inspired Lives."

This book and all other Destiny Image, Revival Press, MercyPlace, Fresh Bread, Destiny Image Fiction, and Treasure House books are available at Christian bookstores and distributors worldwide.

For a U.S. bookstore nearest you, call 1-800-722-6774.
For more information on foreign distributors, call 717-532-3040.
Reach us on the Internet: www.destinyimage.com.

ISBN 13 TP: 978-0-7684-4198-7
ISBN 13 Ebook: 978-0-7684-8750-3

For Worldwide Distribution, Printed in the U.S.A.
1 2 3 4 5 6 7 8 / 17 16 15 14 13

Acknowledgments

TO Peggy, my wife and covenant partner of more than 45 years, who has faithfully served the Lord with me with unselfish love and support. Whatever I have been able to accomplish is because of her sacrifices and servant's heart. There are many great women in the world, but Peggy surpasses them all. She is the best Christian I know and a true overcomer who has her name written in the Lamb's Book of Life.

I also want to thank my friends at Destiny Image, especially Don Nori, for being faithful to his vision of "speaking to the purposes of God for this generation and for the generations to come."

I want to acknowledge two of my students, Angela James who gave so much of her time editing the manuscript and Mark Sessions who prepared the map and two charts for this series. Thank you both for your excellent work.

Let us consider one another in order to stir up love and good works, not forsaking the assembling of ourselves together, as is the manner of some, but exhorting one another, and so much the more as you see the Day approaching.

—*Hebrews 10:24-25*

Contents

Preface

When John was on the island of Patmos, the Lord gave him a revelation of Jesus, the exalted Son of Man, and God's people overcoming satanic opposition before the throne of God. In spite of tremendous persecution, John saw *"in the Spirit"* (Rev. 1:10) that the faithful followers of the Lord were victorious. They overcame satan *"by the blood of the Lamb and by the word of their testimony"* (Rev. 12:11). Furthermore, John was given revelation to see spiritual warfare in Heaven that was being played out on the earth. He saw the outcome of this spiritual battle, as well as prophetic events that would take place in the endtimes before the coming of the Lord.

John saw that God would totally and completely destroy His enemies and resurrect His own people to live with Him forever in a new Heaven, a new Earth, and a New Jerusalem. Regardless of the trials and tribulations God's people must endure.

As His people, our destiny is certain. Jesus is returning, and we will rule and reign with Him in a world free of satan, sin, and death. In the challenging days ahead, we believers can joyfully commit our souls to God, who is faithful to keep His Word of promise.

As John wrote at the end of his vision, "I heard a loud voice from Heaven saying:

Behold, the tabernacle of God is with men, and He will dwell with them, and they shall be His people. God Himself will be with them and be their God. And God will wipe away every tear from their eyes; there shall be no more death, nor sorrow, nor crying. There shall be no more pain, for the former things have passed away (Revelation 21:3-4).

So the Book of Revelation is not a book of doom and gloom but a description of the victory of the Lamb and those who follow Him. The purpose of the Lord's revelation to John was to unveil or disclose to him what John could not know without divine assistance. The Lord gave John his vision to encourage and comfort his immediate readers, as well as believers throughout the ages. What eventually became the Book of Revelation was clearly intended to be understood by John and his first-century readers.

With the passage of time, however, this book that God intended for us to understand has become, without a doubt, the most mysterious book in the Bible. For almost 2,000 years, Christian scholars and everyday believers have tried to understand its message. Because the Book of Revelation is an apocalyptic vision filled with otherworldly symbols and descriptions of strange creatures, God's people have not always agreed on its meaning, leading to many differing interpretations of John's words.

Considering the number of books already written on John's Revelation, with so many differing interpretations, you might ask why I would feel burdened to add to the confusion. It was certainly not my intention to write a book on the Book of Revelation. With more than 38 books in print, I was ready to take a break. I wrote this book only because I saw an urgent need to explain John's revelation with the following four points of view that have not been adequately included in most commentaries.

First, almost all books written to explain the Book of Revelation are written with a Western cultural worldview rather than a biblical worldview. There are some exceptions. What I mean by this is that the writer interprets the Book of Revelation through Western eyes rather than the Hebraic eyes of a Middle Eastern person. John was not a Western theologian. He was a Jewish seer. This means he understood and wrote His Revelation in terms of his own history and culture—the Hebrew Bible or what Christians know as the Old Testament. In this book, I prefer to use the phrase *Hebrew Bible.*

In order to understand the Book of Revelation, we must read it through the eyes of a Jewish man rather than the eyes of a Western theologian. For example, when John sees Jesus in Heaven, he describes Him in Jewish terms, not Western Christian terms. To get the fullest meaning of John's vision of Jesus, we must know Jesus as the Jewish Son of Man. To John, Jesus is the "Cloud Man" of the Book of Daniel (see Dan. 7:13-14).

Second, since the Book of Revelation is the last book in the Bible, we must have a good understanding of all the previous books. We cannot understand the Book of Revelation if we do not have a good understanding of Genesis through Jude as well as some basic knowledge of the literature written between the testaments and of Greek mythology.

We must not read John's Revelation as if it were written in modern times and isolated from the rest of the Bible. The best way to understand the Book of Revelation is to begin with Genesis. For instance, in the last two chapters of the Book of Revelation, John explains the eternal home of believers, and assumes that his readers are familiar with the first two chapters of the Book of Genesis.

Third, in order to understand the Book of Revelation, we must be aware that it was written in an apocalyptic literary style. Apocalyptic literature flourished in the period in which John was writing, and it has certain characteristics that John's readers readily understood. I explain these characteristics in chapter one. Because this is not a normal style of writing in our times, we may have difficulty interpreting it.

By that I mean Western readers often have a tendency to interpret apocalyptic literature as if it were a literal narrative written chronologically like a Western textbook. This can easily lead to wrong conclusions about John's statements. For example, when John says that he saw an open door into Heaven and heard a voice calling him to Heaven, he did not mean that he saw a literal door and was literally taken to Heaven. He meant that God opened his spiritual eyes so that he could see realities in Heaven that he would not have known otherwise. Physically speaking, John never left Patmos.

Fourth, to properly understand the Book of Revelation, we must know the historical context in which it was written. Jesus gave John letters for seven literal congregations that existed in the first century. Since the biblical meaning of the English word *church* means something different to modern readers than its biblical meaning, I have used the word *congregation*, which is more accurate. I could have used the words *assembly* or *community*. These congregations or communities were challenged daily to live out their new faith in a hostile environment— one in which their neighbors worshiped Greek gods and goddesses and Roman emperors, practiced gross immorality, and pressured them to compromise their faith and witness. Each day, they were faced with life-and-death decisions.

In addition, each of the cities where the seven congregations were located had their own unique physical circumstances that Jesus acknowledged in His letters to them. Without knowledge of their spiritual and physical circumstances, it is impossible to understand why Jesus said what He did to each congregation.

For instance, unless we know that Laodicea had a drinking problem (water, not alcohol), we cannot understand why Jesus preferred believers to be cold or hot rather than lukewarm (see Rev. 3:16).

I have the greatest appreciation for scholars and ministers who have spent years studying the Book of Revelation and have labored to help us understand its mysteries. While some of the views presented in this book may not be familiar to many ministers and everyday believers, my intention is not to be critical of what others have written or believe. We must all walk in love and humility and be gracious to one another, especially when we see things differently.

You may be challenged by some of my explanations, especially those that are contrary to your preconceived ideas and traditional teachings. It's OK if you don't agree with everything I have written. My desire is to glorify our Lord, encourage God's people to be steadfast and faithful as we face challenging days ahead, and provide a fresh, exciting, and more balanced understanding of the Book of Revelation. If I accomplish these goals, I will be most grateful to our Lord. May God's people be blessed and His name praised forever.

For ease of reading and understanding, the publisher has wisely organized my writing on the Book of Revelation into a three-volume series entitled *Understanding the Book of Revelation*. Volume 1 covers Revelation chapters 1 through 3, and is entitled *The Overcomers*. Its first three chapters contain information that I feel is necessary to understanding the historical events that prompted the Lord's letters to the seven congregations.

In order to properly understand the Book of Revelation, we must know the context in which it was written. I have also included a chapter on the literary style in which the book was written, as well as a survey of the book. I then explain the letters to the seven congregations within their historical, geographical, archeological, and Hebraic context and perspective, along with my view of their prophetic and personal significance. This background information is often missing or inadequately explained in books written about Revelation; but I feel it is critical to full and proper understanding.

Volume 2 is entitled *The Lamb and the Seven-Sealed Scroll*. This volume opens with John's vision of Heaven and the throne room of God. John witnesses the greatest drama in human history as he watches the Lamb of God take the seven-sealed scroll and open the seals. I explain the unfolding story including: the opening of the first six seals, God's seal of protection, Israelites and Jews, the multitude of the redeemed, the opening of the seventh seal, the mighty angel and the little book, the two witnesses, the proclamation of the Kingdom of God, and the war in Heaven and on Earth.

Volume 2 covers Revelation chapters 4 through 12. We learn along the way that the Book of Revelation actually ends with the close of chapter 11. The rest of the book is an "instant replay" giving more details and different views of the same information.

Volume 3 is entitled *The Victorious Kingdom*. This volume includes an explanation of the two false messiahs; a preview of the end; preparation for blowing the seventh trumpet-shofar; the blowing of the seventh trumpet-shofar; the destruction of the anti-God, one-world religious and political systems; the second coming of the true Messiah; the Battle of Armageddon; the Messianic Kingdom; the new Heaven and new Earth; and Paradise restored. Volume 3 covers Revelation chapters 13 through 22.

These volumes are designed to be read along with the Book of Revelation. Each discussion in the text is keyed to a specific chapter and verse in the Book of Revelation. To get the most from the text, first read from the Book of Revelation and then read my explanations and comments in the books.

I want to say one more time that the Book of Revelation is not about doom and gloom. While it may describe harsh realities and much suffering, it is first and foremost a book about God's faithfulness to Himself, His Word, and His people. It is about God defeating His enemies, and His people overcoming *"by the blood of the Lamb and by the word of their testimony"* (Rev. 12:11).

The outcome is certain and the victory is sure. As you read the Book of Revelation and this three-volume series, may the Lord encourage your heart that our God is sovereign over world conditions and uses them to move forward His awesome plan of redemption for His people. We will live with Him forever in the full manifestation of His blazing glory and dazzling beauty. We will look upon Him as He is for we shall be like Him.

Let us make the following prayer from Jude our own personal praise and worship to our God:

> *Now to Him who is able to keep you from stumbling* [falling], *and to present you faultless before the presence of His glory with exceeding joy, to God our Savior, who alone is wise, be glory and majesty, dominion and power, both now and forever. Amen* (Jude 24-25).

Chapter 1

The Anti-Messiah

REVIEW OF VOLUME 2—*THE LAMB AND THE SEVEN-SEALED SCROLL*

IN Volume 2, we learned that the Lord opened a prophetic door for John to enter the throne room of God. He then called John to *"Come up here..."* (Rev. 4:1). John did not see a literal door nor was he literally caught up to Heaven. These are apocalyptic statements that refer to a spiritual vision the Lord gave him. While John was literally on the island of Patmos, spiritually he was able to observe realities and activities in Heaven that he would have otherwise been unable to see.

John saw the glory of God, the exalted Son of Man, the angels, and the redeemed of all ages around the throne of God. The Lord was showing John this heavenly scene so that he could write down what he saw and distribute his writings to persecuted believers in the seven congregations of the Roman province of Asia Minor. Reading John's Revelation would encourage them to resist the temptations and pressures of emperor worship, idolatry, and immorality from which they had been saved.

While the Book of Revelation was written specifically to believers in the first century, John's prophetic vision is for all believers throughout history, including modern times. As the world becomes more and more anti-God and the West becomes post-Christian, believers today need the same encouragement the Lord gave to those first-century believers. God has a place of eternal glory in His presence for all of His people; therefore, we can have the faith and courage not to "fix our sandals"[1] before an increasing anti-God, one-world system.

Jesus has conquered the Caesars, Zeus, and all the false gods of the Greco-Roman world. Because of His victory, those who follow Him will also be victorious. Understanding that God has a place of glory for us in Heaven, gives us the faith and courage we need to overcome by the blood of the Lamb and the word of our testimony (see Rev. 12:11), even if that means being martyred for our faith.

The Lord then gave John further revelation, which he referred to as being *"in the Spirit"* (Rev. 1:10; 4:2). This is his human way of saying that the Lord opened his spiritual eyes to see additional prophetic activities in Heaven that would be manifested on the earth. When John said he saw things *"which must take place after this"* (Rev. 4:1), he did not mean that the rest of the Book of Revelation was chronological (although some of it is). He was referring to his next sequence of revelations.

John saw God holding a seven-sealed book containing information about prophetic events that would take place in his own time, as well as in the endtimes of history—or as the Bible calls them "the latter days." A powerful angel called for someone to take the scroll from God and open the seals. When no one was found worthy, John wept! (See Revelation 5:2-4).

Just when it seemed that the scroll would forever remain sealed, leaving prophecy unfulfilled, Jesus was recognized as One *"worthy to take the scroll"* (Rev. 5:9). Because Jesus lived a perfect life without sin and died as our innocent substitutionary sacrifice, He was the only Worthy One who could take the scroll and open it. At the same time,

He is the conquering Lion of the Tribe of Judah and the sacrificial Lamb of God. When Jesus took the scroll, the 24 elders representing the company of the redeemed, the four archangels, and all the angels of Heaven gave glory to God and the Lamb.

In this heavenly scene, John sees Jesus opening the seven seals that reveal the judgments of God on the earth. The seventh seal opens the seven trumpet-shofar judgments, and the seventh trumpet-shofar judgment opens the final seven bowl judgments. Each judgment is progressively more severe. As God demonstrates His sovereign power through these judgments, He is destroying His enemies while offering mercy to those who choose to repent.

This is not a time of doom and gloom for believers. It is a time of victory. The judgments are God's answer to the prayers of His people as they plead for justice. They are not judgments against God's people but against those who oppose Him. While evil rulers persecute faithful believers, the Lord seals His own to protect them against His judgments.

The Lord then gives John further revelation by telling him to eat a book that contains additional information about future events. Of course, we should not think that John literally ate a book. It was an apocalyptic way of telling John to spiritually digest more of God's Word. (See Revelation 10.)

John learns about God's two powerful prophetic witnesses on the earth. The Lord gives these two witnesses the power to perform signs and wonders and prophesy for the last three-and-one-half years of the Great Tribulation. The Lord supernaturally protects these two witnesses until their ministry is finished. Satan is given permission to kill the two witnesses, but after three-and-a-half days, the Lord resurrects them and takes them to Heaven. (See Revelation 11.)

When the angel blows the seventh trumpet-shofar, loud voices in Heaven announce the final demise of the kingdoms of this world and the imminent coming of the Kingdom of God on the earth. With this declaration, John has a flashback and sees the spiritual warfare in the heavens when lucifer rebelled against God. The fallen angel lucifer, now called satan, makes war on the earth against God's chosen people and His Messiah, the male Child born to the woman, Israel. (See Revelation 12.)

In his vain attempt to stop God's plan to redeem humankind, satan makes a bid to destroy Israel and kill the Messiah at His birth. But God protects the Messiah, resurrects Him, and establishes Him in a place of honor to await the time when He will return to earth and rule the nations with a rod of iron. His time is *now* as His Kingdom is announced.

As the Great Tribulation begins, John sees satan finally cast out of Heaven. In his rage, he makes one last attempt to destroy the Jews and the believers aligned with them. Satan is relentless in his pursuit of God's people, but God frustrates his efforts to destroy them. While there will be many martyred for their faith, God will preserve a remnant of believers. Whether believers live or die, they will be victorious through their faithful witness.

With this review, we now continue to read John's amazing revelation. May God's name (YHVH), the God of Abraham, Isaac, and Jacob, be praised forever.

THE TWO FALSE MESSIAHS (REVELATION 13:1-10)

In Revelation 13, John has an apocalyptic vision of two strange creatures. He calls the first one the Beast From the Sea and the second one the Beast From the Earth. At this time, satan has been cast out of Heaven. Knowing that his time of final judgment is near, he empowers two world leaders who will serve as his human agents on the earth.

As the Lord had two witnesses, so satan has his counterfeit witnesses through whom he hopes to fulfill his desire to be worshiped in the place of God. Most Bible scholars believe that the Beast From the Sea is the false political messiah known as the antichrist or anti-Messiah. He establishes himself as the leader of an anti-God, one-world *government* system. So the person and the system are both thought of as "the Beast." Scholars consider the Beast From the Earth to be the false religious messiah who heads up an anti-God, one-world *religious* system.

Whether knowingly or not, these two leaders will receive their power from satan and act on his behalf. They are the ultimate embodiment of evil. While their intentions may or may not be good, the results of their actions will only bring more death and destruction to the world.

As we will see, most of the world follows these two human beasts and their political and religious systems. The only exceptions are the worshipers of the One True God who follow Jesus and another group of people who have refused the Mark of the Beast but have yet to repent. These are the people who eventually repent and are judged as righteous when Jesus returns. (See Matthew 25:31-46.) Because God's people refuse to acknowledge the Beasts, satan sees them as a threat to his plans and purposes. Working through his two false messiahs, satan attacks the believers. This action ushers in the final chaos on the earth that leads to the coming of Jesus. This is the time Jesus was speaking of when He said the following:

> *Then there will be great tribulation, such as has not been since the beginning of the world until this time, no, nor ever shall be. And unless those days were shortened, no flesh would be saved; but for the elect's sake those days will be shortened* (Matthew 24:21-22).

THE BEAST FROM THE SEA (REVELATION 13:1-2)

In this chapter we will learn what John says about the first beast—the Beast From the Sea. We have previously noted in Volumes One and Two that Daniel also had an apocalyptic vision, but he did not understand it, so the Lord sent an angel to explain the vision to him. The angel told Daniel that his vision was about prophetic events that would take place in the *"time of the end"* or *"latter days"* (Dan. 8:17; 2:28; 10:14).

The angel then told Daniel that the revelation of his vision would be a sealed or closed book until the endtimes (see Dan. 12:4,9). This means the actual occurrences and the understanding of what Daniel saw would not be revealed to us until the last days of history prior to the coming of Jesus. We are living in those last days.

The Book of Revelation describes and explains the opening of Daniel's closed book or scroll. When Jesus took the seven-sealed scroll and loosened the seals, His action was the fulfillment of the prophecy given to Daniel. In other words, the seven-sealed scroll of the Book of Revelation is the same as Daniel's closed book. Because Jesus is the Worthy Redeemer who is able to open the seals, its contents and actions are now made known.

In view of the fact that the seven-sealed scroll is the same revelation given to Daniel, we should expect to see a connection between Daniel's vision and John's. We are not disappointed. As we will soon realize, Daniel's fourth beast (see Dan. 7:19-25) is the same as John's Beast From the Sea. In fact, Daniel 7 and Revelation chapters 13, 17, and 18 refer to the same characters and events. While Daniel received a general outline of the prophecy, the Lord has given John the details.

Using apocalyptic symbolism, John sees a beast coming out of the sea. Ancient people, including John's readers, were terribly frightened by the sea. To them, the sea was synonymous with the bottomless pit (see Rev. 11:7; 13:1; 17:8).

People living in Bible times did not understand that there was a bottom to the sea. When they dropped an anchor, it never reached bottom. When a ship sank, people believed it descended forever into a bottomless watery darkness. They were also frightened by Leviathan, a sea monster or beast that stirred up the ocean causing chaos and death (see Job 41).

In John's Greco-Roman world, the Greeks worshiped the mythical Poseidon as the god of the sea. He was a fierce god with a violent and vengeful temperament. He is depicted carrying a three-pronged spear called a trident.

A popular American movie called *The Poseidon Adventure* is about a luxury liner called the *Poseidon* that is caught in a great storm at sea. The movie gets its name from the ancient Greek god of the sea. It's also interesting to note that the United States Navy has a class of submarines called Trident submarines because they carry Trident ballistic missiles.

It was the practice of the Romans to adopt Greek gods and give them Roman names. The Roman name for Poseidon was *Neptune.* Before people went to sea, they made sacrifices to Poseidon/Neptune as a means of pacifying him and asking for a safe journey. In a similar way, today's believers ask the One True God for His traveling mercies when making long flights over the ocean.

When John says he saw a beast coming out of the sea, it was for his first-century readers, the most frightening symbolism he could possibly use. Like Poseidon/Neptune and Leviathan, the first false messiah empowered by satan will be a frightening figure who will cause great chaos and destruction on the earth. Speaking apocalyptically, he and the Beast From the Earth, will stir up the sea; that is the masses of people on the earth.

Revelation 17:15 confirms this as the correct interpretation. It reads: *"He said to me, 'The waters which you saw, where the harlot sits, are peoples, multitudes, nations, and tongues.'"* Furthermore, his fierce and violent nature will take vengeance against the believers for not submitting to him.

John says this Beast From the Sea has seven heads, ten horns, and ten crowns on the ten horns. He also has a blasphemous name on his heads. We will study this further in Revelation 17. John observes that the Beast is like a leopard, his feet like a bear, and his mouth like a lion (see Rev. 13:2). So that God's people will not be deceived, John clearly states that satan (the dragon of Revelation 12:3) is the one empowering this false messiah.

Daniel and John

Since Daniel and John had the same apocalyptic vision, we need to read what the Lord showed Daniel, as background for John's Revelation. As we review Daniel's dreams and visions, the connection to John's Revelation will be obvious.

Daniel's dream interpretation recorded in Daniel 2 is further clarified in Daniel 7, which in turn, is explained in detail in Revelation 12–20. Therefore, we can overlay Daniel 2 and 7 with Revelation 12–20. While we do not fully understand some of the details (and shouldn't argue over them), the overall picture connecting these two apocalyptic writings should be clear enough. Furthermore, it is OK that we don't understand all the details. God will help us "connect the dots" in His own time and way. It is more important to understand the function of the characters in the Book of Revelation (what they do) than it is to know everything about their form (what they look like).

We should not get frustrated in trying to figure it all out. Neither should we learn just for the sake of showing our acquaintances how much we know. We should study as an act of worship out of reverence for God. More important than having knowledge is living in right relationship with our Lord and each other so that we might remain faithful and overcome in these difficult times.

Daniel's Dream Interpretation (Daniel 2)

In Daniel 2, the empires of history are seen from man's view as being great and glorious. In Daniel 7, the Lord gives His view of these same empires but calls them "beasts" just like John does in the Book of Revelation. To better understand John's vision, it would be most helpful for you to pause now and read Daniel 2 before continuing with John's Revelation. Then after a brief explanation, we will pause and read Daniel 7.

(For a quick visual presentation of Daniel's dream and its connection to John's vision, please review the chart at the end of this chapter.)

Bible students will recall that Nebuchadnezzar attacked Jerusalem in 606 B.C., at which time Daniel was deported to Babylon. Shortly thereafter, Nebuchadnezzar had a dream that troubled him. He would not describe his dream to his advisors because he knew they would fabricate an interpretation. However, the Lord showed Daniel the dream and gave him the interpretation as well. Now that you have read Daniel 2, let's review the dream and the interpretation. This will be a short summary as we will only review enough to help us overlay Daniel with John.[2]

First, Daniel tells Nebuchadnezzar that the God of Heaven has revealed the dream to him (Daniel), and then he describes what the king saw. Nebuchadnezzar saw a great and glorious image. (This is how world leaders view themselves, their rule, and their power.) The head of the image was fine gold, its chest and arms were silver, its belly and thighs were bronze, its legs were iron, and its feet were partly iron and partly clay. Then, according to Daniel, the king saw a stone strike the image on its feet and destroy it. Daniel says the king saw that the stone was cut out without hands, meaning the image was destroyed by a sovereign act of God, bringing an end to man's empires and vain attempts to rule without Him.

After that, Daniel provides the interpretation. He explains to Nebuchadnezzar that the image represents four successive kingdoms or empires with a fifth empire—the Kingdom of God—coming to the earth.

The head of gold represents King Nebuchadnezzar and the Babylonian Empire (606–536 B.C.). Ancient Babylon is modern Iraq. The chest and arms of silver represent the Medo-Persian Empire (536–333 B.C.) which succeeded Babylon.

While Daniel does not specifically mention the Medes and Persians at this time, he does identify them in Daniel 5:22-31; 8:1-7,20; and 11:1-2. As a side note, the Persians became more powerful than the

Medes and basically displaced them as the next empire. (Ancient Persia is modern Iran.)

The belly and thighs of bronze represent the third empire of Alexander the Great and Greece (333–323 B.C.), which succeeded the Persians. Daniel identifies this empire in Daniel 8:1-7,21 and 11:3. The legs of iron represent a fourth kingdom or empire that Daniel does not identify. However, we know from history that this fourth empire was Rome (30 B.C.–A.D. 364).

Daniel explains that Rome, the fourth kingdom represented by legs of iron, will be divided as indicated by the feet of iron and clay. Rome was divided in A.D. 364 into the western and eastern divisions. Rome was the capital of the western division and Constantinople was the capital of the eastern division. The western division fell to the Mongol invaders in the middle of the fifth century. The eastern division lasted another 1,000 years until the Muslim Turks conquered Constantinople in A.D. 1453.

Because the Roman Empire was divided before it fell, some scholars believe it will be revived in some form in the endtimes as a United States of Europe, which we see today as the European Union. They see this as the Beast system of Revelation 12–18 ruled over by the anti-Messiah. Others believe that a revived Islam led by the Mahdi will be the end-time power because it was the Muslim Turks who conquered Constantinople. Still other scholars believe Revelation chapters 12 through 18 describe the anti-God, one-world political, economic, military, and religious system united against the One True God and His people. We also see this today in the European Union. Since the Bible does not clearly identify the end-time world power, it is best not to be dogmatic in stating our views. God will show us in His own time. I believe He is doing this now. As previously mentioned, it is better to emphasize the function (world domination) than it is the form (the *who* and *what* of the structure).

The feet with their ten toes represent a world empire that will be ruling the nations when God smashes it with the smiting stone, which is His own Kingdom coming to the earth. The ten toes are the same as the ten horns. The destruction of the ten toes/ten horns empire is the prophetic symbolism fulfilled when the seventh trumpet-shofar is blown to announce that the *"kingdoms of this world have become the kingdoms of our Lord and of His Christ* [Messiah]," which John mentions in Revelation 11:15.

Daniel's Dream in Chapter 7

With this brief summary, let's now connect Daniel's dream interpretation in Daniel 2 with God's perspective of these same kingdoms, which is recorded in Daniel 7. Before proceeding with this study, pause and read Daniel 7, noticing how both chapters talk about the same empires. Notice also that Daniel's dream is recorded in 7:1-14 and the interpretation is recorded in 7:15-28.

In Daniel 7, we learn that Belshazzar is the king of Babylon. During his reign, Daniel has an apocalyptic revelation through a dream and vision. He sees the same empires he saw in chapter 2, but now he sees them from God's point of view. To humankind, the empires are glorious, but to God they are beasts and their beastly descriptions characterize the empires.

Notice in Daniel 7:2-3 that Daniel, like John, sees a stirring or chaos in the Great Sea with four great beasts coming out of the water. Remember that this is an apocalyptic way of saying that the four empires or kingdoms will be inspired by and controlled by evil spirits coming out of the bottomless pit, which is synonymous with the sea. They are anti-God, world empires, which is why God refers to them as *beast* empires. While the beasts are said to arise out of the sea, the rulers or empires themselves are said to arise out of the earth (see Dan. 7:17). This means they are human agents of the beasts from the sea.

In the next few verses, Daniel and John use the same words to describe these beast empires. John adds that in the endtimes these former empires become united as one Beast empire (see Rev. 13:2) under the control of the dragon (satan).

In Daniel 7:4, Babylon, represented by the head of gold, is referred to as a lion with eagle's wings, which is the ancient symbol of Babylon. In Daniel 7:5, Medo-Persia, represented by the chest and arms of silver, is likened to a bear. Later, in Daniel 8:3-4, it is likened to a ram with two horns (Medes and Persians). The one horn that is higher represents the Persians displacing the Medes.

In Daniel 7:6, Alexander and Greece, the belly and thighs of brass, are referred to as a leopard with four wings and four heads. In Daniel 8:5-7 they are seen as a goat with a large horn (Alexander) that destroyed the ram. In Daniel 11:3-4 Alexander is called *"a mighty king."* Without getting bogged down in details, let us say that when Alexander died his kingdom was divided between his four generals. They are represented by the four heads on the leopard and four horns on the goat.

In Daniel 7:7, Rome (the legs of iron) is represented by the fourth beast that was fiercer than the others and devoured or conquered all the previous empires. This certainly describes the Roman Empire.

In Daniel 7:7-8, Daniel explains further that this fourth beast is different from the other beasts in that it has ten horns (rulers or governments). Daniel then sees a little horn (ruler) coming out of the ten horns. This little horn disposes of three of the ten horns. This may explain why John's Beast has only seven heads with ten horns. He is more powerful than the other horns and persecutes God's people for three-and-one-half years until God Himself destroys him. At this time, God establishes His literal Kingdom on the earth with His people ruling with Him over a restored Israel and the nations of the world.

As I just noted, the ten toes of the image in Daniel 2 correspond to the ten horns in Daniel 7. They represent the end-time world government under the control of the anti-Messiah (the little horn) who is persecuting God's people as described in Revelation 12–18. The smiting stone from Daniel 2 is clearly the same as the vision of the Ancient of Days and the Son of Man mentioned in Daniel 7:9-14 and 26-28. This connects to John's vision in Revelation 19–20.

Two years after his dream recorded in chapter 7, Daniel has a further apocalyptic dream of the same revelation, which is recorded in Daniel 8. In this dream, he is given more details and mentions a little horn that comes out of the four horns on the goat. Remember that the four horns represent the four generals who inherit Alexander's empire. Historically, this little horn is different from the little horn that comes out of the ten horns. However, prophetically, they seem to merge as the same person—the anti-Messiah described in the Book of Revelation.

Many scholars understand this little horn to represent Antiochus Epiphanes who came from the Syrian horn (general) of the four. Antiochus represented himself as a manifestation of Zeus. He issued coins with an image of Zeus, but it was his picture on the coins. Antiochus fulfilled much of the prophecy in Daniel 8. He forbade the Jews to practice their ancient faith or in any way worship the One True God.

Antiochus went on a rampage against the Jews. From 167–164 B.C., Antiochus stopped the Temple rituals and ordered the burning of the Torah. In the Temple, he erected a statute of Zeus bearing his own image. He built a new altar, dedicated to Zeus, on which he offered a sacrificial pig. He then poured the pig's blood over the Torah.

Antiochus erected shrines and altars throughout Israel and forced the people to make sacrifices to the Greek gods. Those who disobeyed were tortured, killed, or both. This period of time was one of the most gruesome in the long, sad history of the persecution of the Jewish people. Without God's intervention, they would have surely perished from the earth. The festival of Hanukkah celebrates the defeat of Antiochus.[3]

These actions of Antiochus Epiphanes certainly are a fulfillment of the Abomination of Desolation Daniel writes about in Daniel 9:27.

However, in His summary of end-time events, Jesus points to a later and final fulfillment at the beginning of the Great Tribulation:

> "When you see the 'abomination of desolation' spoken of by Daniel the prophet, standing in the holy place" (whosoever reads, let him understand),... "For then there will be great tribulation, such as has not been since the beginning of the world until this time, no, nor ever shall be. And unless those days were shortened, no flesh would be saved; but for the elect's sake those days will be shortened" (Matthew 24:15, 21-22).

To John's readers, the Beast with its many heads and horns and crowns and blasphemous names clearly symbolized the anti-God Roman Empire and the Roman emperors who were persecuting the believers in the seven congregations. They understood what and who John meant by these apocalyptic symbols. This is why some scholars believe the Book of Revelation was written only about Rome and events that took place in the first century. But with the passing of time and history, John's meaning has become less clear. Over the centuries, Christian leaders have tried to connect these symbols to world leaders who seemed to fulfill these prophetic visions, but they have all been proven wrong.

While we may not clearly understand the historical references of the first century, it is clear that what Daniel and John saw reached far beyond anything that happened in the first century or any other period in world history. They were also looking to the endtimes of history prior to the coming of the Son of Man, who will judge those who oppose God, vindicate God's people who have suffered for their faith, and fully establish God's Kingdom on the earth.

When we compare what Daniel says about the little horn with what John says about the anti-Messiah, we certainly get the impression that they are talking about the same person and the same terrible events during the last three-and-one-half years of the Great Tribulation. This is humankind's last desperate attempt to rule the world without God. While this ruler and his coalition of nations empowered by satan think they are achieving their goals, their attempts are futile as God destroys them with the coming of His Kingdom on the earth. May His name be praised forever!

Since the rest of the Book of Revelation provides the details of Daniel's dreams and visions, we will examine this further in the next chapters. For now, let's continue with our study of Revelation 13. Once again, remember that function is more important than form. Let's do our best not to get bogged down in the details but focus on the bigger picture of *what* rather than *whom*. As the author, I am also seeking this balance in what I am writing.

The Dragon and the Beast (Revelation 13:3-10)

In his attempts to deceive the world, the Beast appears to be resurrected from a mortal wound to one of his heads. Since satan does not have the ability to resurrect people from the dead, this is clearly a deception.

Throughout history, scholars and historians have tried in vain to identify this person or empire. Some believe John was referring to Nero or one of the other Roman emperors. There were always rumors, particularly regarding Nero.

In times past, whenever a powerful, charismatic world leader died, students of the Bible watched carefully to see if the person or the empire he ruled would miraculously recover. For example, when President Kennedy died of a head wound, Bible prophecy students wondered if he might somehow survive causing people to consider his recovery a miracle.

We don't know if John is referring to the anti-Messiah himself or the resurrection of the ancient Beast system of Babylon/Rome in the form of an anti-God, one-world system. The Beast system seems to be personified in the Beast person, the anti-Messiah. As world leaders represent their governments, the anti-Messiah and the system he leads merge as one. Satan uses this deception as a counterfeit of the true resurrection of Jesus and the two witnesses.

The way the world responds to this counterfeit miracle is self-condemning. When the Beast kills the two witnesses, those who oppose God celebrate (see Rev. 11:10). When they are resurrected, the people are frightened but do not turn to God. However, when the people believe the Beast has been resurrected, they marvel at the supposed miracle and follow him. The people not only follow the Beast, they worship him saying, *"Who is like the beast? Who is able to make war against him?"* (Rev. 13:4).

This adoration of the Beast is in direct contrast to the worship of the One True God expressed in the Song of Moses: *"Who is like You, O LORD, among the gods? Who is like You, glorious in holiness, fearful in praises, doing wonders?"* (Exod. 15:11).

Instead of glorifying God, the people glorify the Beast. John notes that by worshiping the Beast, the people are actually worshiping the dragon (satan) who gives power to the Beast. It is at this time that satan believes he has finally dethroned God. He is killing the believers while at the same time deceiving the world into worshiping him. In his mind, this is his ultimate triumphant over God and the Lamb.

This supposed victory by satan takes us back to when he tempted Jesus in the desert. In that story, satan showed Jesus all the kingdoms of the world and offered them to Him if He would bypass the cross and worship him (satan) instead. Jesus rebuked satan by quoting the Scripture that says only the One True God is to be worshiped. (See Matthew 4:8-11; Deuteronomy 6:13.)

In the Book of Revelation, satan believes he has accomplished through the anti-Messiah what he failed to accomplish with Jesus, the true Messiah. But satan, the master of deceit, is deceived himself as his apparent victory is short-lived.

At this time in history, satan's agent, the anti-Messiah, embodies the ultimate in ego, arrogance, self-deception, and self-exaltation. Inspired by satan, he really does believe he is the true messiah who will solve the world's problems. To further his own worship in place of God, satan fills the anti-Messiah with hatred for the One True God. With his heart and soul controlled by satan, the anti-Messiah speaks blasphemous words against God, God's name, God's abode in Heaven, and God's people in Heaven who worship the One True God.

The apostle Paul seems to be speaking of this end-time anti-Messiah in Second Thessalonians 2:1-12. Paul calls him the lawless man of sin who exalts himself even above God. He is empowered by satan to perform counterfeit miracles and deceives those who reject the truth of God's Word.

Daniel's visions were probably partially fulfilled in historical personalities such as Antiochus Epiphanes and later in the Roman emperors of John's time. But this anti-Messiah is the final prophetic manifestation of Daniel's little horn who also speaks great words of blasphemy, as we learn in Daniel 7 (verses 8,11,20,25).

John adds, for our understanding, that satan's efforts to be worshiped and rule over humankind through his anti-Messiah lasts for 42 months, or three-and-one-half years. This is the same amount of time that the Gentiles occupy Jerusalem, that the two witnesses prophesy, and that God protects the woman from satan (see Rev. 11:2-3; 12:6,14). This is when satan is cast out of Heaven, which begins the last three-and-one-half years of the Great Tribulation leading up to the coming of Jesus.

Since satan has now been denied access to Heaven, he works through the anti-Messiah to kill God's people on the earth, as we learned in

Revelation 12. We might say that this is his "jihad" against true believers. While the One True God providentially protects Israel and believers who identify with the Jewish people, the anti-Messiah attacks any and all believers he can find. (See Revelation 12:17; 13:7.)

Although satan working through the anti-Messiah is able to overcome many believers and kill them, the believers are the real overcomers. While satan can kill their bodies, he cannot kill their souls, which John has already seen in Heaven before the throne of God.

Jesus gave the following words of encouragement to believers being persecuted for their faith: *"Do not fear those who kill the body but cannot kill the soul. But rather fear Him who is able to destroy both soul and body in hell"* (Matt. 10:28).

To further confirm that Daniel's little horn is ultimately fulfilled in John's anti-Messiah, Daniel was told that the little horn he saw would also persecute and overcome God's people for three-and-one half years until he is destroyed at the coming of the Son of Man. (See Daniel 7:25, where three-and-one-half-years are referred to as *"a time and times and half a time."*)

Tragically, satan's deception is worldwide. Everyone worships the anti-Messiah except believers (those whose names are written in the Lamb's Book of Life) and a remnant of independent-minded survivalists. So it seems there are three groups distinguished during this time. Those who have the mark of God, those who have the Mark of the Beast, and as Gordon Ladd explains: "There is a third group 'who had not worshiped the Beast or its image and had not received its mark on their foreheads or their hands'"[4] Many in this third group will survive the tribulation and be alive when the Lord returns. Jesus will rule over them in His Messianic Kingdom.

To review the earlier explanation of the Lamb's Book of Life, see the chapter in Volume 1 on the Lord's letter to the congregation at Sardis. God's Word is clear. Everyone living at this time will sooner or later have to choose whether to worship satan through the anti-Messiah or the One True God through the real Messiah, the exalted Son of Man, the Lion of the Tribe of Judah, Jesus of Nazareth.

John concludes this part of his vision by exhorting people to hear (which includes to heed) his words. He warns those who are persecuting God's people that they will pay the same consequences for their evil actions. God is sovereign. He will judge satan, his false messiahs, and those who follow and worship the Beast. Just as God's judgments are sure and true, so are His promises to His people. Believers can persevere in faith knowing that they will overcome *"by the blood of the Lamb and by the word of their testimony"* (Rev. 12:11). Amen!

REVIEW QUESTIONS

1. Write a summary of what you have learned in this lesson. Write the summary in clear, concise words as if you were going to present it to another person.

2. Describe how you can apply what you have learned in this lesson to your life.

3. Share what you have learned with your family, friends, and members of your study group.

NOTES

1. "…Citizens of Ephesus were required to bow in worship to the image of Domitian as lord god. Those who refused were either exiled or put to death. Some believers hoped to pretend to bow…by bending over to fix their sandals when they got to the front of the statue.…They didn't want to bow to the image but did not have the courage not to." From Dr. Richard Booker, *The Overcomers* (Shippensburg, PA: Destiny Image, 2011), 41.

2. For more information on this subject, you can order my book, *The End of All Things Is at Hand: Are You Ready?* (Alachua, FL: Bridge-Logos, 2008). It is available at my online bookstore at www.rbooker.com.

3. If you want to learn more about Hanukkah and all the Feasts of the Lord, you can order my book, *Celebrating Jesus in the Biblical Feasts* (Shippensburg, PA: Destiny Image, 2009). It is available at my online bookstore at www.rbooker.com.

4. George Eldon Ladd, *A Theology of the New Testament* (Grand Rapids, MI: Wm. B. Eerdmans, 1993), 679.

THE KINGDOMS

IMAGE	KINGDOM	MAN'S VIEWPOINT (DANIEL 2)	GOD'S VIEWPOINT (DANIEL 7)
	BABYLON 606-536	HEAD OF GOLD (DAN. 2:36-38)	LION WITH EAGLES WINGS (DAN. 7:4)
	MEDO-PERSIA 536-333	CHEST OF SILVER (DAN. 2:39; 5:22-31; 8:1-7, 20; 11: 1-2)	BEAR (DAN. 7:5)
	GREECE 333-323	BELLY & THIGH OF BRASS (DAN. 2:39; 8:1-7, 20;11: 1-2)	LEOPARD (DAN. 7:6)
	ROME 30-364	LEGS OF IRON (DAN. 2:40; 9:26)	BEAST (DAN. 7:7)
	ANTI-MESSIAH	10 TOES OF IRON & CLAY (DAN. 2:41-43; 9:27)	10 HORNS - LITTLE HORN (DAN. 7:8; MATT. 24:15; 2 THESS. 2:1 - 4; REV. 13:1-8)
	JESUS	SMITING STONE (DAN. 2:44-45)	KING OF KINGS (DAN. 7:9 - 14; MATT. 25:31; MATT. 26:64; REV. 19: 11-21)

Chapter 2

The False Prophet

REVELATION REVIEW

AS the time for the coming of the Lord draws near, satan is banished from God's presence, where he actively accused and condemned God's people in the courtroom of Heaven. With satan now denied this access, he vents his rage on the earth against believers in the One True God. Since satan cannot defeat God, he seeks to destroy God's people. His strategy is to empower two world leaders and work through them to establish an anti-God, New World Order. This diabolic act takes place at the beginning of the last three-and-one-half years leading up to the coming of Jesus to establish His literal presence and Kingdom on the earth.

One of satan's chosen is a political leader whom John calls the Beast From the Sea. This is the infamous anti-Christ or anti-Messiah— archenemy of the real Messiah, Jesus of Nazareth. Using apocalyptic language, John sees him as the head of a unified world order that is the final culmination of previous anti-God empires. The anti-Messiah is the personification of this unified Gentile world power called the Beast. As it is in modern times, the person and the system he leads are so closely identified with one another that they are basically one and the same. Both are the Beast From the Sea.

To John's readers, the strange creature with its many heads, horns, and crowns represented the Roman Empire and Roman emperors. However, John's description of the Beast From the Sea and its connection to Daniel's visions clearly go beyond just the first century and point to the future in what the Bible calls the endtimes or the latter days of history. The Beast and the Beast system he leads represent the final efforts of humankind to rule the earth without God in what Jesus called *"the times of the Gentiles"* (Luke 21:24).

Even though he has lost the battle to dethrone God, satan still wants to be worshiped. He believes he can accomplish this by establishing an anti-God, one-world system with his representative as the leader. He manipulates and deceives most of the masses into believing that his chosen one has been resurrected from a mortal wound to the head. Whether they know it or not, they are really worshiping satan who is inspiring and empowering his human agent.

At this time, satan motivates and energizes the anti-Messiah to kill every believer he can find. While God protects many of His people, others are martyred. John gives a word of comfort to the believers saying that God will judge their persecutors and vindicate His people. Those martyred are seen in Heaven before the throne of God, which is infinitely more glorious than that of any Roman emperor.

Since satan knows that human beings are religious by nature, he chooses a religious counterpart to the anti-Messiah. This person, whom John calls the Beast From the Earth, is the final and ultimate embodiment of all false prophets throughout history. This false prophet is also demonically anointed and empowered by satan. He works with the anti-Messiah to further deceive the people of the world into following and worshiping satan.

Let's now open our spiritual eyes with John to see what he sees in his vision of this evil prophet of satan.

The Beast From the Earth
(Revelation 13:11-12)

As if his vision of the Beast From the Sea was not terrifying enough, John now sees another beast. His intention is for us to understand that this other beast, like the first, is empowered by satan. John sees this beast coming out of the earth, meaning a human counterpart to the satanic anti-Messiah.

Whereas the anti-Messiah is described as one having political power, John describes this beast in religious terms. He says that the beast coming out of the earth has two horns like a lamb but speaks like a dragon.

We should be able to understand what John means by this description. This is a person who pretends to be a "man of God" but is in reality a "man of satan." He is a false prophet, or as we say, a "wolf in sheep's clothing." At this point, John assumes that we understand his meaning, but later specifically calls him the *"false prophet"* as recorded in Revelation 16:13; 19:20; 20:10.

When Jesus first began His ministry, He warned those listening about false prophets: *"Beware of false prophets, who come to you in sheep's clothing, but inwardly they are ravenous wolves"* (Matt. 7:15).

Jesus goes on to say in the same sermon that we can know whether people are from God by the spiritual fruit in their lives. Paul refers to this inward character as the *"fruit of the Spirit"* and contrasts it with the *"works of the flesh"* (Gal. 5:22,19; see also 5:16-23).

The devil can counterfeit charisma, but he cannot counterfeit character manifested as the fruit of the Spirit. It is vital that believers refrain from following charismatic personalities who do not have character. There will be many such people in the endtimes.

In His prophetic outline of the endtimes, Jesus warned us against false prophets:

Many false prophets will rise up and deceive many (Matthew 24:11).

If anyone says to you, "Look, here is the Christ [Messiah]*!" or "There!" do not believe it. For false christs* [messiahs] *and false prophets will rise and show great signs and wonders to deceive, if possible, even the elect* (Matthew 24:23-24).

John's readers understood his warnings in the context of their times. The Roman Empire was vast and powerful, but what united the empire was emperor worship. As I explained in Volume 1 of this series, bowing down to the statue of the emperor was not so much a religious act as it was a political act.

The emperor represented the empire—its policies, its gods and goddesses, its way of life, etc. Bowing down to the statue of the emperor was the way one showed loyalty to the empire. This was not a problem for the pagans as they simply added the emperor to their list of deities. But, of course, believers in the One True God could not bow down to the statue of the emperor. They could not "fix their sandals" in front of the statue or at the altar dedicated to the emperor.

These believers' refusal to bow before the emperor was considered an act of disloyalty to the empire. Those who refused to do so were persecuted, exiled, or martyred. As I explained in great detail in Volume 1, this is what caused the crisis among the seven congregations. The believers were being persecuted over this issue, which is why Jesus gave this revelation to John encouraging them to endure to the end.

The situation in Rome is being repeated in this last-days, anti-God, one-world system. Just as satan inspired emperor worship to unify the Roman Empire, he is using the same strategy to unite this last representation of all the ancient empires that opposed God.

Thus, the New World Order political system must have a New World Order religious system. The false prophet is the leader of this global religion. He is the counterpart to the priests who served the imperial cult of emperor worship. He is the ultimate embodiment of all previous false prophets in that he is fully and completely anointed by satan. His demonically inspired "job description" is to get the people to worship the anti-Messiah. As previously noted, when the people worship the anti-Messiah, they are really worshiping satan. Since true believers cannot do this, they are considered to be enemies of the state.

The apostle Paul looked into the future and saw this time in the latter days when many professing believers will fall away from the One True God, at which time the anti-Messiah will appear. Paul writes,

> *Let no one deceive you by any means; for that Day will not come unless the falling away comes first, and the man of sin is revealed, the son of perdition, who opposes and exalts himself above all that is called God or that is worshiped, so that he sits as God in the temple of God, showing himself that he is God* (2 Thessalonians 2:3-4).

The False Prophet

Here is a summary of the activities of the false prophet. He:

- Presents himself as a religious figure (see Rev. 13:12).

- Forces everyone to worship the Beast (see Rev. 13:12).

- Performs signs and wonders (see Rev. 13:13).

- Deceives the people (see Rev. 13:14).

- Can only do what God allows (see Rev. 13:14).

- Calls for the making of an image of the Beast (see Rev. 13:14).

- Seems to make the image come alive (see Rev. 13:15).

- Attempts to murder those who refuse to worship the Beast (see Rev. 13:15).

- Forces people to take the Mark of the Beast (see Rev. 13:17).

DECEPTIVE SIGNS AND WONDERS
(REVELATION 13:13-15)

John is careful to note that this false prophet "is granted" the power to perform miraculous signs and wonders. This means that God allows him to have this power to deceive the people, because they do not want truth. They prefer to believe lies, so God providentially allows this deception as their judgment. This we must understand—if we reject the truth of God's Word, He will allow us to be deceived as our judgment. This is just and right.

The apostle Paul explains:

> *The coming of the lawless one is according to the working of Satan, with all power, signs, and lying wonders, and with all unrighteous deception among those who perish, because they did not receive the love of the truth, that they might be saved. And for this reason God will send them strong delusion, that they should believe the lie, that they all may be condemned who did not believe the truth but had pleasure in unrighteousness* (2 Thessalonians 2:9-12).

Since satan is a very powerful being, he can perform some mighty acts that seem to humans to be miracles. But God has limited what satan can do. We recall that when Moses performed miracles before Pharaoh, the ruler's magicians were able to duplicate some but not all of them (see Exod. 7:10–8:19). This is why believers must not follow signs and wonders. The deceiver, satan, has the ability to duplicate some of them.

Just because someone is able to perform miracles does not necessarily mean that person is from God. We must test the spirits and know those who labor among us so we will not be deceived. We must follow those who have demonstrated the fruit of the Spirit and not just the gifts of the Spirit. This is especially important in these endtimes when many false prophets are among us.

John says that satan empowers the false prophet to do great signs, including making fire come down from Heaven. This miracle reminds us that Elijah brought fire down from Heaven on several occasions. One was when he challenged the prophets of Baal, and on another occasion when King Ahaziah sent groups of 50 men to seize Elijah (see 1 Kings 18:36-38; 2 Kings 1:9-12).

For three-and-one-half years, God's two witnesses breathe fire out of their mouths to destroy those who seek to kill them. They also do miracles such as preventing rain, turning water to blood, and striking the earth with plagues (see Rev. 11). Now satan works his "fire-miracle" and other signs and wonders through the false prophet.

In Bible times, it was important for the pagan priests to strike fear in the hearts of the masses so they would fear and worship the local deity. One of the many ways they did this was to deceive the people into thinking the god or the image of the god was speaking to them. They used demonic utterances, magic, concealed speaking tubes, crude sound machines, gravity, pulleys, levers, and other simple mechanical devices that seemed to cause the god or the image to speak. Of course, it was all a deception.

John records that satan is going to use this same deception. He puts the idea in the mind of the false prophet to tell the people to make an image of the Beast. Using demonic trickery, satan makes the image appear to come alive and speak. By now, the people are so completely deceived that they obey the command to worship the image of the Beast. Once again, this is satan's way of getting the people to worship him since he is the power behind the image. Those who refuse to worship the Beast are to be killed.

John refers to the image four times in this chapter and six more in the Book of Revelation (see Rev. 14:9,11; 15:2; 16:2; 19:20; 20:4). While those who worship the image may prolong their lives for a season, God will judge them with further devastation and cast them into hell with the anti-Messiah and false prophet, where they will be in their own torment forever (see Rev. 14:9-11).

John's first-century readers were used to seeing statues of the emperor and the many Greco-Roman gods throughout the empire. They were used to "the gods" speaking to their worshipers. Because our modern world is so different from the world of the Bible, it is sometimes hard for us to understand that worship practices described in the Bible were the norm. For example, all ancient empires promoted the belief that the emperor was the human incarnation of the high god the people worshiped. How convenient for the emperor. Making statues of the emperor and forcing people to worship the statue was not new to the Romans, although they perfected the practice.

We return to the Book of Daniel for an example. Bible students will recall that King Nebuchadnezzar made an image of gold that was about 90 feet high (see Dan. 3:1). We don't know if the image was of Nebuchadnezzar himself or the Babylonian high god commonly called Ba`al. It doesn't really matter since Nebuchadnezzar was considered the representative of Ba`al. Worshiping the emperor was the same as worshiping the god.

Nebuchadnezzar sent out a decree that at a certain time everyone was to bow down and worship the image. The call to worship was announced by the sound of a great symphony of music. Anyone who refused to bow down to the image would be thrown into a fiery furnace.

Daniel writes:

> *Then a herald cried aloud: "To you it is commanded, O*
> *peoples, nations, and languages, that at the time you hear*
> *the sound of the horn, flute, harp, lyre, and psaltery, in*
> *symphony with all kinds of music, you shall fall down and*
> *worship the gold image that King Nebuchadnezzar has*
> *set up; and whoever does not fall down and worship shall*
> *be cast immediately into the midst of a burning fiery fur-*
> *nace"* (Daniel 3:4-6).

In one of the best known stories of faith and courage in the Bible, three Jewish men—Shadrach, Meshach, and Abed-Nego—refused to bow down to the statue. Some informers told the king about their disobedience. King Nebuchadnezzar went into a rage. He had the three men brought before him and told them that they would be thrown into the fiery furnace unless they bowed before the statue. He even bragged that there was no god who could help them if they refused.

This is how Shadrach, Meshach, and Abed-Nego answered the king:

> *O Nebuchadnezzar, we have no need to answer you in*
> *this matter. If that is the case, our God whom we serve is*
> *able to deliver us from the burning fiery furnace, and He*
> *will deliver us from your hand, O king. But if not, let it*
> *be known to you, O king, that we do not serve your gods,*
> *nor will we worship the gold image which you have set up*
> (Daniel 3:16-18).

Nebuchadnezzar went into another rage. He commanded that the fiery furnace be heated seven times hotter. He then commanded some of his officers to bind Shadrach, Meshach, and Abed-Nego and throw them into the furnace. By this time, it was so hot that the flames consumed the officers as they threw the three men into the inferno.

Keeping a safe distance, Nebuchadnezzar looked into the furnace and was astonished by what he saw. He turned to his advisors and said:

"Did we not cast three men bound into the midst of the fire?" They answered and said to the king, "True, O king." "Look!" he answered, "I see four men loose, walking in the midst of the fire; and they are not hurt, and the form of the fourth is like the Son of God" (Daniel 3:24-25).

Nebuchadnezzar got closer to the mouth of the furnace and called to Shadrach, Meshach, and Abed-Nego. He instructed them to come out and he acknowledged that they were indeed servants of the Most High God. When they got out of the furnace, the king's servants saw that the fire had not touched them.

The satraps, administrators, governors, and the king's counselors gathered together, and they saw these men on whose bodies the fire had no power; the hair of their head was not singed nor were their garments affected, and the smell of fire was not on them (Daniel 3:27).

King Nebuchadnezzar praised the God of Shadrach, Meshach, and Abed-Nego, threatened anyone who spoke against their God, and promoted all three men. Hallelujah!

Shadrach, Meshach, and Abed-Nego believed the One True God would deliver them from death in the furnace. But regardless of the outcome, they would continue to worship the One True God and no other. Because of their faith and courage, the One True God was exalted and Shadrach, Meshach, and Abed-Nego were honored.

The lesson for us is clear. In John's time, as well as in the endtimes of the Book of Revelation, God will deliver some and not others. This is according to His sovereign plan for our lives. Whether He chooses to deliver us or not, we must have the same faith, courage, and commitment as Shadrach, Meshach, and Abed-Nego. We must not "fix our sandals" before the anti-God, one-world system in an attempt to save our lives.

Whether we live or die, we do so "as unto the Lord." The way we face this choice will bring glory to God. When people see our faith and courage in times of persecution, this will be our greatest testimony. Furthermore, when Jesus returns, He will destroy all those who spoke against His Father, and we will be promoted and honored to serve Him in His Kingdom. That is a far more glorious future than denying our Lord to escape a little persecution. God will be with us as He was with Shadrach, Meshach, and Abed-Nego. He will give us the faith and courage to stand strong. We will overcome by the blood of the Lamb and the word of our testimony (see Rev. 12:11).

Paul adds the following word of encouragement:

> *Nevertheless the solid foundation of God stands, having this seal: "The Lord knows those who are His," and, "Let everyone who names the name of Christ* [Messiah] *depart from iniquity"* (2 Timothy 2:19).

The Mark of the Beast (Revelation 13:16-18)

As a final act of worship inspired by satan, the false prophet forces everyone to take a mark, identifying them as followers and worshipers of the anti-Messiah. As previously noted, God's people and a remnant of an independent-minded group refuse the mark. This mark will distinguish those who take it from those who have God's mark, which John explained in Revelation 7. The mark of God protects believers from His judgments on the unbelievers while the Mark of the Beast protects the unbelievers from being persecuted by the anti-Messiah. Before this terrible time is over, people will have to choose to either worship God or the devil.

Since the anti-Messiah will be the head of a brutal totalitarian anti-God, one-world system, only people who have his mark will be able to buy and sell anything. As mentioned previously, there will be some who do not take the Mark of the Beast, but neither will they have accepted Jesus as their Savior, Lord, and Redeemer. This will be a great opportunity for God to supernaturally provide for His people. What an awesome time it will be for the people of God. It will be as it was when the Lord supernaturally provided for Elijah, and when Jesus multiplied the loaves and fishes (see 1 Kings 17:1-7; John 6:1-14).

John explains that people will take this mark on their right hand, forehead, or both. This is a further satanic counterfeit and copy of God's original command to the Jewish males in Bible times. God instructed the people to "wear" His words: *You shall bind them as a sign on your hand, and they shall be as frontlets between your eyes* (Deut. 6:8).

The Mark of the Beast is also a perversion because Jewish men bind God's Word on the left hands and arms (not the right) symbolically keeping God's Word near their hearts. As an observant Jew, Jesus would have kept this commandment and worn these symbols of God's Word and prayer.

John explains that the mark is the name of the Beast or the number of his name. This is another attempt to counterfeit what the Lord has promised His people.

In Revelation 3:12, the Lord made the following promise to the overcomers at the Philadelphia congregation:

> *He who overcomes, I will make him a pillar in the temple of My God, and he shall go out no more. I will write on him the name of My God [YHVH] and the name of the city of My God, the New Jerusalem, which comes down out of heaven from My God. And I will write on him My new name.*

We learned in Revelation 7:3 and 9:4 that God put His seal on the foreheads of the believers. Revelation 22:4 adds that God's people *"shall see His face, and His name shall be on their foreheads."*

Those who choose the mark and name of the Beast will be judged by God and separated from Him for eternity in their own hell. Those who choose the mark and name of God will be persecuted by the Beast but will overcome in life and in death and live forever in the presence of God.

John expects his first-century readers to know the identity of the Beast. The number of his name is 666. In Hebrew and Greek, the letters of the alphabet have numeric values. For example, in Hebrew the *alef* is 1, *bet* is 2, *gimel* is 3, *dalet* is 4, etc.

In the first century, Nero was the only Roman emperor whose name in Greek may have equaled the number 666. Nero certainly persecuted the believers unmercifully. Furthermore, there were many who believed that Nero would come back to life after he died in A.D. 68. However, if John received his Revelation around A.D. 96, this would have been much too late for anyone to believe that Nero would be resurrected. And this one thing we do know for sure—Nero did not come back to life.

The identity of any person this number represented has been lost in time. And yet, throughout history, scholars have tried to connect the number to certain leaders, institutions, and world organizations. Christian authors have written numerous books on the subject, all based on speculation. While books and sermons on this subject can be sensational and appeal to the masses, they don't help anyone in their walk with God. We would be better served to live a life that pleases God, provoke one another to love and good works (see Heb. 10:24-25), and prepare for the difficult days ahead. This should be our priority.

REVIEW QUESTIONS

1. Write a summary of what you have learned in this lesson. Write the summary in clear, concise words as if you were going to present it to another person.

2. Describe how you can apply what you have learned in this lesson to your life.

3. Share what you have learned with your family, friends, and members of your study group.

Chapter 3

Preview of the End

REVELATION REVIEW

TO his first-century readers, John's apocalyptic vision of "otherworldly" beings most likely referred to Rome, the Roman emperors, and the imperial cult worship of the emperors. The believers understood that John was talking about them. They were the ones being persecuted for their faith. However, John's Revelation certainly seems to go far beyond the near-term view of just Rome.

Since God's Word is timeless for all generations, biblical scholars and historians have had a long-term view of the Book of Revelation. It doesn't make sense that the rest of the Bible would be relevant for our lives today, but this book would not. Read that last sentence again closely.

Throughout history, theologians have certainly disagreed on how to interpret this mystifying book. Some see John's prophecy completely fulfilled in the Roman Empire of his day while others have attempted to apply it to important world leaders and nations that have arisen during the last 2,000 years.

Most biblical scholars understand the Book of Revelation to have both a past and a future. That is, they understand the historical context in which John was writing but they also believe that John's Revelation is prophetic.

When considering the whole context of the Bible, the Book of Revelation certainly refers to real historical events, while also explaining events that will take place in the latter days of history. These events will culminate in the coming of Messiah Jesus, the glorious Son of God-Son of Man who will defeat satan and his followers. Jesus will literally establish the Kingdom of God on the earth by which He will usher in the golden age spoken of by the prophets.

Of course, the coming of Jesus will mean the downfall of satan. His lifelong goal to be worshiped as god will come to an end. Using apocalyptic language, John sees satan cast out of Heaven to the earth three and-one-half years prior to the coming of Jesus. This is the prelude to satan's final time on the earth before he is consigned forever to the lake of fire.

Knowing that his time is short, satan is frantic. In one last effort to achieve his goal of world dominance and glory, he empowers two human agents through whom he will be worshiped as god. John describes one of these demonic representatives as a beast coming out of the sea and the other as a beast coming out of the earth.

The Beast From the Sea is the anti-Messiah whom satan will put in place as the political leader of the final confederation of the anti-God, one-world government. Since satan knows that human beings are religious by nature, he brings forth another beast like the first one. This Beast From the Earth is the false prophet who will perform signs and wonders to deceive the people into worshiping the anti-Messiah and his image. They prove their allegiance by taking the Mark of the Beast.

The mark of God provides divine protection for God's people against His judgments on those who oppose Him. The Mark of the Beast is satan's copy of the mark of God. Only those who have this mark will be able to conduct business in the anti-God, one-world economic system. This mark also is to identify the followers of the anti-Messiah so they won't be persecuted in the anti-Messiah's police state.

The anti-Messiah and false prophet seek to kill everyone who does not take the Mark of the Beast. God will supernaturally protect many of His people, but He will allow many others to be martyred. This demonic attack against God's people is the beginning of the end for satan, the anti-Messiah, the false prophet, and all who oppose God. This is the subject of Revelation chapter 14. It is the preview of the end.

Preview of the End (Revelation 14)

As we study, we see that Revelation 14 is divided into four parts. In the first part, John sees 144,000 souls redeemed from the earth and standing in the presence of God in Heaven. Next, he sees and hears three powerful angels proclaiming God's judgments against those who oppose Him. In the third part, John sees "One like the Son of Man" reaping the earth. Finally, an angel comes forth to further reap the earth in what is known as the "Judgment of the Grapes of Wrath."

Let's begin our study with this chapter that offers hope for believers, but destruction for those who oppose God.

The Lamb and the 144,000 (verses 1-5)

In a vision, John sees the Lamb standing on Mount Zion. Of course, the Lamb is Jesus, who conquered satan, sin, and death. Why does John say he sees Jesus standing on Mount Zion? In the Bible, Mount Zion symbolizes the place of God's dwelling. So when John says he sees Jesus standing on Mount Zion, his readers understand him to mean that Jesus is standing in the place where God rules over the nations from Jerusalem.

There is a literal, earthly Mount Zion in Jerusalem that we call the Temple Mount. Unfortunately, this is the place where the Dome of the Rock is currently located. This may soon change as God may destroy it with an earthquake. But for now, its presence is certainly a dramatic symbol of the spiritual battle for Jerusalem and God's holy mount.

However, long before there was an Islamic structure, Mount Zion was the place God chose to reveal Himself to the Hebrews and later to the world. This is the place where Abraham offered Isaac as a sacrifice to God (see Gen. 22). In Abraham's time, Mount Zion was referred to as Mount Moriah. This is the place David purchased for 50 shekels of silver and built an altar to the Lord (see 2 Sam. 24:24). Mount Zion is the place where Solomon built the Temple to the God of Israel (see 1 Kings 6) It is the place where Jesus taught as recorded in the Gospels (see John 10:22-30). It is the same area where Jesus had His Passover meal with His disciples and where He was arrested, tried, and crucified (see Matt. 26–28).

Incredibly, since Israel liberated Jerusalem in 1967, Muslim religious leaders claim there never was a Jewish Temple on the Temple Mount. There is some humor here. If there never was a Jewish Temple on the Temple Mount, why do they (and the world) refer to the location as *the Temple Mount?*

In 1925 the Supreme Moslem Council published an official Muslim guide to the Temple Mount called *A Brief Guide to Al-Haram Al-Sharif.* Page four of this document asserts:

> The site is one of the oldest in the world. Its sanctity dates from the earliest (perhaps from pre-historic) times. Its identity with the site of Solomon's Temple is beyond dispute. This, too, is the spot, according to universal belief, on which "David built there an altar unto the Lord, and offered burnt offerings and peace offerings."[1]

While not specifically named, Mount Zion is also the place where the Holy Spirit came to the disciples on the Day of Pentecost (see Acts 2). This outpouring of the Spirit of God most likely took place at Solomon's Porch on the Temple Mount. Jesus is going to return to this sacred place from which He will rule over the nations (see Ps. 2). God's people, those who follow the Lamb, will rule with Him from this holy mount (see Rev. 20:1-4). Wow! No wonder John sees Jesus standing on Mount Zion.

In addition to a literal place in Jerusalem, Mount Zion is also a spiritual symbol of God's presence in Heaven and the New Jerusalem that will one day come to Earth. As God's people will rule with Jesus from the literal Mount Zion on Earth, John sees them already in place in the heavenly representation of the earthly Mount Zion.

The writer of Hebrews explains:

> *You have come to Mount Zion and to the city of the living God, the heavenly Jerusalem, to an innumerable company of angels, to the general assembly and church* [congregation] *of the firstborn who are registered in heaven, to God the Judge of all, to the spirits of just men made perfect, to Jesus the Mediator of the new covenant, and to the blood of sprinkling* [the Lamb's blood] *that speaks better things than that of Abel* (Hebrews 12:22-24).

Psalms 2 speaks about the Son of God ruling over the nations from Mount Zion. It is a wonderful psalm to read in its entirety. The psalmist tells how God is laughing at the puny counsels of world leaders conspiring to overthrow Him. He then explains God's plan to exalt His Son to rule over the nations from Mount Zion.

Meditate on these words that will certainly fill your heart with joy:

> *He who sits in the heavens shall laugh; the LORD shall hold them in derision. Then He shall speak to them in His*

wrath, and distress them in His deep displeasure: "Yet I have set My King on My holy hill of Zion. I will declare the decree: the LORD has said to Me, 'You are My Son, today I have begotten You [bringing you forth]. Ask of Me, and I will give you the nations for Your inheritance, and the ends of the earth for Your possession. You shall break them with a rod of iron; You shall dash them to pieces like a potter's vessel'" (Psalms 2:4-9).

Alongside Jesus, John sees 144,000 Jewish and grafted-in Gentile believers, which he introduced to us in Revelation 7:1-8. In my view, 144,000 is a symbolic number referring to a representative group of Jews from each of the 12 tribes along with the non-Jewish believers who are part of the Commonwealth of Israel (see Eph. 2). When John says he sees them standing on Mount Zion, he wants his readers to be encouraged that he sees them (and us) standing with the Lord in the place of victory over satan and those who seek to kill them.

We learned in Revelation chapter 7 that the Lord sealed this company of people in order to protect them from His further judgments. John says they are sealed on their foreheads (see Rev. 7:3), but he did not identify the seal. Here and in other places, we learn that this seal is God's name (YHVH). (See Revelation 14:1.) In fact, all of God's people will have God's name written on their foreheads (see Rev. 9:4).

I noted previously that the Lord promised to write God's name, the name of God's city (the New Jerusalem), and a new personal name on each of the believers (see Rev. 3:12). Also, the Lord promises His people that we will see His face and His name will be on our foreheads (see Rev. 22:4). This is an apocalyptic way of saying that God knows those who belong to Him and are citizens of His holy city. They will have a new name—a name that will be an expression of their unique radiance of the glory of God in them and out of them for eternity.

Although this "marking of believers" in honor of a deity is foreign to Western people, it was a common practice in Bible times as we learned from Deuteronomy 6:8. It is still practiced by people living in the East. For example, people in India wear a mark on their foreheads as an expression of their devotion to a particular deity.

We realize that scholars have differing interpretations of some of the details of John's writings. And that is OK. What is clear is that John sees God's people overcoming the anti-Messiah and living with and in the presence of God and the true Messiah both in Heaven and on the earth. This is what we must keep in mind as we continue in our study of this wonderful, but mysterious book.

As John is contemplating this most incredible scene, he hears a heavenly voice so loud he likens it to the sound of many waters and loud thunder (see Rev. 14:2). Think about this for a moment. The sound of many waters is deafening. The sound of loud thunder is ear-splitting. Compared to the awesome power of the voices in Heaven, the voices of those calling people to worship the emperor are no more than a whisper. Better to worship the One True God than to "fix your sandals" before the emperor (the anti-God, one-world system).

Responding to the call to worship, John hears the sound of harps, which was the instrument King David used to praise the Lord. Heaven is getting ready for a great big praise and worship service.

When the heavenly call to worship is heard, 144,000 souls sing a new song of redemption to the Lord. Put yourself in this scene as you join your voice with those of God's people, and the harps of Heaven provide musical accompaniment. You are giving praise and worship to the Creator of the universe while those around the throne serve as your audience. Try to imagine singing before the throne of God and the Redeemer with an audience that includes the four special beings and the 24 elders. Just contemplating this should stir your spirit to want to start practicing so you will be well rehearsed and ready for this glorious moment.

Let us praise the Lord together both now and forevermore!

John gives further information about this company of the redeemed. He did not mean for us to understand his statements literally. He is describing their moral character and spiritual life. John says four things about them:

First, he says they are virgins who have not defiled themselves with women. By this statement, John does not mean that these are all men who never had sex with a woman. This is not a statement about gender and celibacy. He is using spiritual language to tell us they had kept themselves from idolatry, which the Bible calls spiritual adultery and fornication. In other words, they are spiritually pure. Using the language of the Book of Revelation, they had not defiled their garments.

When God gave the Ten Commandments to the Hebrews, He said, *"You shall have no other gods before Me"* (Exod. 20:3). Worshiping other gods or loving the things of the world more than we love God defiles us morally and spiritually. Whenever the Children of Israel committed this sin of idolatry, God spoke of it in terms of infidelity to Him, as a spouse would be unfaithful in marriage.

For example, when the Lord called backsliding Israel to repentance, He expressed Himself with these words:

> *...She has gone up on every high mountain and under every green tree, and there played the harlot....So it came to pass, through her casual harlotry, that she defiled the land and committed adultery with stones and trees"* (Jeremiah 3:6,9).

You can find this type of terminology throughout the Hebrew Bible—in Hosea as well as Ezekiel 16 and 23, for example. It can also be found in the New Testament, in Second Corinthians 11:2 and James 4:4, for example. It is the common expression used in the Bible in reference to worshiping idols or anything of the world that we desire more than God. John uses these phrases repeatedly in the Book of Revelation when he refers to the act of spiritual immorality (see Rev. 14:8; 17:2,4; 18:3,9; 19:2).

The apostle Paul had this spiritual purity in mind when he wrote:

> *I beseech you therefore, brethren, by the mercies of God, that you present your bodies a living sacrifice, holy, acceptable to God, which is your reasonable service. And do not be conformed to this world, but be transformed by the renewing of your mind, that you may prove what is that good and acceptable and perfect will of God* (Romans 12:1-2).

This same John wrote in one of his letters:

> *Do not love the world or the things in the world. If anyone loves the world, the love of the Father is not in him. For all that is in the world—the lust of the flesh, the lust of the eyes, and the pride of life—is not of the Father but is of the world. And the world is passing away, and the lust of it; but he who does the will of God abides forever* (1 John 2:15-17).

Second, John says that they follow the Lamb wherever He goes. Once again, John did not mean that they were literally walking behind Jesus. He meant that they were His disciples. Jesus explained this in the following way:

> *Most assuredly, I say to you, unless a grain of wheat falls into the ground and dies, it remains alone; but if it dies, it produces much grain* [fruit]. *He who loves* [prefers or puts first] *his life* [psuche] *will lose it, and he who hates* [does not prefer or put first] *his life* [psuche] *in this world will keep it for eternal life* [zoe]. *If anyone serves Me, let him follow Me; and where I am, there My servant will be*

also. If anyone serves Me, him My Father will honor (John 12:24-26).

The Greco-Roman (Western) version of Christianity teaches that salvation by grace means that believers are free to live their lives apart from the constraints of the Law. This is a perversion of the biblical meaning of grace. God's grace is His provision that sets us free from ourselves, not from the commandments of God. The Adam-like nature in believers resists such a statement because it wants to live its own rebellious, self-centered life. Furthermore, the biblical meaning of *Law* is not legalism, as it is in the West, but teaching or instruction. Do believers need teaching and instruction on how to walk with God?

Yes, we are saved by grace but if our salvation is real, it will be evidenced by covenantal works of Spirit-inspired loving-kindness. Although we have been taught and believed differently, Jesus was very clear on this matter. He said:

> *If you love Me, keep My commandments....He who has My commandments and keeps them, it is he who loves Me. And he who loves Me will be loved by My Father, and I will love him and manifest Myself to him* (John 14:15,21).

God manifests Himself to those who obey Him. If we don't want to obey the commandments of the Lord, why do we say we are His followers?

Third, John says that this company of people is the firstfruits of the redeemed. We know what he means by being redeemed. We have been bought out of slavery to satan, sin, and death by the precious blood of Jesus. But what does he mean by the word *firstfruits*? In the Bible, God told the Hebrews to bring the firstfruits of their harvest to Him (see Exod. 23:19). This was the way God chose for the people to dedicate their harvest to Him.

In the midst of the Feast of Unleavened Bread, there was a Feast of Firstfruits (Yom HaBikkurim) of the barley harvest to God. The Feast of Shavuot (Pentecost) was a Feast of Firstfruits of the wheat harvest. (See Leviticus 23.) The people would wave their offerings before the Lord. In this way, they acknowledged that the whole of the harvest belonged to Him. By accepting their firstfruits-wave offering, the Lord promised that He would bless the rest of their harvest. So the idea of firstfruits is dedication.

This company of the redeemed was wholly and completely dedicated to God. May we who claim to follow Jesus be so dedicated to our Lord that we would give ourselves to Him as a human wave offering. Or as Jesus said: *"Seek first the kingdom of God and His righteousness, and all these things shall be added to you"* (Matt. 6:33). As we give ourselves and all that God has given us to Him first, He promises to bless the rest of our labors with fruitfulness. If we seek God, we don't have to seek "all these other things." God automatically provides them for us.

Fourth, John says these redeemed have no deceit or false confession of faith. They are what they say in that they live their faith and convictions in their everyday lives. They don't act worldly some of the time and spiritual at other times. They have not embraced a false religion. They have not compromised by "fixing their sandals," and they have not taken the Mark of the Beast in order to save their lives. As a result, John says they are without fault before the throne of God.

May the same be said of us today. May it be said that we live out what we believe in our everyday lives: that we do not compromise our convictions in order to be accepted by the world; that we are not content with a watered-down religious version of our faith that entertains us, tells us what we want to hear, or makes us feel good; that we also will be found faultless when we appear before the throne of God.

As Jude writes:

> *Now to Him who is able to keep you from stumbling* [falling]*, and to present you faultless before the presence of His*

glory with exceeding joy, to God our Savior, who alone is wise, be glory and majesty, dominion and power, both now and forever. Amen (Jude 24-25).

The Proclamation of the Three Angels (verses 6-13)

John now sees and hears three angels giving God's last warnings of impending judgment. The first angel proclaims the everlasting Gospel to all who have survived the previous judgments. The everlasting Gospel is not the Western Gospel of salvation. It is the Gospel of the Kingdom, as we learned in Revelation 11:15-19 and Psalms 145:13. The Gospel proclamation is a last warning to fear God, give glory to God, and worship the Creator of the universe.

The seventh trumpet-shofar judgment proclaims that the kingdoms of this world are judged and replaced with the Kingdom of God, which is coming to the earth. Before the Lord gives John the vision of what this judgment entails, He gives John more information about people and events recorded in Revelation 12–15. This information does not advance the story in time; it only provides more information.

After telling us about the people and events, John describes the contents of the judgments that take place at the blowing of the seventh trumpet-shofar. What this means is that Revelation 11:15-19 is an introduction and general overview of the details given later beginning in Revelation 14:6 and continuing through Revelation chapters 15, 16, 17 and 18.

In other words, the overall story of the Book of Revelation actually ends at Revelation 11:15-19 when the blowing of the seventh trumpet-shofar is announced. John is then given the details, which he records in the rest of the Book of Revelation. As I have explained in the previous volumes, this is an instant replay, and in my view, a major key to understanding the Book of Revelation.

Following the proclamation that God's final judgment is at hand, John sees and hears a second angel who adds to the first proclamation with a more specific statement about this judgment. He identifies the end-time, anti-God, one-world system with Babylon. John mentions the name Babylon five additional times, all in the context of judgment (see Rev. 16:19; 17:5; 18:2,10,21). Then, as recorded in Revelation 17–18, the angel pronounces God's imminent judgment on Babylon.

Ancient Babylon was established by Nimrod. It was the first empire, and the satanic religion Nimrod established became the mother of all future pagan religions. (See Genesis 11.) We will study this later in Revelation chapters 17 and 18. But for now, what we need to know is that the Babylon of Daniel's time was an evil empire and an evil city with an evil religion. It is the empire we discussed previously when studying Daniel's prophecies. Nebuchadnezzar was the head of gold and the one who set up the image people were forced to worship.

Babylon was the archenemy of Israel and the Jewish people. When Nebuchadnezzar was king, Babylon attacked Judah in 606 B.C. and finally conquered Jerusalem in 586 B.C. To the Hebrews, the Babylonian empire, civilization, and religion represented the epitome of satan's world system. Because Babylon was Judah's worst enemy and the mother of all pagan, anti-God religions, Isaiah and Jeremiah prophesied its destruction. It is significant that the angel pronouncing God's judgment on the Babylon of the Book of Revelation uses the identical words Isaiah and Jeremiah used.

Isaiah's prophecy is recorded in Isaiah 21. Toward the end of his prophecy, Isaiah wrote: *"Babylon is fallen, is fallen! And all the carved images of her gods He has broken to the ground"* (Isa. 21:9).

Jeremiah's prophecies against Babylon are recorded in Jeremiah 50–51. He warns God's people to flee Babylon before the coming judgment:

> *Flee from the midst of Babylon, and everyone save his life!*
> *Do not be cut off in her iniquity, for this is the time of*

the LORD's vengeance; He shall recompense her. Babylon was a golden cup in the LORD's hand that made all the earth drunk. The nations drank her wine; therefore the nations are deranged. Babylon has suddenly fallen and been destroyed. Wail for her! Take balm for her pain; perhaps she may be healed (Jeremiah 51:6-8).

John says that this Babylon is a city, but he doesn't say *which* city—and for a good reason. In John's day, it was not wise to speak against Rome. When someone wanted to write something negative about Rome or the Roman Empire, they used the code word, *Babylon*. Believers often do the same today when speaking of the established world system.

In the first century, Jews and the early Christians saw the Roman Empire and the city of Rome in the same light as ancient Babylon. The empire and the city were one and the same. It was the most powerful and cruel empire in history. It was a pagan system that promoted emperor worship and persecuted Jews and Christians. Like Babylon of old, Rome was the archenemy of God and His people.

When the apostle Peter wrote his first letter, he used the code word *Babylon* to refer to Rome (see 1 Pet. 5:13). John does the same. He is talking about the Rome of his day. It was a city that opposed God and God's people. However, John's words are clearly more far-reaching than first-century Rome. Because of its satanic nature, its power, and its persecution of God's people, the word *Babylon* became the word of choice to describe anti-God civilizations throughout history. John is not only writing about first-century Rome but also the final anti-God, one-world system that is in place in the endtimes.

Not only is God now ready to administer the final judgment on this end-time Babylon, He will also judge those who are part of it. John sees and hears a third angel proclaiming God's judgment on those who worship the Beast and take his mark. The angel uses graphic language to describe God's judgment. First, he says they will drink of the cup of the wrath of God *"poured out full strength"* (Rev. 14:10). What did he mean by the phrase *full strength?*

Because good drinking water was not always available, people in Bible times drank wine at their meals and festive occasions. However, they didn't want to get drunk so they diluted their wine with water. They normally mixed three parts water with one part wine. This is where we get the term *watered-down.* The people knew that drinking wine that was not diluted with water could lead to drunkenness and drunkenness could lead to idolatry and immorality. This behavior could lead to the judgment of God. In view of this natural cause and effect, when people wanted to talk about the judgment of God, they often referred to a cup of undiluted wine. It was a figure of speech that everyone understood. (Review Jeremiah 51:6-8; see Jeremiah 25:15-32.) The angel in the Book of Revelation uses the same expression in his pronouncement of God's impending judgment. It is repeated in Revelation 16:19; 17:2; and 18:3.

With this knowledge, we are able to understand what the angel means when he says the people will drink the cup of God's wrath in full strength. He means that God's judgment will not be diluted or watered down with His mercy. For those who took the Mark of the Beast, the time for God's mercy is over. There is no point in God continuing to offer it to the people. They have already drunk—full strength—the cup of the anti-Messiah's Babylon. Now they will drink, full strength, the cup of God's wrath.

In language anyone can understand, the angel gives graphic details of the horrible fate of those who drink the undiluted cup of God's wrath. The word is *tormented* (see Rev. 14:10). The angel uses biblical imagery to describe this torment as one of fire and brimstone, which is burning sulfur.

The universally-known example in the Bible of this form of God's judgment is Sodom and Gomorrah. Genesis reads: *"Then the LORD rained brimstone and fire on Sodom and Gomorrah, from the LORD out of the heavens"* (Gen. 19:24).

When Abraham saw God's judgment, *"he looked toward Sodom and Gomorrah, and toward all the land of the plain; and he saw, and behold, the smoke of the land which went up like the smoke of a furnace"* (Gen. 19:28). In my many trips to Israel, I have personally seen sulfur still burning and emitting smoke at the southern tip of the Dead Sea.

Jesus connected God's holy judgment on Sodom and Gomorrah with God's final judgment on the wicked:

> *...On the day that Lot went out of Sodom it rained fire and brimstone from heaven and destroyed them all. Even so it will be in the day when the Son of Man is revealed* (Luke 17:29-30).

As the smoke ascended from Sodom and Gomorrah in Abraham's time, the angel says the smoke from this final judgment will ascend forever and ever. From this clear language, we learn that God's final judgment on those who reject Him will be unending. It is the place of the lake of fire we know of as hell and the second death (see Rev. 21:8).

Since Heaven is forever, so is hell. While Heaven is a place of endless joy and rest in the presence of God, hell is a place of endless suffering. There will be no relief—*ever.* As Abraham saw God's judgment on Sodom and Gomorrah, so Jesus, the Lamb of God, and His holy angels will see the consequences of this judgment on the wicked. This is a real place of torment and separation from God. We will study this in more detail later on.

Our time in this life is short, and it passes quickly. Eternity is forever. Using human words, we could say that eternity passes by very slowly. In view of the fact that God's people will live with God for eternity while the wicked suffer the consequences of their sins forever, surely God's people can patiently endure short-term hardship and persecution—can't we?

The apostle Paul us gives the following words of assurance: *"I consider that the sufferings of this present time are not worthy to be compared with the glory which shall be revealed in us"* (Rom. 8:18; see also 8:35-39).

John further substantiates that salvation by grace does not mean believers are free from the obligation to live holy lives. He specifically says this word of encouragement is for those who keep the commandments of God and their faith in Jesus. Since God's judgment is imminent, those who die in the Lord are blessed, for they will no longer suffer. While God's righteousness is a free gift of God to those who accept it, John adds that the works of the believers will follow them to Heaven. James said that *"...faith by itself, if it does not have works, is dead"* (James 2:17).

Please, let us get beyond the Western Christian teaching of cheap grace and live our lives fully dedicated to the will and the ways of God.

Reaping the Earth's Harvest (verses 14-16)

Continuing the theme of God's final judgment, John sees the exalted Son of Man ready to reap the spiritual harvest of the earth. He is sitting on a white cloud and wearing a crown of gold. He has a sharp sickle in His hand with which He will reap the harvest of human souls. An angel comes from the throne of God with the message that it is time for the Son of Man to reap the harvest.

John's vision connects to Daniel's, which pictured the Son of Man coming with the clouds of Heaven (see Dan. 7:13). Jesus Himself connected John's vision with Daniel's when He said to Caiaphas, *"It is as you said. Nevertheless, I say to you, hereafter you will see the Son of Man sitting at the right hand of the Power and coming on the clouds of heaven"* (Matt. 26:64).

In these closing verses, it seems that the angels are announcing two different harvests. In my view, the first harvest in verses 14-16 is the harvest of the righteous, while the second harvest in verses 17-20 is the harvest of the unrighteous. Although John records what he sees in

Revelation 14, these harvests don't actually take place until the end of Revelation 18, just prior to and at the coming of the Lord. Jesus explains this for us in one of His teachings about the great end-time judgment when God's people are separated from the wicked.

In Matthew 13, Jesus told two parables about sowing and reaping. As He always did, Jesus put His teachings in terms of the culture and the everyday life experiences of the people, so they could relate to what he was telling them. Since his listeners were agricultural people, Jesus often used agricultural expressions to teach them spiritual truths.

In the second parable, Jesus likened the righteous to wheat and the unrighteous to tares (see Matt. 13:24-30). While growing in the field, tares look so much like wheat that, until the wheat matures, it's hard to tell one from the other. It is wise to wait until the grain appears on the wheat before trying to separate the two.

Jesus said that He and the angels will separate the righteous (human wheat) from the unrighteous (human tares) in the great end-time harvest of souls. The righteous are those who have the mark of God and the unrighteous are those who have the Mark of the Beast.

Matthew records these words of Jesus:

> Let both grow together until the harvest, and at the time of harvest I will say to the reapers, "First gather together the tares and bind them in bundles to burn them, but gather the wheat into my barn" (Matthew 13:30).

Jesus further explained:

> The enemy who sowed them [the tares] is the devil, the harvest is the end of the age, and the reapers are the angels. Therefore as the tares are gathered and burned in the fire, so it will be at the end of the age. The Son of Man will send out His angels, and they will gather out of His kingdom all things that offend, and those who practice lawlessness,

and will cast them into the furnace of fire. There will be wailing and gnashing of teeth. Then the righteous will shine forth as the sun in the kingdom of their Father. He who has ears to hear, let him hear! (Matthew 13:39-43)

Jesus repeats His teaching:

So it will be at the end of the age. The angels will come forth, separate the wicked from among the just, and cast them into the furnace of fire. There will be wailing and gnashing of teeth (Matthew 13:49-50).

The Hebrew prophets used similar biblical imagery to speak of God's judgments. Jeremiah wrote: *"The daughter of Babylon is like a threshing floor when it is time to thresh her; yet a little while and the time of her harvest will come"* (Jer. 51:33).

In my opinion, it is at this time that the rapture or "catching up" of the saints takes place. In keeping with Jewish marriage customs, this is when the Father in Heaven will tell His Son to go get His Bride. (See Matthew 22:1-14; 25:1-13; John 14:1-3.) It seems to me that this is the only interpretation consistent with what the Bible actually says.

So what does the Bible say?

Daniel prophesied about this end-time separation of the righteous from the unrighteous. He says that God's people will be delivered after Michael fights on their behalf. John sees Michael engaged in this fight at the middle of the tribulation period, which is recorded in Revelation 12. This means that God's people will not be delivered until after that time. Daniel also sees the reaping of the harvest of the righteous in Revelation 14:14-16 and the reaping of the harvest of the unrighteous grapes of wrath in Revelation 14:17-20. This takes place at the end of the Great Tribulation. Believers will be caught up to meet the Lord in the air and return with Him as described in Revelation 19.

The angel says to Daniel:

At that time Michael shall stand up, the great prince who stands watch over the sons of your people; and there shall be a time of trouble, such as never was since there was a nation, even to that time. And at that time your people shall be delivered, every one who is found written in the book. And many of those who sleep in the dust of the earth shall awake, some to everlasting life, some to shame and everlasting contempt (Daniel 12:1-2).

If this is the correct interpretation of Daniels words, it will be confirmed in the New Testament as there are no contradictions in the pages of the Bible.

So what does the New Testament say?

When Jesus' disciples asked Him about these great end-time events, Jesus said He would send His angels to blow the trumpet-shofar and gather His own after the tribulation. Since Jesus said this would happen after or at the end of the tribulation, it was not necessary for Him to tell them this was the last trumpet-shofar. The Jewish sages taught that Messiah would come after much tribulation, and Jesus' disciples understood what He meant.

Even Islam, borrowing from Judaism and early Christianity, teaches that the Mahdi (Islamic messiah) will appear after a period of tribulation. This is why the leader of Iran wants to cause war and turmoil in the world. In his mind, this is necessary for the Mahdi to appear.

Matthew records these words of Jesus:

Immediately after the tribulation of those days the sun will be darkened, and the moon will not give its light; the stars will fall from heaven and the powers of the heavens will be shaken. Then the sign of the Son of Man will appear in heaven, and then all the tribes of the earth will mourn, and they will see the Son of Man coming on the clouds of heaven with power and great glory. And He will send His angels with a great sound of a trumpet [the last trumpet-shofar], *and they will gather together His elect from the four winds, from one end of heaven to the other* (Matthew 24:29-31).

Paul writes to the believers at Corinth and Thessalonica about the same event. His Corinthian letter says the following:

Behold, I tell you a mystery: We shall not all sleep, but we shall all be changed—in a moment, in the twinkling of an eye, at the last trumpet [shofar]. *For the trumpet* [shofar] *will sound, and the dead* [believers] *will be raised incorruptible, and we shall be changed* (1 Corinthians 15:51-52).

Notice that Paul says this will happen at the blowing of the last trumpet-shofar.

Paul writes to the Thessalonians:

I do not want you to be ignorant, brethren, concerning those who have fallen asleep [died], *lest you sorrow as others who have no hope. For if we believe that Jesus died and rose again, even so God will bring with Him those who sleep in Jesus. For this we say to you by the word of the Lord, that we who are alive and remain until the coming of the Lord will by no means precede those who are asleep. For the Lord Himself will descend from heaven with a shout, with the voice of an archangel, and with the trumpet* [last trumpet-shofar] *of God. And the dead in Christ* [Messiah] *will rise first. Then we who are alive and remain shall be caught up together with them in the clouds to meet the Lord in the air. And thus we shall always be with the Lord. Therefore comfort one another with these words* (1 Thessalonians 4:13-18).

It should be clear that all of these Scriptures are talking about the same event. It is also clear that they all say God's people will be caught up to meet the Lord in the air when He returns at the last trumpet-shofar. The last trumpet-shofar is sounded at Revelation 11:15-19 to announce the destruction of the kingdoms of this world and the coming of the Kingdom of God. Since the story of the Book of Revelation actually ends at the close of Revelation 11, the last trumpet-shofar is sounded at the end of the tribulation period. John gives more details in Revelation 12–13, provides an instant replay in Revelation 14, and then gives the final details in Revelation 15–19. God's people are caught up to meet the Lord in the air just before His final judgment on the nations.

I love, bless, and honor my friends who have a different understanding of some of these details. We do not have to agree on all of these end-time issues. It isn't important and shouldn't be our priority.

The writer of Hebrews tells us what should be important to us. Please take it to heart. Let his words be the topic of discussion when we meet and the subject of our lecturers at our prophecy conferences:

> Let us consider one another in order to stir up love and good works, not forsaking the assembling of ourselves together, as is the manner of some, but exhorting one another, and so much the more as you see the Day approaching (Hebrews 10:24-25).

As true believers, our unity and friendship should be based on Kingdom relationships rather than theology and doctrine. Our passion should be focused on Jesus rather than full agreement on issues in the Bible that are open to opinion. We should be exhorting one another to love and good works. Let this be our basis of fellowship and common interest.

Regardless of our differing views, let's do our best to read the Bible and accept the plain truth of what it says. If we read the Bible through the eyes of others, no matter how well-meaning or popular their teachings, we will read into it what they have told us it means rather than what it actually says. There is often a big difference between what the Bible says and what we think it says. More times than not, we teach the latter instead of the former.

The Bible is not that hard to understand. It only seems complicated when we read it through other people's eyes.

Reaping the Grapes of Wrath (verses 17-20)

The second harvest is the reaping of the souls of the unrighteous. John sees another angel coming from the throne of God with a sharp sickle in his hand. Then another angel comes forth with the message from God for the first angel: It is time to reap the harvest.

The biblical imagery of this harvest relates to the harvest of grapes. The angel says that the clusters of grapes are ready to be harvested. They are fully ripe, meaning their time has come. While literal grapes at the harvest are full of juice, these human grapes are full of evil.

During the grape harvest, the reapers would cut the clusters of grapes and bring them to a winepress, a pit lined with rock and sealed with a hard substance such as plaster. Workers would pile the grapes on the winepress and then stomp on the grapes to press out the juice. The juice would flow through a hole near the bottom into the vat.

At harvest time, this stomping on the grapes to turn out the new wine was a joyous celebration that included singing and literally dancing on the grapes. Wineries still do this today and often invite their patrons to participate in their "wine-stomping festival."

While God's harvest of the righteous is a time of great joy, His harvest of the grapes of the unrighteous is not. It is a time of God's wrath. Joel used similar words when he prophesied about God's great judgment at the end of the age:

> *Let the nations be wakened, and come up to the Valley of Jehoshaphat; for there I will sit to judge all the surrounding*

nations. Put in the sickle, for the harvest is ripe. Come, go down; for the winepress is full, the vats overflow—for their wickedness is great (Joel 3:12-13).

John learns that this winepress is outside the city. While John identified Rome as the city connected to Babylon, he does not identify this city. However, because Joel tells us that God's final judgment is in the valley of Jehoshaphat, we believe that John is talking about Jerusalem. The valley of Jehoshaphat is thought to be the Kidron Valley or the valley of Hinnom, both of which are just outside Jerusalem. We will study this further in a later chapter.

This judgment is unimaginably great. John learns that the blood crushed from the human grapes reaches the horses bridles and covers about 180 miles. While John describes this carnage in first-century terms, we certainly understand his words to mean a devastating judgment of God at the very end of the Great Tribulation.

Because Jesus suffered God's winepress of judgment for us, those who oppose Him must suffer in their own winepress. While all good people hate to think of humans suffering in this way, this judgment, detailed in the next chapters, is God's answer to the prayers of His people. God is a God of mercy but those who will not accept His mercy must experience His just judgments. We must all decide—holy wrath or holy mercy.

What will you choose?

REVIEW QUESTIONS

1. Write a summary of what you have learned in this lesson. Write the summary in clear, concise words as if you were going to present it to another person.

2. Describe how you can apply what you have learned in this lesson to your life.

3. Share what you have learned with your family, friends, and members of your study group.

NOTE

1. The Supreme Moslem Council, *A Brief Guide to Al-Haram Al-Sharif,* (Jerusalem: 1925), 4, http://www.templeinstitute. org/1925-wakf-temple-mount-guide.pdf (accessed July 17, 2012).

Chapter 4

Preparing to Blow the Seventh Trumpet-Shofar

REVELATION REVIEW

THE One True God has revealed Himself to us in the Bible, and He makes it clear that He desires to have a relationship with us. He has supremely demonstrated this by becoming one of us in the person of Jesus of Nazareth, and then paying the ultimate price by dying for our sins so this relationship would be possible. Since Jesus never sinned, He triumphed over the grave and has been exalted in Heaven as the glorious Son of God-Son of Man. He is returning to the earth as God's divine-human representative to rule over the nations with justice and righteousness. This will be the golden age about which the prophets spoke.

As in human relationships, God gives us a free will to accept or reject His desire to share His life with us. For example, a man pursuing a woman cannot make her love him. Love is an act of the will that comes from the heart. Likewise, God will not make us love Him. We have to choose for ourselves. If we accept His reaching out to us, we greatly benefit because His very own life comes into us. Since God's life is eternal, those who receive Him will receive eternal life and will rule with Him over the rebellious nations.

Unfortunately, not everyone wants this relationship with the Creator. Not only do they oppose God but they also oppose those who have a relationship with Him. As believers live to please God, their holy lives remind nonbelievers of the ever-present reality of the God they have rejected. The holy lives of the believers are like salt in a wound or a bright light in the spiritually-darkened eyes of nonbelievers. Nonbelievers feel a spiritual irritation that they very much want to remove from their lives. The result is persecution against believers.

Furthermore, there is a real satan who desires that we have a relationship with him rather than God. In his great need to be worshiped "like the Most High" (see Isa. 14:14), satan has established a world system that opposes God and deceives those who reject Him. Unwittingly, they become followers of satan and his world system. Together, they resist God and seek to rid the world of God's people. Although this has been happening throughout history, the Book of Revelation tells us about this spiritual war between Rome and the first-century believers, as well as the final war at the end of the age.

Forever banished from God's presence in Heaven, satan knows he has limited time on the earth to achieve his goal. He handpicks two world leaders as his agents to bring the world under his rule. This evil adversary of God works through the anti-Messiah and the false prophet to deceive the world into worshiping him. Their plan, instigated by the false prophet, is the final solution to the "believers problem." Those who refuse to take the Mark of the Beast are to be killed.

This onslaught against God's people greatly advances God's judgments against satan and his followers. Furthermore, God has His own mark for the believers. The mark of God will protect God's people from the judgments He releases against those who oppose Him. While many of God's people will be martyred during this time, they will overcome by the blood of the Lamb and the word of their testimony (see Rev. 12:11). John sees them before the throne of God, in the place satan lost. Hallelujah!

With believers sealed and shielded from God's final judgments, three angels proclaim that the Kingdom of God is now going to be revealed. This results in the final downfall of the Babylonian anti-God, one-world system and those who have opposed God (taken the Mark of the Beast). The time for God's mercy has come to an end.

John is given a preview of two harvests that take place when Jesus returns at the end of God's judgments. In his visions that follow, John sees the details of these final judgments, which are recorded in Revelation 15–18. The first harvest seems to symbolize the rapture or "catching up" of God's people so that they can return with Him. The second harvest is God's judgment on the unrighteous culminating in the coming of Messiah Jesus.

As Jesus said, this all takes place at the very end of the Great Tribulation:

> *Immediately after the tribulation of those days the sun will be darkened, and the moon will not give its light; the stars will fall from heaven, and the powers of the heavens will be shaken. Then the sign of the Son of Man will appear in heaven, and then all the tribes of the earth will mourn, and they will see the Son of Man coming on the clouds of heaven with power and great glory. And He will send His angels with a great sound of a trumpet, and they will gather together His elect from the four winds, from one end of heaven to the other* (Matthew 24:29-31).

With this review, let's continue to see and hear what John sees and hears as God prepares to pour out His final seven judgments on the earth. May His Kingdom come and His will be done on Earth as it is in Heaven. Amen!

PREPARING TO BLOW THE SEVENTH TRUMPET-
SHOFAR JUDGMENT (REVELATION 15)

Remember that the story of the Book of Revelation really ends at the close of chapter 11. John is then given the "instant replay" recorded in the rest of the chapters.

What this means is that the scene in Revelation 15 is a detailed replay of what John saw only in part in Revelation 11:15-19. It is the same scene with the details added. When we read Revelation 11:15-19, we see clearly how it overlays Revelation 15. Because God's final judgments represent the end of the world as we know it, the Lord devotes an entire chapter to preparing readers for these judgments.

Chapter 15 is a heavenly scene where John is shown the preparation taking place for the destruction of the anti-God, one-world system. For the sake of study and understanding, we can divide the chapter into two sections. In the first section, John sees the overcomers giving glory to God, while in the second section, John sees seven angels being given the bowls of judgment.

The Overcomers Give Glory to God (verses 1-4)

In Revelation 12:1-3, John says that his vision of the woman with child and the dragon was a sign. Throughout history, and even in modern times, people consider unusual happenings in the sky to be signals from God that something important is about to happen on the earth. In Revelation 12 the important event was the birth of the Messiah on the earth. The Gospels also mention the sign of the Star of Bethlehem pointing to the Messiah's birth. The sign in Revelation 12:3 was satan being cast out of Heaven to the earth.

Now John says he sees another sign in Heaven that will affect the earth. This sign is preparation for the last seven judgments on the earth.

When John realizes what he is seeing, he does not call it a sign of doom and gloom, as we are often told. He calls it a great and marvelous sign. Yes, it is certainly doom and gloom for the wicked, but for the righteous, it is great and marvelous. And what is this sign? John sees seven angels with the last seven judgments of God.

John explains that when these seven judgments are released on the earth, they will bring to fulfillment or completion the holy wrath of God against evil. Hallelujah! With this proper perspective, we can join with John in calling this a great and marvelous sign.

While believers can rejoice, the wicked will weep and mourn. The Bible is clear that throughout history, God has taken the initiative by extending His love and mercy to all. It is not His desire that any should perish but that all would come to Him and receive forgiveness for sin and eternal life with Him. However, we also learn in the Bible (as I have shared many times in this writing), that God is also just and must judge those who reject His mercy. In our heart of hearts, we know this is true.

As we study the Bible and history, it seems that God has determined a certain period of time in which He would allow humankind the opportunity to respond to Him. Based on the Feasts of the Lord and God's biblical calendar, conservative Bible scholars believe this time is 6,000 years.

The Jewish sages divide time into three 2,000-year redemptive periods. They refer to the first 2,000 years before the giving of the Torah as the Age of Chaos. The second 2,000 years they call the Age of Torah. The last 2,000 years is called the Age of Messiah. The Age of Messiah is also called the latter days. When Jesus came the first time, it was the beginning of the latter days. His second coming will be the end of the latter days. That time has now come, and God prepares to release His last judgments against those who have made their final choice to reject Him.

In Revelation 4:6, John saw what looked like a sea of crystal glass before the throne of God. In discussing what John saw, I pointed out that he did not see a literal sea. He was using figurative language to describe the limitless splendor and riches and pure holiness of God as opposed to the limited and temporal riches of the emperors.

Once again, John's attention is focused on this sea. Here he adds an incredible observation: fire is now being mingled with the sea of crystal glass. What a sight! It would be like watching lighting flashing on a crystal clear body of water. I have seen a rainbow skip across the ocean, but never fire. The fire represents God's holy fire of judgment to be poured out. Even more remarkable, John sees the overcomers actually standing on the sea.

What is that about?

This whole scene takes us back to when God delivered His people from Pharaoh. When God parted the Red Sea, the Children of Israel were able to pass through the sea on dry ground with walls of water to their right and left. Put yourself in that setting and try to imagine being one of those Hebrews. God held back Pharaoh and his army with a pillar of cloud and fire until the Hebrews had passed through. When they were safely on the other side, Pharaoh and his army followed them. But God allowed the waters to return, and all the Egyptians drowned.

The Children of Israel watched this awesome scene—victorious and in their place of safety—as the blazing glory of God in the pillar of fire mingled with the waters of the Red Sea and brought them crashing down on Pharaoh and his army (see Exod. 14). What an incredible sight!

Just as the Lord helped the Children of Israel have a great victory over Pharaoh, He will help the children of God overcome the evil one. He will bring them to the place of safety and victory over the Beast—that is, satan, the anti-Messiah, the false prophet, and the anti-God, one-world system. No matter what difficulties the believers experience (even martyrdom), victory is certain.

Paul wrote to the believers at Thessalonica:

> *God did not appoint us to wrath, but to obtain salvation*
> *through our Lord Jesus Christ* [Messiah], *who died for us,*
> *that whether we wake or sleep, we should live together with*
> *Him. Therefore comfort each other and edify one another,*
> *just as you also are doing* (1 Thessalonians 5:9-10).

As John continues, we see even more clearly the connection of this heavenly scene to the Exodus story. Notice that these overcomers have all learned to play the harp. If you are not musically inclined in this life, you will be when you enter the throne room of God. Everyone will become skilled on King David's favorite instrument. Can you imagine being on King David's harp team along with millions of other believers?

John hears this great company of God's people (Jews and Gentiles) singing the Song of Moses and the Song of the Lamb. This company is the ultimate fulfillment of God's plan of redemption to make Jews and Gentiles to be "one new man" in the Messiah (see Eph. 2:14-22).

There are two Songs of Moses in the Hebrew Bible. The first one is recorded in Exodus 15:1-18. This is the great song of praise to God for delivering the people from Pharaoh. The second is recorded in Deuteronomy 32:1-43, when Moses was preparing to give his final blessing to the Children of Israel before he died. This Song of Moses ends with the following remarkable exhortation:

> *Rejoice, O Gentiles, with His people* [the Jews]; *for He will*
> *avenge the blood of His servants, and render vengeance to*
> *His adversaries; He will provide atonement for His land*
> *and His people* (Deuteronomy 32:43).

The scene that John sees in Revelation 15 is clearly the ultimate fulfillment of the closing words of this song as both Jews and Gentiles give glory to God, singing of His judgments on their adversaries and the atonement provided by the Lamb—just as they had sung earlier in Revelation 5:8-14. Wow! Our God is an awesome God.

Each line they sing comes from a corresponding passage in the Hebrew Bible. I have quoted just a few below. There are many similar verses. As we read these, let us praise our God for His greatness and goodness and His mighty acts of wonder and awe and redemption on the earth.

Who is like You, O LORD, among the gods? Who is like You, glorious in holiness, fearful in praises, doing wonders? (Exodus 15:11).

I proclaim the name of the LORD: ascribe greatness to our God. He is the Rock, His work is perfect; for all His ways are justice, a God of truth and without injustice; righteous and upright [just] is He (Deuteronomy 32:3-4).

Sing praise to the LORD, you saints of His, and give thanks at the remembrance of His holy name (Psalms 30:4).

Let all the earth fear the LORD; let all the inhabitants of the world stand in awe of Him (Psalms 33:8).

Among the gods there is none like You, O Lord; nor are there any works like Your works. All nations whom You have made shall come and worship before You, O Lord, and shall glorify Your name. For you are great, and do wondrous things; You alone are God (Psalms 86:8-10).

Oh, sing to the LORD a new song! For He has done marvelous things; His right hand and His holy arm have gained Him the victory....Shout joyfully to the LORD, all the earth; break forth in song, rejoice, and sing praises. Sing to the LORD with the harp, with the harp and the sound of a psalm (Psalms 98:1,4-5).

Exalt the LORD our God, and worship at His footstool— He is holy (Psalms 99:5).

I will meditate on the glorious splendor of Your majesty, and on Your wondrous works. Men shall speak of the might of Your awesome acts, and I will declare Your greatness. They shall utter the memory of Your great goodness, and shall sing of Your righteousness (Psalms 145:5-7).

Inasmuch as there is none like You, O LORD (You are great, and Your name is great in might), who would not fear You, O King of the nations?... (Jeremiah 10:6-7).

The LORD is the true God; He is the living God and the everlasting King. At His wrath the earth will tremble, and the nations will not be able to endure His indignation (Jeremiah 10:10).

The Tabernacle of the Testimony (verses 5-8)

As John continues to observe this incredible scene in Heaven, he sees the Temple of God and the Holy of Holies. The English wording in verse 5 could be clearer. The phrase, *"the temple of the tabernacle of the testimony"* means the inner room of the Temple, the Holy of Holies, which housed the Ark of the Covenant. This is the same scene that John saw in Revelation 11:19. The wording is clearer in that verse which says: *"The temple of God was opened in heaven, and the ark of His covenant was seen in His temple..."* (Rev. 11:19). The significance of the statement is that the Holy of Holies is open when it would normally be closed or concealed by a thick curtain (see Exod. 40:21).

This scene takes us back to the time when God told the Hebrews to make a tabernacle, or tent, where He would dwell among them. We read in Exodus where God said, *"Let them make Me a sanctuary, that I may dwell among them"* (Exod. 25:8).

Bible students will recall that the Tabernacle was divided into three sections: 1) the Outer Courtyard, 2) the first room called *the Holy Place,* and 3) the inner room called *the Holy of Holies.* When God gave Moses the Ten Commandments (called *the Testimony*), He needed a place to preserve them. So He instructed Moses to make a small chest to house them. This chest would be kept in the Holy of Holies. The chest is the Ark of the Covenant.

Exodus reads: *"You shall put into the ark the Testimony which I will give you"* (Exod. 25:16). We learn in the New Testament that the pot of manna and Aaron's rod that budded were also placed in the Ark of the Covenant (see Heb. 9:4).

God gave Moses specific instructions for making the Ark of the Covenant. The lid or top of the Ark was called *the Mercy Seat.* Statues of two cherubim angels were made and attached to the two ends of the Mercy Seat. God told Moses that He would meet with him in the Holy of Holies above the Mercy Seat.

Exodus reads:

> *You shall put the mercy seat on top of the ark, and in the ark you shall put the Testimony that I will give you. And there I will meet with you, and I will speak with you from above the mercy seat, from between the two cherubim which are on the ark of the Testimony, about everything which I will give you in commandment to the children of Israel* (Exodus 25:21-22).

(See Exodus 25–40 for the details God gave Moses regarding the Tabernacle.)

The Tabernacle was a portable structure that the Hebrews could carry with them in their 40 years of wandering through the desert. Later, when they settled in the land, King David wanted to build a permanent Temple as the central place of worship. However, since King David was a man of war, God did not allow him to build the Temple. His son, King Solomon, was given the assignment.

As we see the Temple worship scenes in Heaven, we realize that both the earthly Tabernacle and Temple were copies of the heavenly dwelling of God. They were "made according to the pattern" God gave Moses and later King David. They would be visuals or pictures on the earth of the eternal reality in Heaven.

In Revelation 15, John sees the seven angels coming out of the Holy of Holies. Their garments symbolize their purity and undefiled nature. One of the four special living beings gives them the seven golden bowls that John says are *"full of the wrath of God"* (Rev. 15:7). This is John's way of saying there is no more mercy coming from the Mercy Seat of God. There is only judgment as those who have opposed God have rejected His mercy.

These bowls, or basins, are the same kind of vessels used in the Tabernacle and Temple for catching the blood of the sacrifices offered to God. They represent both the mercy and the judgment of God.

On Yom Kippur, the Great Day of Atonement, the High Priest would sprinkle the blood on the Mercy Seat at the Tabernacle and Temple (see Lev. 17). God, looking down from His glory cloud, would see the blood covering the Ark of the Covenant. For that one day each year, He did not see the evidence of the people's sins represented by the pot of manna, Aaron's rod, and the stone tables. The innocent blood sacrifice changed God's throne from one of judgment to one of mercy. That was the administration of the blood covenant before the time of Jesus.

The blood of Jesus began the administration of the blood covenant that did away with the need for animal sacrifices. Whereas the blood of bulls and goats can only cover sin, the blood of Jesus takes sin away to be remembered no more. This is why the believers are singing the Song of Moses and the Song of the Lamb.

The slain but resurrected Lamb of God now sits at the right hand of God on the throne of the universe. It is His blood that the earthly sacrifices pictured. It is His blood that changes God's heavenly throne from one of judgment to one of mercy. Those who accept the blood of the Lamb of God as their innocent sacrifice for sin, receive God's mercy. Those who reject it receive God's judgment.

John sees the glory and power of God, like smoke, filling the Holy of Holies and the Temple. This manifestation of God was so awesome and holy that no one could enter the Temple until the judgments were complete.

John's vision again takes us back to the Tabernacle and Temple when God's glory appeared to the people. Exodus reads:

> The cloud [the manifested presence of God] *covered the tabernacle of meeting, and the glory of the* Lord *filled the tabernacle. And Moses was not able to enter the tabernacle of meeting, because the cloud rested above it, and the glory of the* Lord *filled the tabernacle* (Exodus 40:34-35).

Later, when the Temple was dedicated, the presence of God so filled the place that the priests could not even stand to minister.

> *The priests brought in the ark of the covenant of the* Lord *to its place, into the inner sanctuary of the temple, to the Most Holy Place, under the wings of the cherubim.... And it came to pass, when the priests came out of the holy place, that the cloud filled the house of the* Lord, *so that the priests could not continue ministering because of*

the cloud; for the glory of the LORD *filled the house of the* LORD (1 Kings 8:6,10-11).

As we contemplate the greatness and goodness of our God, may His glorious presence also fill our bodies and souls—each personal house of God. May we experience the cloud of God's glory so that we cannot stand under the weight of His manifested presence. May the worship of Heaven become our ever-present reality. Let this be our prayer today.

REVIEW QUESTIONS

1. Write a summary of what you have learned in this lesson. Write the summary in clear, concise words as if you were going to present it to another person.

2. Describe how you can apply what you have learned in this lesson to your life.

3. Share what you have learned with your family, friends, and members of your study group.

Chapter 5

The Seventh Trumpet-Shofar Judgment

REVELATION REVIEW

Our God is an awesome God. In His majestic greatness, He is sovereign over His handiwork, all-knowing, all-powerful, everywhere present, and unchanging in His being. In His moral character, He is perfectly holy, loving, just, and good.

God is all that He is as a unit. He is a "collective one." This means that He is not a component; He is not one part of Himself sometimes and other parts at other times. Because God transcends time and space, whatever He was, He is; and whatever He is, He will be. He is the "I AM."

God has always extended the fullness of who He is to us. From the time Adam and Eve sinned in the Garden until the final destruction of satan and evil, God reaches out to us in His complete self. His relationship to us comes from who He is and is not conditioned on or influenced by us. This means that God is always holy, just, loving, good, and merciful toward sinners—while simultaneously, his moral, holy anger, called *wrath,* burns against sin. His wrath is not a passing emotion as with humans. It comes from within His nature and is eternal, just as He is eternal.

Because God is morally perfect, His holy nature requires that the judgment for sin must be separation from Him. Since God is life, separation from Him is death. God's just nature requires that the judgment be paid. Yet, God's goodness and mercy do not desire us to pay the judgment ourselves. God's love came to earth and paid the judgment for us in the person of Jesus of Nazareth. This is the story of the Bible, from beginning to end.

This means that God's mercy is holy, loving, just, and good; and God's just judgment is holy, loving, merciful, and good. As we continue to study these horrific judgments, we must understand that they not only represent the justice of God, but also His mercy. God's judgments are not against sinners; they are against sin.

When we respond to God's mercy, His mercy is holy, loving, just, and good. This is because Jesus paid the just judgment for us, making God's just mercy available to us. When we do not respond to God's mercy, His just judgment of our sin is also holy, loving, merciful, and good. This is also because Jesus paid the just judgment of sin for us. God's justice and mercy meet at the cross of Jesus.

Because God's just mercy is within His nature, it is eternal. Those who respond to His just mercy will live with God in eternity. Those who reject His just mercy will live separated from Him for eternity in the realm of His just judgment.

The great example of God's just mercy in the Hebrew Bible is His dealings with Pharaoh. As noted in previous chapters, God's just mercy gave Pharaoh ten opportunities to repent. However, as we know, Pharaoh hardened his heart each time. Since Pharaoh refused to accept God's mercy, he experienced ever-increasing levels of God's just judgments. The final was death to the firstborn of Egypt.

The Book of Revelation is the great example in the New Testament of God offering His just mercy to those alive during this period of time in history. Instead of giving the people ten opportunities to repent, God gives them 21 opportunities to repent. These are manifested in the three seven-part judgments on the earth. Like with Pharaoh, each judgment is more severe than the previous one.

As we have explained, the seven seals are the first of the three seven-part judgments. They are described in Revelation 6:1-17; and 8:1-5. The seventh seal opens the seven trumpet-shofar judgments described in Revelation 8:6–9: 21; and 11:15-19. The seven trumpet-shofar judgments open the seven bowl judgments described in Revelation 16:1-21. Together, these judgments represent the just mercy of God extended to the people.

Also, as with Pharaoh, when the people harden their hearts to the place where they will never repent, God's just mercy is no longer offered to them. The unrepentant wicked bring God's just judgments on themselves. This is not what God desires, but He gives us a free will to accept or reject Him. So please, let us not ask the question, "How can a loving God allow such horrible things?" The better question is "How can a just God give us so many chances to repent?"

I am not the judge of any person. If people seek God with their whole heart, they will find Him. If they love God and want a relationship with Him more than they love their religious traditions, God will reveal Himself to them. God is bigger than religious doctrines, theology, and traditions. He looks at the heart rather than outward religious rituals.

The kind of relationship people have with God is between them and God. God loves everyone the same but only reveals Himself to people who truly want to know Him. I do not believe in nor embrace a "convert or die" theology as some teach. Having said that, during the Great Tribulation period, it will be clear whether someone truly has a relationship with God. Those who take the Mark of the Beast reject God and bring His just judgments on themselves.

As we will see in the following chapters, these judgments expose the hardness of the people's hearts toward God. Instead of repenting, they curse Him. This is the tragic end of the three seven-part judgments described in Revelation 16 (with further details given in Revelation 17–18).

These judgments climax with the coming of Jesus described in Revelation 19. Let's join John now as he explains the seven bowl judgments.

THE SEVEN BOWL JUDGMENTS (REVELATION 16)

In Revelation 15, John is told that one of the four living beings gave the seven bowls to seven angels. John learns that these bowl judgments contain the just judgments of God, for in them the wrath (holy anger) of God is fulfilled. Because God's just mercy has been rejected, His moral perfections require that He administer His just judgments on those who oppose Him. God administers these bowl judgments through the seven angels who pour them out on the wicked.

While these horrific judgments are being poured out on the earth, John sees the people of God who were martyred for their faith before the throne of God giving Him glory. Unlike those of us who often question God's judgments on the earth, these believers acknowledge that God's judgments are just and true. They know that God is not a cosmic Santa Claus. They know He is not a sentimental heavenly Father who can condone sin. He is a holy God who is not willing that any should perish. However, once His mercy is forever rejected, He must administer His just judgments.

These believers are not asking God for further mercy for their enemies. They are asking Him for justice. These bowl judgments are the final answer to their prayers.

The Command to Administer the Judgments (verse 1)

John hears a loud voice from the Temple. Although he does not identify the voice, it is most likely the Lord's voice. Isaiah said that he heard a voice from the Temple, which he identified as the voice of the Lord who fully repays His enemies (see Isa. 66:6).

The voice commands the seven angels to pour out the bowls of the wrath of God on the earth. Believers can take comfort in knowing that these judgments are not for them but are intended for those who took the Mark of the Beast.

In my opinion, these terrible judgments are poured out one right after the other in rapid succession. This happens right at the end of the Great Tribulation leading up to the coming of the Lord. These judgments most likely take place in just a few days' time or even on the last day, during which God completely destroys the anti-God, one-world system, which John sees happening in Revelation 17–18.

With this satanic kingdom destroyed, Jesus will come and establish the full measure of the Kingdom of God on the earth. Hallelujah! Our God reigns.

The First Bowl: Devastating Sores (verse 2)

The first bowl judgment is described as *"a foul and loathsome sore."* While the exact nature of this sore is not clear, it is extremely painful and repulsive in appearance. It obviously causes great physical suffering.

Because this judgment parallels the sixth plague in Egypt, it may be that the sore is a boil. The Lord instructed Moses and Aaron to take some ashes from a furnace and toss them toward Heaven while Pharaoh watched. The Lord then scattered the ashes throughout Egypt and they caused boils on the Egyptians. Exodus reads:

> *They took ashes from the furnace and stood before Pha-*
> *raoh, and Moses scattered them toward heaven. And they*

caused boils that break out in sores on man and beast (Exodus 9:10).

The text continues:

The magicians could not stand before Moses because of the boils, for the boils were on the magicians and all of the Egyptians. But the LORD hardened the heart of Pharaoh; and he did not heed them, just as the LORD had spoken to Moses (Exodus 9:11-12).

The English text that says *"the LORD hardened the heart of Pharaoh"* can be misleading. It means that God created a circumstance to test Pharaoh. However, Pharaoh would not repent but hardened his own heart against God because of the plague.

It is interesting to note the parallels between this plague in Egypt and the one in the Book of Revelation. Both are described as a sore. Both are done in the presence of the anti-God leaders (Pharaoh and the anti-Messiah). Both afflict only those who reject God. And in both instances, those who were judged had hardened their hearts against God instead of repenting.

The Second Bowl: The Sea Turns to Blood (verse 3)

The second bowl judgment is similar to the first plague in Egypt as well as the second trumpet-shofar judgment. John explains that the sea became like the blood of a dead man and everything in the sea died.

God's first plague against Pharaoh turned the Nile River and all the fresh water in Egypt to blood (see Exod. 7:14-25). It did not include the sea (most likely the Mediterranean). Of course, this made the water unfit to drink and killed all the fish. This is similar to the third bowl judgment.

There are parallels between God's judgments against Pharaoh and His judgments against the anti-Messiah. God poured out His judgment in sight of Pharaoh. The judgment was only against Pharaoh and the Egyptians, not the people of God. (Notice God's people were not raptured, they were protected. God's people are delivered only at the end of the judgments.)

Likewise, the bowl judgments in the Book of Revelation are poured out in the sight of the anti-Messiah, the false prophet, and the entire world which, like Egypt, is the anti-God empire. The judgment is only against those who have the Mark of the Beast. Like Pharaoh, the people harden their hearts against God.

In the second trumpet-shofar judgment, only a third of the sea became blood so that only a third of the creatures living in the sea died (see Rev. 8:8-9). Since that was only a partial judgment, people had the opportunity to repent. However, the bowl judgment is a total devastation of the sea. This is God's way of telling us that, because the people will not repent, His mercy is no longer possible.

The Third Bowl: The Fresh Waters Turn to Blood (verses 4-7)

As just noted, the third bowl judgment is also similar to the first plague in Egypt as well as the third trumpet-shofar judgment.

Exodus reads:

> *Moses and Aaron did so, just as the LORD commanded. So he lifted up the rod and struck the waters that were in the river, in the sight of Pharaoh and in the sight of his servants. And all the waters that were in the river were turned to blood* (Exodus 7:20).

The Scripture goes on to say that Pharaoh hardened his heart against God (see Exod. 7:22-23).

John explains that (in the third bowl judgment) all the fresh water turns to blood. Because God was judging Pharaoh and the gods the Egyptians worshiped, only the fresh water in Egypt turned to blood.

But in Revelation 16, God is judging the whole world. Therefore, all the fresh water on the whole earth turns to blood.

In the third trumpet-shofar judgment, only a third of the fresh water became bitter (see Rev. 8:10-11). God was giving the people an opportunity to repent. But since they refused to turn to Him, He now pours out the fullness or completeness of His just judgment (His holy wrath).

As John beholds this terrible judgment, he hears the angel who poured out this bowl worshiping God. Contrary to worldly people who refuse to accept or be accountable to a moral Creator, the angel proclaims God's righteousness in this judgment. The angel acknowledges the "rightness" of God's judgment. Because the wicked have shed the blood of God's people, God will judge them with blood.

In the Bible, this is known as the Law of Reciprocity or the Law of Sowing and Reaping. As Paul explains in Galatians: *"Do not be deceived, God is not mocked; for whatever a man sows, that he will also reap"* (Galatians 6:7). The angel notes that this judgment is the just due of the wicked. Where there is no more mercy, the wicked get just what they deserve.

As if to say, "Amen," John hears a voice from the altar also declaring God's judgments to be true and righteous (see Rev. 16:7). Whose voice did John hear? In my mind, he heard the voice of the martyrs from the altar in Heaven. We heard their voices in Revelation 6:10:

> *They cried with a loud voice, saying, "How long, O Lord, holy and true, until You judge and avenge our blood on those who dwell on the earth?"*

The Lord told them to wait until the time was right, and He would vindicate them (see Rev. 6:11). The pouring out of the seven bowl judgments is the time God had in mind. He is fully vindicating His people who were faithful even unto death. As they see these final judgments, they acknowledge God's faithfulness to them. He is the Lord God Almighty and His judgments are true and righteous.

The Fourth Bowl: The Scorching Sun (verses 8-9)

In the fourth bowl judgment, God continues to demonstrate His sovereignty over His creation. In this instance, it is the sun. In the fourth trumpet-shofar judgment, God darkened the sun, the moon and the stars for a third of the day and night. This judgment is just the opposite. He heats up the sun so hot that it scorches those who have the Mark of the Beast.

God has used the sun in times past to accomplish His purposes. Joshua and his army were fighting, and winning. But Joshua became concerned that the sun would go down before they could completely destroy their enemy. According to the Bible, Joshua commanded the sun to stand still. God honored his faith by stopping the sun until the enemy was fully defeated.

Joshua reads:

> *Joshua spoke to the LORD in the day when the LORD deliv-*
> *ered up the Amorites before the children of Israel, and he*
> *said in the sight of Israel: "Sun stand still over Gibeon; and*
> *Moon, in the Valley of Aijalon." So the sun stood still, and*
> *the moon stopped, till the people had revenge upon their*
> *enemies* (Joshua 10:12-13).

Tragically, instead of repenting, the people in Revelation 16 reveal what is in their hearts by cursing God. They demonstrate that they have the same character and hatred of God as the anti-Messiah they are following. They are one in that they both blaspheme God as we learned earlier:

> *They worshiped the dragon who gave authority to the*
> *beast; and they worshiped the beast, saying, "Who is like*
> *the beast? Who is able to make war with him?" And he*
> *was given a mouth speaking great things and blasphe-*
> *mies, and he was given authority to continue for forty-two*

months. Then He opened his mouth in blasphemy against God, to blaspheme His name, His tabernacle, and those who dwell in heaven (Revelation 13:4-6).

Many people think that if God would just reveal Himself clearly to people, they would believe in Him. Oh, how I wish this were true. Instead, it is a very naïve understanding of the human heart. Do not be deceived, we can harden our hearts to the point that we become completely irrational in our thinking regarding God. We can go so far as to lose any ability to repent and seek Him.

The Bible warns us about this spiritual condition:

As the Holy Spirit says: "Today, if you will hear His voice, do not harden your hearts as in the rebellion, in the day of trial in the wilderness, where your fathers tested Me, tried Me, and saw My works forty years" (Hebrews 3:7-9).

The Hebrews saw God perform mighty signs and wonders on their behalf for 40 years. Yet, most still did not worship Him. So they perished in the desert. There are millions of people like this today. Because they are amoral and secular, they cannot see the connection between national and personal tragedies and their sinful behavior. When their situations go from bad to worse, they curse God rather than repent. When godly leaders point out this connection, they curse them as well and marginalize them as being religious fanatics.

The Fifth Bowl: Darkness (verses 10-11)

The fifth bowl judgment is similar to the fourth trumpet-shofar judgment except, with this judgment, there is total darkness. John specifically mentions that the darkness is directed toward the throne of the Beast. To John's first-century readers, this would be Rome. For those of us living in the endtimes, the throne of the Beast is the center of the anti-Messiah's one-world political and religious system. Exactly where that is will become clear as events unfold.

This judgment is a repeat of God's ninth plague against Pharaoh and Egypt. In a Scripture we referenced previously, we read: *"The LORD said to Moses, 'Stretch out your hand toward heaven, that there may be darkness over the land of Egypt, darkness which may even be felt'"* (Exod. 10:21). The darkness in Egypt lasted three days. It was so dark, the people couldn't see anything. But the Children of Israel had light in their dwellings (see Exod. 10:22-23).

Can you imagine being in such total darkness that you cannot see your hand in front of your face? As in Egypt, this is a selective judgment on those who oppose God. It is not a judgment against God's people. As pointed out previously, God seals His people to protect them from His wrath.

This total natural darkness corresponds to the total spiritual darkness of those who oppose God. They cannot see physically or spiritually. John notes that the people are already suffering greatly as a result of the previous judgments. Yet, like Pharaoh, they do not repent. They continue to blaspheme God. There are no human words to describe the depths of the horror of rejecting God. It is too painful to contemplate.

The Sixth Bowl: Euphrates River Dries Up (verses 12-16)

In this next to last bowl judgment, John sees the Euphrates River dry up. Why the Euphrates River? And why is it dried up?

In the sixth trumpet-shofar judgment, we learned that the Euphrates River was the most important river in Bible times. In the Hebrew, its name means to "break forth."[1] Beginning in the mountains of Turkey, the Euphrates River, along with the Tigris, broke forth from the mountains and provided the necessary water for the whole region to prosper. These rivers were important in the development and prosperity of Ur, the biblical city where Abraham lived (see Gen. 11:31).

With its life-giving waters traversing 1,780 miles from Turkey to the Persian Gulf, the flow of the Euphrates River enabled the forming of ancient civilizations such as the Assyrians, Babylonians, Sumerians, and others. The Euphrates and Tigris rivers run parallel to each other before coming together to empty into the Persian Gulf. In fact the word *Mesopotamia* is a Greek word meaning "the land between the rivers."[2] (Euphrates and Tigris).

The Garden of Eden was located near the Tigris and Euphrates Rivers (see Gen. 2:14 NASB). It was also the boundary of the land God promised to Abraham, Isaac, Jacob, and their descendants (see Gen. 15:18). Because of its prominence, the Bible sometimes refers to the Euphrates simply as *"the river"* or *"the great river"* (Deut. 11:24; Gen. 15:18). Everyone in Bible times knew which river was being referred to.

Because of its greatness, no one in John's time would ever have imagined the Euphrates River drying up. What a crazy idea! What was John thinking when he wrote this? His first-century readers must have shaken their heads in disbelief. They would not shake their heads if they were living in our times, because the great river is indeed drying up.

The Euphrates flows through Turkey, Syria, and Iraq. (Iraq is geographically located in the area of ancient Babylon.) These three countries compete with each other for the river's precious water. Because the Euphrates originates in Turkey, it has the upstream advantage over Syria and Iraq when it comes to using the waters for its own needs. Syria has the upstream advantage over Iraq.

Both Turkey and Syria have built numerous dams to harness the waters of the Euphrates for irrigation and hydroelectric power. By the time the Euphrates reaches Iraq, much of its waters have already been diverted. Furthermore, the Iraqi government and Iraqi farmers along the Euphrates have greatly mismanaged the use and conservation of the river. To make matters worse, there has been a severe drought in the region for several years. Where there was once an abundance of water, some areas are now mud and hard clay. This situation is having a devastating effect on the farmers who depend on the Euphrates for their livelihood. Concerned officials are fearful that the great river will soon be half what it is today.

Yes, the great Euphrates River is clearly drying up. The only possible way John could see this prophetically is if God showed it to him in his apocalyptic vision. The fulfillment of this vision is one of the most important signs that we are living in the end days of history before the coming of the Lord.

John explains that the drying up of the Euphrates River enables the kings from the east to "break forth" across it, bringing their armies to gather with the armies of the world in the battle of the great day of God Almighty. When discussing the sixth trumpet-shofar judgment, I noted that the Euphrates River formed the boundary between East and West and was the Eastern limit of the Roman Empire. In the first century, Rome's most feared enemy east of the Euphrates was the Parthians. John, however, sees a worldwide battle when God gathers the armies of all the nations in a central place to destroy them. This is why the battle is called the battle of that great day of God Almighty.

God allows demonic spirits coming from the mouth of the dragon, the anti-Messiah, and the false prophet to persuade world leaders to gather for this last great battle, which will end in their own destruction. Much like the demonically empowered magicians in Egypt (see Exod. 8:7-19), the demonic spirits work through satan, the anti-Messiah, and the false prophet to entice and deceive the leaders, convincing them to bring their armies into the *great winepress of the wrath of God*" (Rev. 14:19).

There is a story in the Hebrew Bible that serves as a precedent for these lying spirits deceiving world leaders. It also involves an apocalyptic vision like John's.

Here's what happened in First Kings 22:

King Ahab was the King of Israel (the northern kingdom). He asked King Jehoshaphat (king of the southern kingdom) to join with him to attack Syria. God was going to convince King Ahab to attack Syria because He planned to use the Syrians to kill Ahab, because he was so wicked. God put a lying spirit in the mouths of 400 false prophets to tell King Ahab that he would defeat the Syrians. Now King Jehoshaphat knew these were false prophets, so he asked for a true prophet of God to prophesy.

King Ahab reluctantly sent for the prophet Micaiah, who at first mocked the king by telling him what he wanted to hear. When the king told Micaiah to tell him the truth, Micaiah said, *"Hear the word of the LORD: I saw the LORD sitting on His throne, and all the host of heaven standing by, on His right hand and on His left"* (1 Kings 22:19).

When you read this verse do you really think Micaiah was raptured to Heaven? Of course not, he had a vision just like John did, which he described in Revelation 4:1.

Micaiah then explains a conversation he heard between God and a spirit:

> *The LORD said, "Who will persuade Ahab to go up, that he may fall at Ramoth Gilead?" So one spoke in this manner, and another spoke in that manner. Then a spirit came forward and stood before the LORD, and said, "I will persuade him." The LORD said to him, "In what way?" So he said, "I will go out and be a lying spirit in the mouth of all His prophets." And the LORD said, "You shall persuade him, and also prevail. Go out and do so." Therefore look! The LORD has put a lying spirit in the mouth of all these prophets of yours, and the LORD has declared disaster against you* (1 Kings 22:20-23).

Because of the wickedness of world leaders, God has declared disaster against them. He is going to destroy them all in the last great battle at the coming of Jesus. In view of the hardness of their hearts and their rejection of truth, God allows them to be deceived by the lying spirits calling them to come to this battle.

The apostle Paul wrote of this end-time deception:

> *The coming of the lawless one is according to the working of Satan, with all power, signs, and lying wonders, and with all unrighteous deception among those who perish, because they did not receive the love of the truth, that they might be saved. And for this reason God will send them strong delusion, that they should believe the lie, that they all may be condemned who did not believe the truth but had pleasure in unrighteousness* (2 Thessalonians 2:9-12).

John informs us that the armies of the world will come together at Armageddon. In Hebrew this word is *Har Megiddo* or *Har Megiddon*, which essentially means "the Mount or Hill (*Giva*) of Megiddo."[3]

The Hill of Megiddo overlooks the town of Megiddo and the vast Jezreel Valley, where many scholars believe the armies will assemble for this battle. Furthermore, the Hill of Megiddo is located strategically at the junction where the ancient main road from Egypt (*Via Maris* or Way of the Sea) makes a northeast turn toward Syria. Ancient trade caravans as well as armies traveled this route. Whoever controlled the Hill of Megiddo controlled the entire region.

Historically, many battles have taken place in this area. The Hebrew Bible tells us that Deborah and Barak defeated the Canaanites in the Jezreel Valley. Gideon defeated the Midianites here as well. (See Judges 4–8.) Due to its strategic location, King Solomon made the Hill of Megiddo a fortress for defending the pass and the valley (see 1 Kings 9:15-19). Pharaoh Necho defeated King Josiah at Megiddo (see 2 Kings 23:29). In more modern times, both Napoleon and General Allenby defeated the Turks near Megiddo. In fact, General Allenby was given the title, "Earl of Megiddo." Today, the Hill of Megiddo is a major archeological dig and a must-stop for tourists.

It seems that Megiddo is the staging area for these armies as they make their way toward Jerusalem, where the climax of the battle against God will take place. Zechariah prophesied about this battle when Messiah comes. He says that the inhabitants of Jerusalem will mourn when they realize that it is Jesus, the "pierced One" they had rejected (see Zech. 12:10). He compares their mourning to the time when Pharaoh Necho defeated King Josiah, saying: *"In that day there shall be a great mourning in Jerusalem, like the mourning at Hadad Rimmon in the plain of Megiddo"* (Zech. 12:11).

Zechariah further says:

> *Behold, I will make Jerusalem a cup of drunkenness to all the surrounding peoples, when they lay siege against Judah and Jerusalem. And it shall happen in that day that I will make Jerusalem a very heavy stone for all peoples; all who would heave it away will surely be cut in pieces, though all nations of the earth are gathered against it....In that day the LORD will defend the inhabitants of Jerusalem; the one who is feeble among them in that day shall be like David, and the house of David shall be like God, like the Angel of the LORD before them. It shall be in that day that I will seek to destroy all the nations that come against Jerusalem* (Zechariah 12:2-3;8-9).

Before pouring out the last bowl judgment, Jesus warns the people one last time to be watching for His return. He compares His coming to a thief who comes when no one expects it. He reminds them to be awake and sober as watchmen and keep their garments handy. By this, He means they should be dressed spiritually in pure garments. The Lord had already given this warning to the congregations at Sardis and Laodicea. (See Revelation 3:2-5; 3:18.)

In His teaching recorded in Matthew 24, Jesus said:

Watch therefore, for you do not know what hour your Lord is coming. But know this, that if the master of the house had know what hour the thief would come, he would have watched and not allowed his house to be broken into. Therefore you also be ready, for the Son of Man is coming at an hour you do not expect (Matthew 24:42-44).

The apostle Paul gave the same instructions with these words:

Concerning the times and the seasons, brethren, you have no need that I should write to you. For you your-selves know perfectly that the day of the Lord so comes as a thief in the night. For when they say, "Peace and safety!" then sudden destruction comes upon them, as labor pains upon a pregnant woman. And they shall not escape. But you, brethren, are not in darkness, so that this Day should overtake you as a thief. You are all sons of light and sons of the day. We are not of the night nor of darkness. Therefore let us not sleep, as others do, but let us watch and be sober (1 Thessalonians 5:1-6).

The Seventh Bowl: The Earth Is Shaken (verses 17-21)

The seventh bowl is the last judgment against the anti-God, one-world system. In Revelation 16:1, John heard a loud voice from the Temple telling the seven angels to pour out the bowl judgments. Now, John again hears a loud voice from the Temple and the throne. No doubt, this is again the voice of God Himself announcing the end.

When the voice declares, *"It is done!"* (Rev. 16:17), this clearly connects to when Jesus said, *"It is finished!"* (John 19:30). Both refer to the final act of divine judgment against sin. Jesus took the judg-ment for us on the cross. Now, those who reject Him must bear the judgment themselves.

When God opened the seventh seal, He announced it with *"noises, thunderings, lightnings, and an earthquake"* (Rev. 8:5). Now for the pouring out of the seventh bowl judgment, the Creator of the universe once again announces His final judgment with noises, thunderings, lightnings, a great earthquake, and this time, hailstones (see Rev. 16:17-21). These are God's weapons of mass destruction.

Since the physical earth is cursed because of sin, it has experienced many natural upheavals in its long history. The earth itself suffers due to humankind's rebellion against God. This is why there are earthquakes, tornadoes, hurricanes, tsunamis, and many other natural disasters on the earth. Jesus prophesied this in His teaching about future events on the earth (see Matt. 24). The apostle Paul wrote that all of creation groans and labors with birth pangs waiting to be delivered from the curse of sin it has endured (see Rom. 8:20-22). Now that time of waiting is coming to an end.

But first, there will be one last earthquake. This will be the "mother of all earthquakes" as it will destroy Babylon and all its cities, as well as sink every island and level every mountain. Wow! This is beyond our ability to comprehend.

John says that the earthquake will split Babylon into three parts (see Rev. 16:19). As I have noted before, to John's first-century readers, Babylon meant Rome. To his last-century readers (us), it means the revived Babylonian-Roman, anti-God, world system. We are not sure what city John is specifically referring to, but he is clear that the capital city of the anti-Messiah and all the cities of the nations aligned with him will be destroyed.

In Revelation 11:15-19, the seventh angel announced that the seventh trumpet-shofar was about to be blown. This was the proclamation that the Kingdom of God was coming to destroy the kingdoms of this world. In Revelation 14:6-10, an angel repeated the proclamation and added some details regarding the fall of Babylon.

The seventh bowl judgment is the fulfillment of those proclamations. It is the "instant replay" with more details. Revelation 17–18 provides the final details. All of these pronouncements and proclamations are telling about the same event—the final judgment of God's undiluted, "full-strength" wrath (righteous anger) against satan and his human followers.

God finishes off whatever is left standing from the earthquake with a rain of 100-pound hailstones. The Lord used this same weapon in His seventh judgment against Pharaoh and to aid Joshua when He also made the sun stand still (see Exod. 9:13-35; Josh. 10:11-13).

How did the people respond? Did they repent and cry out to God for mercy? No, they continued to blaspheme God just as Pharaoh hardened his heart (see Exod. 9:34-35). How ironic that God decreed that the judgment for blaspheming His name was stoning (see Lev. 24:16). Here God stones them from Heaven. (See Joel 3 for a prophetic description of God's final judgment of the nations.)

In the next two chapters, John is shown the details of God's judgment on the anti-God, one-world system. It is the last "instant replay" of the fall of those who oppose God. Their fall ushers in the coming of Jesus and the establishment of the literal Kingdom of God on the earth. May His name be praised forever.

Review Questions

1. Write the summary in clear, concise words as if you were going to present it to another person.

2. Describe how you can apply what you have learned in this lesson to your life.

3. Share what you have learned with your family, friends, and members of your study group.

NOTES

1. Biblesoft's New Exhaustive Strong's Numbers and Concordance
    with Expanded Greek-Hebrew Dictionary. CD-ROM. Biblesoft,
    Inc. and International Bible Translators, Inc. (© 1994, 2003,
    2006) s.v. "Perath," (OT 6578).

2. Ibid., s.v. "Aram Naharayim" (OT 763).

3. *Blue Letter Bible,* Dictionary and Word Search for
    "Harmagedōn" (Strong's 717), Blue Letter Bible, 1996-2012,
    < http:// www.blueletterbible.org/lang/lexicon/lexicon.
    cfm?Strongs=G717&t=KJV > (accessed July 18, 2012). Also
    Biblesoft's New Exhaustive Strong's Numbers and Concordance,
    s.v. "har" (OT 2022); s.v. "Megiddown" (OT 4023); and s.v.
    "gib`ah" (hill) (OT 1389).

Chapter 6

The Destruction of the World Religious System

REVELATION REVIEW

THE Book of Revelation is not a book of doom and gloom, though it is often presented that way. It is not a book about the anti-Messiah, the Mark of the Beast, or 666. It is a book about the exalted Son of Man—Jesus the Messiah, Savior, Lord, and Redeemer of humankind.

Jesus promised that He would return to the earth at which time His Jewish brethren would rule and reign with Him in the Kingdom of God. Until that time, God would call out a people among the Gentiles who would embrace His eternal covenant through a personal relationship with Jesus.

During this long period of time, the Jewish people would be scattered among the nations. However, God promised them that He would preserve a remnant of the descendants of Abraham, Isaac, and Jacob. Then in the latter days, God would bring these descendants back to their ancient land. He would make Israel the head of nations under the righteous rule of the Messiah. This would be the golden age about which the prophets spoke.

Throughout history, satan, the adversary of God, has worked to hinder the fulfillment of God's plan. His primary strategy for achieving this has been his efforts to destroy the Jews. Apparently, satan believes he can defeat God by keeping the Jews from fulfilling their God-given destiny. Inspired by satan, one dictator after another has sought to rid the world of the "Jewish problem." Yet, every last one has failed. The Book of Revelation describes satan's last attempt to usurp God's authority by destroying the Jews and Israel. This evil effort will hasten his demise and the return of Jesus.

The Jews are an eternal people because God has made an eternal covenant with Himself to bless them. His covenant blessings include all the non-Jews (Christians) who have put their faith in Jesus. They have been adopted into the Jewish family of God and become part of the Commonwealth of Israel. God has made both Jew and believing Gentile one new man in the Messiah (see Eph. 2:15). One day soon both Jewish and non-Jewish believers will join their voices and cry out to God, *"Baruch HaBa B'Shem Adonai,"* which means "Blessed is He who comes in the name of the Lord" (see Matt. 23:39).

The period of time between the first and second coming of Jesus is known as the Times of the Gentiles. Jesus said, *"...Jerusalem will be trampled by Gentiles until the times of the Gentiles are fulfilled"* (Luke 21:24).

Revelation chapters 17 and 18 describe the end of the Times of the Gentiles. This is the culmination of the seventh seal, the seventh trumpet-shofar, and the seventh bowl judgment. As mentioned, these judgments are not for God's people but against those who oppose Him. They are God's answers to the prayers of His people, asking Him to vindicate them and judge the unrighteous.

This final judgment on the nations is preceded by great upheavals in the heavens and on the earth. There is great suffering by those who take the Mark of the Beast. Instead of repenting, they curse God and His followers. While we grieve when people suffer, this is all necessary as the Kingdom of God comes to the earth. God must destroy the evil kingdoms of this world in order to establish His Kingdom. His judgments are true and righteous. While this is a time of great fear and dread for those who oppose God, it is a time of great hope and expectation for God's people who are waiting for the Messiah.

Jesus said it this way:

> *There will be signs in the sun, in the moon, and in the stars; and on the earth distress of nations, with perplexity, the sea and the waves roaring; men's hearts failing them from fear and the expectation of those things which are coming on the earth, for the powers of the heavens will be shaken. Then they will see the Son of Man coming in a cloud with power and great glory. Now when these things begin to happen, look up and lift up your heads, because your redemption draws near* (Luke 21:25-28).

DESTRUCTION OF THE WORLD RELIGIOUS SYSTEM (REVELATION 17)

With this brief review, let's now join John as he learns the fate of the anti-God, one-world system. In Revelation 17, John sees the final destruction of the religious system. His vision continues in Revelation 18, where he is given understanding about the final destruction of the political system. As the Times of the Gentiles come to an end, John sees the coming of the Messiah to judge and make war against the followers of satan and the anti-Messiah. Revelation 19 describes this glorious event when the Lamb of God returns as the Lion of the Tribe of Judah. Hallelujah!

The Great Harlot and the Beast (verses 1-6)

As noted in the previous chapter, Revelation 17–18 are the final "instant replays" of the destruction of the anti-God, one-world system. Revelation 17 has two parts. In the first part (verses 1-6), John is given a spiritual vision of the great harlot. In the second part (verses 7-18), John is told the meaning of the vision. He is made to understand the mystery of the harlot and the Beast.

As we study Revelation 17–18, keep in mind that John is using apocalyptic symbolism to describe earthly empires, events, structures, and leaders. He explains some of his symbolism and leaves some unexplained. But even when he does explain, he does so in guarded terms using code words in order to disguise his meaning from the prying eyes of the authorities.

John's first-century readers would have understood his symbolism, but it isn't as clear for us today. While we want to understand John's meaning, we don't want to focus on the symbolism but rather on the spiritual realities they represent for our times. It is important that we keep this perspective and priority.

One of the angels who had the seven bowls shows John the great harlot and the Beast in their evil splendor, drunk with the blood of God's people. The great harlot is the religious counterpart of the anti-Messiah's political system. Working in alliance with the anti-Messiah, it is the religious world power ruling over the souls of humankind. Filled with riches and arrogance, it has martyred many of God's people and appears to have been victorious. To the natural eye, it seems the wicked have prevailed over the righteous. Where is God in all of this? Where is there hope for His people?

The angel provides the answer that cannot be seen with the natural eye. He shows John God's final judgment on the harlot that results from the outpouring of the seven bowl judgments. The angel mentions that the harlot sits on many waters. In Revelation 17:15, the angel explains that the many waters symbolize the nations and people of the world. The clear idea the angel is communicating is that the religious system is ruling over and influencing the souls of the people of the world—those who have taken the Mark of the Beast.

The angel further explains that both the world leaders and the people have committed fornication with this religious system. We have previously explained that the Bible calls idolatry a type of spiritual adultery. We recall that this was the problem with the congregation at Thyatira. They were allowing a woman referred to as Jezebel to seduce believers into worshiping idols and committing immorality. The Lord severely rebuked the congregation for accepting this unholy teaching and practice.

The religious system is called the great whore because it is serving as a spiritual prostitute to the wicked. They have not just taken a sip of the wine of her fornication; the angel says they are drunk with it. They have continued to drink of this cup with the prostitute. Like alcoholics, they want more and more until they have lost all control of their spiritual senses. In their spiritually drunken state, they have taken the Mark of the Beast, cursed God, and persecuted the believers. There is no "politically correct" way to say this. They have sold their souls to satan. They are beyond redemption and the mercy of God.

The angel wants John to have another view of the harlot to help him better understand what he is seeing. Using apocalyptic language, John says that the angel carries him away in the Spirit into the wilderness (desert). John uses the phrase *"in the Spirit"* four times in the Book of Revelation (1:10; 4:2; 17:3; 21:10). As I have previously shared about John's "in the Spirit" statements, he does not mean that he literally went into the desert. (See my comments regarding Revelation 4:2 in Chapter 1 of this book.) He means that the Holy Spirit opened his spiritual eyes to see what he could not know in the natural.

From this "in the Spirit-desert view," John sees the harlot sitting on a scarlet Beast. The fact that the harlot is sitting on the Beast implies that the harlot is strongly influencing or perhaps, even dominating, the Beast, but with its willing support. This simply means that the harlot and the Beast need each other at this point. They are using each other for their own purposes but that will soon change.

The Beast was full of names of blasphemy and had seven heads and ten horns. A few verses later the angel explains the seven heads and ten horns to John. We will seek to understand his meaning when we discuss those verses.

We were first introduced to this scarlet Beast in Daniel 7. We can also clearly connect the scarlet Beast to Revelation 12:3, where we see a similar description of the fiery red dragon (satan). The description is repeated in Revelation 13:1, where we learned about the Beast From the Sea (the anti-Messiah and anti-God Beast system). Since these descriptions are all similar, we can understand that they are talking about the same satanically inspired and empowered anti-God, one-world system through different world leaders in different time periods of history. The most prominent are Babylon, Rome, and the end-of-days anti-God, one-world system.

As John mentioned previously in Revelation 13:1, the Beast has blasphemous names written on him. In ancient times, emperors were thought to be the human embodiment of the gods of the nation. Therefore, they had the names of the gods inscribed on their crowns, garments, staffs, statues, etc. In addition, as we have learned, they often deified themselves and were referred to as gods, saviors, lords, masters, rulers of the universe, etc.

Historically, John would be writing about Rome, the Roman Empire, and the Roman emperors. To readers at the end of the age, he is referring to satan, the anti-Messiah, and the anti-God, one-world system. Both the personal Beast and the Beast system would have the Mark of the Beast and other blasphemous names written on them and on everything representing them.

The harlot is dressed as a prostitute would have dressed in Bible times. For example, when God rebuked Israel for giving herself to the gods of the pagans, He said the following:

> *When you are plundered, what will you do? Though you clothe yourself with crimson, though you adorn yourself with ornaments of gold, though you enlarge your eyes with paint, in vain you will make yourself fair; your lovers will despise you; they will seek your life* (Jeremiah 4:30).

As we will soon discover, this is exactly what the Beast does to the harlot in the Book of Revelation.

The dress of the harlot symbolizes her wealth and position. The word *purple* (see Rev. 17:3) should probably be translated as blue or reddish blue. The blue dye was an extremely expensive color to produce in Bible times. The dye came from the blood of a hillazon snail. It took 12,000 of these snails to fill a thimble. In 200 B.C., one pound of blue cloth cost the equivalent of $36,000. By the year A.D. 300, a pound of blue cloth cost about $96,000. It is the same blue dye that God commanded the Hebrews to wear in one of the tassels *(tzitzit)* of their four-cornered garments.

Numbers describes the tassles:

> *Speak to the children of Israel: Tell them to make tassels on the corners of their garments throughout their generations and to put a blue thread in the tassels of the corners* (Numbers 15:38).

Because a garment with this blue dye was so expensive, it was only worn by royalty and priests. Aaron's garment of glory and beauty was made of blue, purple, and scarlet (see Exod. 39:1). This is why the Hebrew males only had one thread dyed blue. The significance of God giving this instruction is that the blue dye was a constant reminder to the people that they were all the royal priests of God.

The garment the harlot is wearing also has scarlet. This color is obtained from the eggs of a certain insect. In Bible times, scarlet was a vibrant crimson color. It was also too costly to be purchased by the average person. Scarlet not only denoted wealth and royalty; it was also a symbol of sin and harlotry. For example, the Lord says: *"Though your sins are like scarlet, they shall be as white as snow; though they are red like crimson, they shall be as wool"* (Isa. 1:18). Even in our modern world, we apply the scarlet color to an immoral woman.

To further clothe herself with majesty and splendor, the harlot wore gold, precious stones, and pearls. Wow! This is really a beautiful and expensive garment, one any woman would be thrilled to wear. It should be clear to us by John's description of her clothing that the harlot is in a position of wealth, power, and prestige. She is wearing satan's counterfeit royal-priestly garment of glory and beauty. In her outward appearance, she is beautiful and alluring and seductive. It is easy to see why the people of the world would follow her.

While John further observes this harlot, he notices that she has a golden cup in her hand. As with her garment, this cup symbolizes her wealth and prominence. She only has the best, and she has it on display for everyone to see. Her followers would certainly be impressed and enticed.

However, as John describes her outward beauty, he sees what she really is on the inside. The golden cup is *"full of abominations and the filthiness of her fornication"* (Rev. 17:4). To first-century readers, this is the most graphic description of evil that John could give. This is what the angel wanted John to see.

The abomination refers to the ultimate act of sacrilege or desecration of that which is holy. When Antiochus Epiphanes set up an altar to Zeus in the Temple of God in 167 B.C., that was an abomination to the One True God. Jesus spoke of *"the abomination of desolation...standing in the holy place..."* (Matt. 24:15). The imperial cult worship was an abomination of desolation. The anti-Messiah and the false prophet taking the place of God is an abomination of desolation. Anytime religion tries to take the place of God, it is an abomination of desolation.

John relates this act of abomination to spiritual fornication. Using highly descriptive language, John says that this harlot, who is so attractive on the outside, is inwardly as unclean spiritually and morally as a prostitute. Yet, because the people have rejected truth, God has given them over to the allure and deception of this deadly harlot. She is a gold cup in God's hand from which the people drink the wine of their own destruction.

John's words echo those of Jeremiah when he spoke of ancient Babylon: *"Babylon was a golden cup in the LORD's hand, that made all the earth drunk. The nations drink her wine; therefore the nations are deranged"* (Jer. 51:7). John revisits this verse in the next chapter when he speaks of political Babylon.

John sees that the harlot has words written on her forehead. As pagan priests and priestesses had marks on their bodies and clothing identifying them with their gods and goddesses, so this harlot is finally identified. Whereas her identity has been a mystery, she is now revealed as the source of all pagan religions originating in ancient Babylon.

A brief review is helpful as a reminder of the connection between the ancient Babylonian religion, Rome, and the harlot of the book of Revelation. I explained this previously in Volume One in the chapter about Pergamos. (Much of the following information is taken from my book, *The End of All Things Is at Hand: Are You Ready?*[1])

We go back to Genesis where we learn about the infamous Nimrod in Genesis 10:8-11 and Genesis 11. Nimrod was the first person we know of in the Bible who started a war. He wanted to conquer his neighbors for the purpose of establishing an empire with himself as the ruler. His first conquest was Babel, which later became Babylon and the great Babylonian Empire of the days of Nebuchadnezzar. Babylon was one of the greatest cities of the ancient world. He also built Nineveh, another great city, which became the capital of the Assyrian Empire.

Now here is where this history really gets interesting. Historians and scholars tell us that Nimrod built what we call the Tower of Babel. It was a ziggurat or temple built in the form of a pyramid for the purpose of worshiping the sun and exalting Nimrod as the high priest of the sun. This temple was to be the center of his empire. Nimrod was a great promoter who presented himself as the human incarnation of the sun god. This was the beginning of sun worship and emperor worship and all pagan religions.

When Nimrod died, his wife, Semiramis, claimed she was impregnated by the sun god and miraculously gave birth to a son named Tammuz. She also was a great promoter. She told the people that Tammuz was the reincarnation of Nimrod. Since she was perceived as the "Mother of God," she and Tammuz were worshiped as the Mother-Son cult. She was the Mother of God and Queen of Heaven, and her son was the reincarnation of the Father.

At this time, all the people spoke the same language. God saw that this powerful idolatry would seduce all the inhabitants so He confused their languages and scattered them. When the people scattered, they took their sun worship and worship of the Queen of Heaven with them. As they formed new empires and civilizations, this became their form of worship. The names were changed to the new languages the people spoke and there were local adaptations of the worship, but it was basically the same sun worship that began with Nimrod. In a similar manner, Mother-Child worship was also an integral part of sun worship and passed from one empire to the next with only the names and local practices differing.

The Chaldean/Assyrians called the sun god by the name of Bel or Ba`al. The Egyptians called him Osiris. Nebuchadnezzar and the Babylonians worshiped the sun god as Bel-Merodach. The Persians called him Mithra. The Greeks called him Zeus (Adonis). The Romans called him Jupiter. This was the religion of Constantine when he established Christianity as the official religion of the Roman Empire.

We learn in the Bible that even God's people were influenced by this all-pervasive religion. Ezekiel tells us that the women were at the Temple in Jerusalem *"weeping for Tammuz"* (see Ezek. 8:14). Jeremiah 7:18 says the women were making cakes for the Queen of Heaven.

Scholars believe that Nimrod's sun worship religion was the origin of all pagan religions that were passed down to succeeding empires. Let's review how this happened. When Persia defeated Babylon, the Persians adopted and adapted Babylonian sun worship into their own religion. Persia became the new world power with a mix of Babylonian and Persian sun worship. Fearing for their lives, many of the Babylonian priests fled to Asia Minor, where they established their spiritual center at Pergamos. Later, local Pergamos kings became the spiritual heirs of Nimrod's Babylonian sun worship.

While Alexander established Greek mythology throughout the Mediterranean region, it did not replace Babylonian-Persian sun worship. It flourished alongside it. Therefore, when Rome became the new power in the Mediterranean world, the center of Nimrod's religion passed from Pergamos to Rome. The Caesars embraced and incorporated the Babylonian form of sun worship into their own blend of paganism, which they assimilated from the cultures they conquered. The Caesars accepted the title and position as the King-Priest of both the Roman government and the Roman version of the old Babylonian religion. Thus, the Roman political order and Roman religious order, while separate entities, were one and the same.

The Roman Emperor Constantine was a sun worshiper. In order to unite the religion of his empire, he made cosmetic changes to Babylonian sun worship, and blended it with the emerging Christian faith. Constantine redefined Christianity into a Greco-Roman religion so it would be accepted by his pagan subjects who also worshiped the sun. While it is certainly good that Constantine stopped the persecution of believers, his actions had tragic consequences for the purity of Christianity and Judeo-Christian relationships.

Constantine and his successors spread his new form of Roman-ized Christianity throughout Europe—with the sword. It is still with us today in various forms and will reestablish itself in some final redefined expression as part of the worldwide, end-time harlot mentioned in the Book of Revelation.

What Revelation 17–18 seems to be describing is the all-embracing, last-days religion that will continue to seduce the world until God finally judges it at the coming of the Lord. It will contain all the ele-ments of ancient and modern religions synergized into a one-world political-economic-religious system. This will certainly include apos-tate Christianity and secular Judaism.

Throughout history, Constantine's form of Christianity has not only persecuted Jews, but also the remnant of true Bible believers. As the politically-correct religious establishment of "Christian" Europe, it has martyred millions of people who did not accept its perversion of biblical Christianity. John sees the end-time harlot still drunk with the blood of the followers of Jesus. John is amazed at the revelation of the true nature of the harlot.

The Explanation of the Vision (verses 7-18)

The angel seems surprised that John was astonished about the nature of the harlot. He explains the mystery of the harlot and the Beast to John. As we learn what the angel has to say, keep in mind that Baby-lon was the code word for Rome. To John's immediate audience (the seven congregations), Babylon meant Rome, the Roman Empire, and the Roman emperors.

Since the Roman religion and the Roman government were united under the emperors, the Babylon of Revelation 17 and the Babylon of Revelation 18 are basically two sides of the same coin. One is the *religious* Babylon while the other is the *political* Babylon. It is hard to separate the two. What is said about one equally applies to the other. This is why the wording in these two chapters is so similar. John is writing about the same Beast system, just different administrations of it. Furthermore, as I have noted, the beast of Rome is seen by scholars and theologians as the model of the final Beast person and system in the latter days of world history.

The angel explains that the seven heads on the Beast are seven mountains upon which the harlot sits. In the Bible, mountains are sometimes used as a figure of speech to mean kingdoms. For example, do you remember when Daniel saw the stone cut out of the mountain in Daniel 2? He explained that the stone became a great mountain (kingdom). (See Daniel 2:34-35;44-45.) That mountain referred to the Kingdom of God coming to the earth.

The angel further confirms that the seven mountains are seven kings. He explains that five of these kings have fallen, one is, and the other is yet to come. The one yet to come will only rule for a short time. The angel also says that the Beast is the eighth ruler or system that will emerge from the seventh. He reminds John that the Beast comes out of the bottomless pit and will *"go to perdition* [be destroyed]" (Rev. 17:8; see also 11:7).

Prophetically, the eighth beast is the anti-Messiah. The people of the world are mesmerized by the presence and power of the Beast. We remember that both the Beast person (the anti-Messiah), and the Beast system are empowered by satan. (See Revelation 13.)

The angel also explains the meaning of the ten horns. He says they are ten kings waiting for their time to rule. Until then, satan working through the anti-Messiah allows them to rule for one hour with the Beast person and system. One hour is also mentioned in Revelation 18, verses 10, 17, and 19. The mention of one hour may be literal or symbolic of a short period of time. Either way, they are only in power for a short time. They recognize the superiority of the Beast person and system and submit themselves to him (it). These ten horns may be the same as the ten toes from Daniel 2. This was discussed previously in Revelation 13 and clearly connects to Revelation 17–18.

The angel states what seems to be the real message of the Book of Revelation. He says of these anti-God rulers:

These will make war with the Lamb, and the Lamb will overcome them, for He is Lord of lords and King of kings; and those who are with Him are called, chosen, and faithful (Revelation 17:14).

The angel clarifies for John that the many waters over which the harlot sits are the people of the world who have been deceived by the false prophet and have taken the Mark of the Beast. Yet, all along, the anti-Messiah and his Beast system have hated the harlot. When he and his political leaders no longer need the harlot to seduce the people, they turn on her.

John describes their satanic hatred in the most graphic terms. He writes: *"The ten horns which you saw on the beast, these will hate the harlot, make her desolate and naked, eat her flesh and burn her with fire"* (Rev. 17:16).

Leviticus 21:9 says that the judgment for the daughter of a priest who becomes a prostitute is to be burned with fire. Even this turn of events is orchestrated by God so that there will be no competition between the false prophet and the anti-Messiah. All will submit to the rule of this evil incarnation of satan himself who will be worshiped as God.

Finally, the angel explains that the woman is the great city that reigns over the kings of the earth. Babylon, the code word for Rome, is also called the *"great city"* in Revelation 14:8 and Revelation 18. The understanding John wants us to have is that the Beast person and system, both political and religious, have their roots in ancient Rome. It will reemerge in the latter days in a one-world system that has the same anti-God culture and character as Rome.

For centuries, scholars have tried their best to identify the seven heads. They have connected them to the Roman emperors beginning with Augustus. Others have connected them to seven ancient empires beginning with Egypt. While John's first-century audience probably knew who and what he was talking about, we don't. The passing of time has obscured his meaning for us. We would all like to be able to understand everything that John wrote about, but God will make it clear to us when we need to know.

I greatly appreciate all the scholars and theologians who have given so much of their lives to help us understand some of the more difficult parts of the Book of Revelation. Sound biblical scholarship is important and needed. However, it grieves my heart when Christian leaders spend so much of their time giving their opinions and speculations about the parts of the Book of Revelation we don't fully understand.

As I have said, the Book of Revelation is not primarily about the rapture, the anti-Messiah, the Mark of the Beast, the false prophet, etc. It is about the exalted Son of Man-Son of God. While these speculations may be interesting to believers, they do not help them in their walk with God. As a result, they do more harm than good. That is why I have not filled this book with the different theories of Christian leaders. We cannot put God in our Western theology charts.

Let us not spend our time debating and arguing about these issues. It is much more important for us to realize that a New World Order is coming, and it is an anti-God, one-world system that seeks to take the place of God and persecute God's people. We would do better to spend our time developing our personal relationships with God and each other and spiritually preparing ourselves to live in such a world. God will show us the meaning of John's words as the events about which he is writing unfold. The most important understanding we need is that God is sovereign, Jesus is Lord, evil will only briefly have its way, God will crush the wicked, and His people will overcome.

Hallelujah!

REVIEW QUESTIONS

1. Write a summary of what you have learned in this lesson. Write the summary in clear, concise words as if you were going to present it to another person.

2. Describe how you can apply what you have learned in this lesson to your life.

3. Share what you have learned with your family, friends, and members of your study group.

NOTE

1. Dr. Richard Booker, *The End of All Things Is at Hand: Are You Ready?* (Alachua, FL: Bridge-Logos, 2008). You can order this book directly from my online bookstore at www.rbooker.com.

Chapter 7

The Destruction of the
World Political System

REVELATION REVIEW

In previous chapters, we have noted again and again that God our Father in Heaven loves us. As human beings, we mirror this relationship of love between parents and children. Human parents love their children because they are their own flesh and blood. The DNA of the parents is in their children. It is only natural, then, that parents love their offspring, even when they misbehave. But good parents will discipline their children when necessary. When I was a child, this was the norm. Today, it is called "tough love."

Because the life of the parents is in the children, the children also naturally love their parents. This love between parents and progeny is not something forced on us. It is natural and comes as a result of our own free will. However, because of our failings as human beings, sometimes parents and children become estranged. They may harden their hearts against one another to the point that they choose to break off further relationship. Sadly, this often becomes a way of life.

God loves us. He loves us because it is His nature to love. Because God created us, His DNA is in us. In other words, God made us in His image and after His likeness (see Gen. 1:26). This does not refer to us looking like God. God does not have a human body. God is spirit. Simply put, to be made in God's likeness and image means that we have an intellect and the ability to make things. Of course, God makes things from nothing, but we need to use something He has already made in order to make new things.

Being made in His image and likeness also means that God made us as moral beings with a free will. We can choose to love God or we can choose to break off relationship with Him.

Like human parents, God loves us even when we misbehave. If He didn't, we would all be in big trouble. However, unlike human parents, God's love is holy and just. God is longsuffering with us and full of mercy. When we go astray, He takes the initiative to encourage us to return to Him. We call this repenting. However, if we harden our hearts so that we will not and cannot repent, God's nature requires that He judge us, and His judgments are true and just. Deep in our hearts we know this is the way of life between God and His human creation.

In the Book of Revelation, we see God extending His love to those who have rebelled against Him. He offers forgiveness and mercy to those who respond. But to those who have hardened their hearts, God must administer His just judgments. We have studied these judgments in the form of the seven seals, the seven trumpet-shofars, and the seven bowls. Each time God released a new judgment, it was His desire that people would respond and repent. But as happened with Pharaoh, there comes a time when God makes it clear that people are not going to repent. Therefore, God must administer His holy and righteous judgments undiluted and without mercy. This is what we see happening in Revelation 17–18.

Earlier, in the fifth seal, God's martyrs cried out for justice. They asked God how long they would have to wait before He would avenge their deaths. The Lord told them to wait just a little longer and He would judge those who had persecuted them. (See Revelation 6:9-11.) In Revelation 17–18, we learn that their wait is over.

In the previous chapter, we discovered the mystery of the religious harlot who was drunk with the blood of the martyrs and the blood of the saints. To first-century readers, the harlot was Rome, the great city that reigns over the kings of the earth.

To believers living in the endtimes, she is the mother of all harlots, incorporating in herself the spiritual idolatry and fornication of all pagan religions of all time but specifically that of Babylon and Rome. Led by the false prophet, she is the religious expression of the anti-God Beast system. She has great wealth and power and influence over the anti-Messiah, the nations, and those who took the Mark of the Beast. Yet, when the anti-Messiah and his political leaders no longer need the harlot, they turn on her and destroy her. John learns that God put this in their hearts.

DESTRUCTION OF THE WORLD POLITICAL SYSTEM (REVELATION 18)

As John marvels at the disclosure and destruction of the harlot, another angel brings revelation about the destruction of the political Beast. This is God's final judgment that ushers in the coming of Jesus to establish His Kingdom on the earth. Since the political and religious nature of Babylon, Rome, and the latter-day Beast have common characteristics; John describes their destruction in terms similar to those used in Revelation 17. Let's join him now as he is a spiritual eyewitness to God's final judgment.

Announcing the Fall of Babylon (verses 1-8)

Throughout the Book of Revelation, the Lord has used angels to communicate His messages to John and administer His judgments on the earth. After seeing the fall of religious Babylon, John sees another angel proclaiming the fall of political and economic Babylon. This angel is so powerful that John says his presence illuminates the whole earth. Wow! This is beyond our natural ability to grasp.

We don't know if John means this literally or if he is using apocalyptic language to describe the brilliant appearance of this angel. Either way, we should be encouraged that God has a spectacular future for us on the other side of this life. As Paul wrote: *"I consider that the sufferings of this present time are not worthy to be compared with the glory which shall be revealed in us"* (Rom. 8:18).

The angel loudly proclaims that Babylon the great is fallen. He repeats the phrase, "is fallen" as if to punctuate his proclamation and infer Babylon's complete and utter destruction. This same proclamation was given in Revelation 14:8 which says: *"Another angel followed, saying, 'Babylon is fallen, is fallen, that great city, because she has made all nations drink of the wine of the wrath of her fornication.'"*

So we will not get bogged down in the details, a review is in order at this point to help us see how this information is presented and recorded in John's Revelation. Revelation 11:15-19 tells us that the seventh angel blows the seventh trumpet-shofar to announce the last judgment. The angel does not give the details; he only announces the judgment. The announcement is that *"The kingdoms of this world have become the kingdoms of our Lord and of His Christ [Messiah]…"* (Rev. 11:15).

This same information is given as an "instant replay" with more details in Revelation 14:6-20. This is the preview of the end we studied earlier in our explanation of Revelation 14. Then John sees and records the final details in a last "instant replay" in Revelation 15–18. This means that we can overlay Revelation 11:15-19 on top of Revelation 14:6-20 and Revelation 15–18. They all tell the same story with a different degree of detail.

The angel explains that, in spite of its appearance to the contrary, Babylon is the abode of demons and everything that is unclean. What an accurate commentary on how the world system perceives itself. The world glories in its riches, its power, its great structures and cities, its music and arts, its knowledge and technology, its beauty and lusts. But to God, it is the abode of demons and unclean spirits. May we also see the world system as God sees it and refuse to live for its pleasures.

Repeating what John was told in Revelation 14:8, the angel informs John that Babylon is now being judged because it has become drunk with the wine of its spiritual idolatry and immorality. It has blasphemed God and persecuted His people. It accepted satan's offer of the riches of the world—the same offer that Jesus rejected (see Matt. 4:8-11). It has sold its soul for wealth and power. It is the final and ultimate embodiment of greed. It is surely Rome of the first century but much more than Rome. It is the final anti-God, one-world system ruled over by satan and his representatives, the anti-Messiah and the false prophet.

Paul warned against the entrapment of materialism with these words:

> *Those who desire to be rich fall into temptation and a snare, and into many foolish and harmful lusts which drown men in destruction and perdition. For the love of money is a root of all kinds of evil, for which some have strayed from the faith in their greediness, and pierced themselves through with many sorrows* (1 Timothy 6:9-10).

How sad that many believers today have not heeded Paul's words.

Before continuing with this part of our study, it would be very helpful to flash back. Pause and read Revelation 11:15-19 and 14:6-20 again. Then read again the comments I made when discussing those Scriptures. I gave the explanation of Babylon and the prophecies about its destruction when commenting on the verses in Revelation 14:6-13. Also, for the full background of the fall of Babylon, read Isaiah 13, Isaiah 21:1-10, and Jeremiah 50–51. These prophecies had an immediate reference to the fall of ancient Babylon, but they also predict the fall of the end-time Babylon of the Book of Revelation.

I was startled when John heard another voice (in Revelation 18), probably God's voice, saying, *"Come out of her, my people, lest you share in her sins, and lest you receive of her plagues"* (Rev. 18:4).

Because of all that John has seen and written to God's people, the Lord Himself gives the warning, telling His people to come out of Babylon or suffer His just judgments along with those who have rejected Him. He who has an ear, let him hear.

The Lord issued the same warning to His people when they were captives in Babylon:

> *Flee from the midst of Babylon, and everyone save his life! Do not be cut off in her iniquity, for this is the time of the LORD's vengeance; He shall recompense her* (Jeremiah 51:6).

In Jeremiah's prophecy, the Lord was calling the people to physically come out of Babylon and return to the land of Israel. In John's prophetic word, the Lord is calling the people to spiritually come out of the world system that is like Babylon and Rome, and turn to Him. If these believers do not heed God's warning, they will partake of the sins and the plagues of this wicked and demonic system God is judging.

Surely believers today must take seriously John's warning in one of the letters he wrote:

> *Do not love the world or the things in the world. If anyone loves the world, the love of the Father is not in him. For all that is in the world—the lust of the flesh, the lust of the eyes, and the pride of life—is not of the Father but is of the world. And the world is passing away, and the lust of it; but he who does the will of God abides forever* (1 John 2:15-17).

The sins of first-century Rome and this latter-day Babylon have reached to Heaven like Nimrod's Tower of Babel (see Gen. 11:4). God can no longer withhold His judgment against her. The angel cried out to God to judge Babylon with a double portion of calamity because of the magnitude of her sins. As she has terrorized the believers, may God give her a double portion of terror. As she has lived in prideful arrogance and self-indulgent luxury and pleasure, may God give her a double portion of sorrow. There is no plea here for mercy. It is too late for mercy; it is time for the full, undiluted judgment of God.

Daniel 5 records the judgment of ancient Babylon because of their pride and blasphemies against God. In this chapter describing the hand writing on the wall, God tells King Belshazzar that his kingdom is finished. That same night Belshazzar was killed and the Medes replaced Babylon, establishing themselves as the new empire. (See Daniel 5:22-31.) In like manner, John learns that God will destroy this end-time Babylon by fire in one day.

This scene reminds us of the time when God warned Lot to leave Sodom before He destroyed it. When Lot was reluctant, the angels forced him to take his family and leave. God then destroyed Sodom and Gomorrah with fire and brimstone in one day. (See Genesis 19.) Here the Lord is again warning His people to leave this wicked anti-God, one-world system before He completely destroys it.

The World Mourns the Fall of Babylon (verses 9-20)

Four times John calls this Beast system the "great city" or the "great city Babylon" (see Rev. 18:10,16,19,21). He had already identified the harlot as *"that great city"* (Rev. 17:18). As I have shared, our best understanding is that this is John's way of naming Rome, but with a prophetic look to the end-time world system that is the ultimate expression of Rome. The harlot and the political-economic world power are seen as one with the Beast system and the great city. In my view, they are one and the same.

John mentions three different groups of people and explains how they react to the fall of Babylon. These are the kings of the earth, the merchants of the earth and the sea, and the people of God. He begins with the kings of the earth.

In modern times, the kings of the earth would be the political leaders of the anti-God, one-world system. John uses the same words he used in Revelation 17:2 when he mentioned that the kings of the earth committed fornication with the harlot. The idea is that both the political leaders and the religious leaders are spiritual adulterers. They worship satan and have sold their souls to him in order to maintain their power, position, and rule over the people. We might say they are greedy, corrupt politicians who will say and do anything to stay in power.

When these godless political leaders see their governmental world capital burning, they distance themselves lest they too be consumed by the judgment fire of Almighty God. However, this action will not save them as the King Messiah will soon destroy them as well. Their response is to wail and mourn as God is bringing to an end the system they worshiped and thought was "too big to fail." These world leaders have given their lives to promote and protect their anti-God, one-world system. Now they see it burning to the ground. Everything they have loved, worshiped, and worked for is destroyed in one hour.

The merchants of the earth respond in the same way the political leaders do. These are the people who took the Mark of the Beast so they could prosper. With the Beast system destroyed, there is no way for them to sell their goods. The economies and financial markets of the nations have collapsed. All the manufacturers, Wall Street, financial markets, service organizations, stores, and shopping malls have been destroyed. The merchants wail and mourn as they realize there is no one to buy their goods.

The products John describes are luxury items, not basic goods people need such as food, clothing, and shelter. The idea John is presenting is a materialistic world of luxury and self-indulgence. Their most important priority is to make money. Now their wealth and prosperity are gone. Their gold and silver could not save them. Like the politicians, they stand at a distance in deep anguish and despair. Their world has come to an end. All they loved, trusted in, and valued—gone in one hour.

John summarizes their loss with these words:

> *The fruit that your soul longed for has gone from you, and all the things which are rich and splendid have gone from you, and you shall find them no more at all* (Revelation 18:14).

John further notes that the merchants of the sea who made their fortunes trading with the Beast system wail and mourn as well when they see the great city on fire. The world system has come to an end and all who have prospered from it are left as desolate as the system itself. Everything they gave their lives for has gone up in smoke in one hour.

This scene is similar to what Ezekiel wrote about when he pronounced God's judgment on the city of Tyre, a wealthy seaport city located in present-day Lebanon. It was a renowned city but it was also an anti-God pagan city that persecuted God's people. Furthermore, like Babylon and Rome, Tyre was a city that embodied the evil of satan himself. When Ezekiel pronounced God's judgment on Tyre, those who profited from its commerce wailed and mourned like the others. (See Ezekiel 26–28.)

Whether it is Tyre, Babylon, Rome, modern nations, or the Beast of the Book of Revelation, the warning is the same. God will eventually judge those who oppose Him and persecute His people. The words of Jesus are certainly appropriate: *"What will it profit a man if he gains the whole world, and loses his own soul?"* (Mark 8:36).

When the city of Rome was the world's capital, it was the center of an incredible amount of economic activity and prosperity. There was full employment and work for everyone. Not only did the local businesses prosper but merchants throughout the Mediterranean world brought their goods to Rome. They became rich doing business with Rome. Not only did they trade goods, but they also bought and sold slaves who did the work that ordinary Romans thought beneath them.

It was a Roman world and everyone who traded with Rome prospered.

When Nero was emperor, he wanted to build a monument to himself in Rome. However the area where he wanted to build was already overbuilt. What did Nero do? In A.D. 64, he burned the buildings to make room for his monument. Historians tell us that the fire lasted for days and burned much of the city. Merchant ships ready to unload their goods and ships at sea waiting their turn saw the smoke as Rome burned and wailed in anguish at the loss of their income. John sees a repeat of this situation with the latter-day Babylon-Rome.

The martyrs in Heaven and the apostles and prophets of God make up the third group John mentions. Their response is certainly different from the others. Instead of weeping and wailing, a voice tells them to rejoice for God has finally avenged them. Their wait for justice is over. The wicked anti-God, one-world system that has persecuted them for so long has come to an end. The kingdoms of this world have been destroyed making way for God's Kingdom to come to the earth.

God's Final Judgment on Babylon (verses 21-24)

As a final statement emphasizing God's judgment against the Beast, John sees a mighty angel pick up a stone that he compares to a great millstone. Millstones were used to grind grain and olives to produce flour and oil. A millstone was a basic tool everyone needed. Symbolically, it represented economic activity and the ability of the people to produce their food.

A large millstone would be so heavy no one could even move it much less pick it up. When John says that an angel picks up a stone that is like a great millstone, he is giving a vivid word picture of the power of this angel. With great force, the angel throws the huge stone (we would say *boulder*) into the sea, and it sinks to the bottom. Likewise, God is going to violently throw down the great city with its anti-God, one-world system. Figuratively speaking, like the unsinkable *Titanic*, it will sink to the bottom of the ocean. Unlike the *Titanic*, there will be no survivors. All will sink with Babylon. The great city, which represents the end-time Beast system, will be silent.

God has used this same prophetic act in the past as a picture of His judgment on Babylon. We earlier noted Jeremiah's prophecy against ancient Babylon recorded in Jeremiah 50–51. Jeremiah wrote God's judgment against Babylon on a scroll and gave it to Seraiah, who went into captivity with King Zedekiah. Jeremiah told Seraiah that when he got to Babylon he was to read the judgments, tie a stone around the scroll, and throw it into the Euphrates River. As the scroll sank to the bottom of the Euphrates, so Babylon would sink, never to rise again.

Jeremiah reads:

> It shall be when you have finished reading this book, that you shall tie a stone to it and throw it out into the Euphrates. Then you shall say, "Thus Babylon shall sink and not rise from the catastrophe that I will bring upon her..." (Jeremiah 51:63-64).

John clarifies again that God has judged ancient Babylon, Rome, and this end-time embodiment of those pagan empires because they killed His people. As we will learn in the next chapter, this action from God causes all of Heaven to give Him glory in response to the exhortation in Revelation 18:20. The wicked world system empowered by satan is destroyed. The way is prepared for the King Messiah, the exalted Son of Man-Son of God to return to earth.

Let the people of God rejoice.

REVIEW QUESTIONS

1. Write a summary of what you have learned in this lesson. Write the summary in clear, concise words as if you were going to present it to another person.

2. Describe how you can apply what you have learned in this lesson to your life.

3. Share what you have learned with your family, friends, and members of your study group.

Chapter 8

The Second Coming of Messiah

In the Book of Genesis, God created Adam and Eve to fellowship with Him and rule over His creation. Genesis 1 explains:

> *God created man in His own image; in the image of God*
> *He created him; male and female He created them. Then*
> *God blessed them, and God said to them, "Be fruitful and*
> *multiply; fill the earth and subdue it; have dominion over*
> *the fish of the sea, over the birds of the air, and over every*
> *living thing that moves on the earth" (Genesis 1:27-28).*

God gave Adam and Eve a free will to obey or not obey Him. Tragically, they chose not to obey God. When they disobeyed God, they lost their God-given authority and right to rule over His creation. Satan usurped their authority and established an anti-God world system that has been in place since Adam and Eve were expelled from the Garden of Eden. In Revelation 17–18, we see that system coming to an end.

Beginning with Abraham, God put in motion His plan to take back control from satan and return it to humankind. The Bible is God's record of how He called a people through whom He would accomplish this task. We learn about how God advanced His plan in history through Moses, King David, and the Hebrew prophets. Because of sin and human failures, none of God's own people were worthy to receive the authority and right to rule for Him as God originally intended Adam and Eve to do.

So God prepared for Himself a body and became one of us in the person of Jesus of Nazareth. In His first coming, Jesus fulfilled His mission as the Lamb of God who died for our sins. After He was resurrected, His followers asked Jesus, *"Lord, will You at this time restore the kingdom to Israel?"* (Acts 1:6).

Jesus replied:

> *It is not for you to know times or seasons which the Father has put in His own authority. But you shall receive power when the Holy Spirit has come upon you; and you shall be witnesses to Me in Jerusalem, and in all Judea and Samaria, and to the end of the earth* (Acts 1:7-8).

Jesus clarified that He would not physically establish God's Kingdom on the earth when He was resurrected. He would establish it spiritually in the hearts of His people instead. However, in God's own time, He would return as the worthy One through whom God would restore His rule over the earth, through a man.

The story in Acts continues:

> *When He had spoken these things, while they watched, He was taken up, and a cloud received Him out of their sight. And while they looked steadfastly toward heaven as He went up, behold, two men [angels] stood by them in white apparel, who also said, "Men of Galilee, why do you stand gazing up into heaven? This same Jesus, who was taken up*

from you into heaven, will so come in like manner as you saw Him go into heaven" (Acts 1:9-11).

Jesus ascended to Heaven to take His rightful place as the exalted Son of God-Son of Man. Throughout history, He has ruled in the hearts of His people. As Jesus prophesied, His people have been His witnesses throughout the world. By His unconditional love and forgiveness, Jesus has conquered the hearts of billions of people who acknowledge Him as their Lord and King. There is no other explanation for this phenomenon except the one given in the Bible.

Now in the Book of Revelation, we learn that it is God's time and season for Jesus to return and establish His literal Kingdom on the earth. But first, He must destroy the anti-God, one-world system of satan. John describes this final clash of kingdoms in Revelation 17–18.

The Second Coming of Messiah
(Revelation 19:1-16)

In Revelation 19, we see the return of Jesus to establish God's physical Kingdom on the earth. Jesus will unite in Himself both the spiritual and literal aspects of this Kingdom. By returning as the Lion of the Tribe of Judah, Jesus will rule over Israel and the nations as King of the Jews, King of kings, and Lord of lords. He will defeat satan and rule as God's righteous representative on the earth.

Let's join John as he describes this glorious appearing of our Lord.

A Celebration in Heaven (verses 1-6)

We can divide Revelation 19 into four parts. They are: 1) A Celebration in Heaven, 2) Announcing the Marriage Supper of the Lamb, 3) The Second Coming of Messiah, and 4) The Battle of Armageddon. We will study the first three parts in this chapter and the last one in the next chapter.

The celebration in Heaven that ended Revelation 18 continues in the first six verses of chapter 19. John hears all of Heaven celebrating the downfall of satan's anti-God, one-world system. While humans often blame God for their suffering, the great company of worshipers in Heaven acknowledges that God's judgment on the harlot system is true and righteous and just. They declare again that God has judged the demonically inspired system for its spiritual fornication and to avenge the blood of the martyrs who cried out for justice. (See Revelation 6:10.)

This worship and acknowledgment of God's righteous judgment is by the same company of people who earlier sang, *"Salvation belongs to our God who sits on the throne, and to the Lamb!"* (Rev. 7:10). It is the same company of people who sang the Song of Moses and of the Lamb, saying:

> *Great and marvelous are your works, Lord God Almighty!*
> *Just and true are Your ways, O King of the saints! Who*
> *shall not fear You, O Lord, and glorify Your name? For*
> *You alone are holy. For all nations shall come and wor-*
> *ship before You, for Your judgments have been manifested*
> (Revelation 15:3-4).

While this was an incredible time of worship and praise, a voice came from the throne exhorting the great multitude, the 24 elders, and the four living beings to even greater heights of praise. Their response was so loud John compared it to the sound of mighty thundering and the roaring sound of many waters. They all shouted, "Hallelujah!" (from the Hebrew) or (from the Greek) *"Alleluia! For the Lord God Omnipotent reigns!"* (Rev. 19:6).

This was the original "Hallelujah Chorus." The word *hallelujah* comes from two Hebrew words: *halal* and *Yah*.[1] When combined, the word means "Praise Yah(weh)," or "Praise God," or the more general phrase, "Praise the Lord."

Yah is the abbreviation of *Yahweh*, the covenant name of God. In regard to the English spelling of God's covenant name, there is no letter "J" in Hebrew. *Yahweh* is mistranslated into English as "Jehovah."

King David used this phrase recorded many times in the psalms. Like the voice exhorting the heavenly host to praise God, King David said:

> *Let the righteous be glad; let them rejoice before God; yes, let them rejoice exceedingly. Sing to God, sing praises to His name; extol Him who rides on the clouds, by His name YAH, and rejoice before Him* (Psalms 68:3-4).

Hallelujah (Alleluia) is only found four times in the New Testament—all in Revelation 19.

Announcing the Marriage Supper of the Lamb (verses 7-10)

The great multitude praising the Lord now begins to celebrate the marriage supper of the Lamb. What is this about? The Bible tells us that God wants to have a personal relationship with us. One of the ways God communicates this to us is through various expressions we can understand in human relationships. In our relationship with God, these are figures of speech that we would not understand literally. The following information is based on what I have written in my book, *Here Comes the Bride.*[2]

For example, in the Hebrew Bible, God calls Israel to be His bride-wife. When God delivered the Hebrews from Egypt, He said to them: *"I will bring you out…I will rescue you…I will redeem you…. I will take you as My people, and I will be your God…"* (Exod. 6:6-7).

God is using marriage talk when He says He will "take" the Hebrews. He means that He will acquire them as a bride.

Isaiah clarifies:

"Your Maker is your husband, the LORD of hosts is His name; and your Redeemer is the Holy One of Israel; He is called the God of the whole earth. For the LORD has called you like a woman forsaken and grieved in spirit, like a youthful wife when you were refused," says your God (Isaiah 54:5-6).

Some scholars see Israel as the wife of *Yahweh* and the followers of Jesus as the Bride of Christ [Messiah] as if they are two separate groups. It is true that spiritually God needs a wife to have a Son. From a covenant standpoint, Israel is that wife and Jesus (Yeshua) is His Son born to Israel. His Son has a Bride, both Jewish and non-Jewish believers. However, these are figures of speech God uses so we can understand that He wants to have an intimate relationship with us.

God's covenant bride-wife is neither Jew nor Gentile. God has made us one with Him and in Him through the marriage covenant in the blood of Jesus. His Spirit in us joins us to Himself and to each other as one company of people. God is in us and we are in Him in a covenant union like a marriage. (Paul makes this very clear in First Corinthians 6:17; Galatians 3:26-29; Ephesians 2:11-22; etc.)

In Bible times, a Jewish marriage had three phases. The first phase was the betrothal. A young man, with help from his father, would prepare a marriage contract for the young woman. This marriage contract was, and still is, called a *ketubah*. It is a formal written document stipulating the terms of the marriage.

Once the contract was prepared, the young man would go to the house of the young woman and present the contract to her (and her father). We would call this his proposal of marriage. This is not as romantic as our modern way of proposing, but the boy and girl are too young to actually have a wedding and live together as husband and wife anyway. That will come later.

The most important part of the proposal was the bride price—the amount of money the young man was willing to pay the father for the right to marry his daughter. The young man would pour a glass of wine and set it on the table. This glass of wine was called the cup of acceptance. It represented the blood covenant union the two would have when they came together as husband and wife. If the young woman drank from the cup, she was saying "Yes" to the marriage proposal.

The couple was then betrothed to one another. The young woman was legally his bride although they were not yet ready or able to live together as husband and wife. The bridegroom would then give the young woman gifts as tokens of his love. The nearest we come to this tradition in modern times is the engagement period.

Before leaving the house of his newly betrothed, the young bridegroom would tell her that he was going to return to his father's house and prepare a place for her. This was usually a room added on to his father's house. It was the wedding chamber or *chuppah*. He assured her that he would come again and bring her to himself that where he was, she would be also. The young man's father decided when the room was complete and when it was time for him to go get his bride. Whenever someone asked him when he was returning for his bride, the young man would reply, "I don't know, only my father knows."

In the meantime, the young bride made herself ready so she would be prepared when her young man came to get her. She used the gifts he had given her to make herself attractive for him. Although she didn't know when he was coming, she wanted to be ready. Her every thought was focused on the day when she would see him face to face. She would set herself apart and resist all other would-be suitors. She had been bought with a price, and she kept herself pure for her one true love.

The second phase in ancient Jewish marriages was the wedding phase. When the young man's father approved the wedding chamber, he would tell his son to go get his bride. Since she did not know exactly the day or hour when he would be coming, the bride made special preparations. She kept an oil lamp beside her bed with plenty of oil in case he came at night. Her bridesmaids would do the same.

When the wedding party got close to the house, the young man would give a shout and blow the shofar to let his bride know he was coming for her. He would take his bride back to the place he had prepared for her and there in the wedding chamber, they would consummate the marriage. In Bible terms this is called "cutting the covenant."

The third and final phase of an ancient Jewish wedding was the celebration phase. Once the young couple had joined themselves as one flesh, they celebrated their union with family and friends. Part of that celebration was a joyous feast called the marriage supper. Many couples today have a meal for family and friends after their wedding service. It is a time to honor the new husband and wife and celebrate their marriage covenant.

Since the New Testament is a Jewish book, we should not be surprised to see these traditions used to explain the relationship Jesus wants to have with His followers. It is as intimate a relationship as we find in a marriage covenant.

John the Baptist said of his relationship to Jesus:

> *You yourselves bear me witness, that I said, "I am not the Christ [Messiah]," but "I have been sent before Him." He who has the bride is the bridegroom; but the friend of the bridegroom, who stands and hears him, rejoices greatly because of the bridegroom's voice. Therefore this joy of mine is fulfilled* (John 3:28-29).

Jesus said to His followers:

> *Let not your heart be troubled; you believe in God, believe also in me. In My Father's house are many mansions [rooms]; if it were not so, I would have told you. I go to prepare a place for you. And if I go and prepare a place*

for you, I will come again and receive you to Myself; that where I am, there you may be also (John 14:1-3).

His followers asked Him when He would come again for them. Jesus responded, *"Of that day and hour no one knows, not even the angels of heaven, but My Father only"* (Matt. 24:36).

Believers are now in the betrothal phase of our covenant relationship with God through Jesus. He paid the price to make us His Bride. That price was His own blood shed for us. When we say yes to Him, we spiritually drink the cup of the New Covenant in His blood showing our union with Him through His indwelling Holy Spirit. We become *"partakers of the divine nature"* of God (2 Pet. 1:4).

Jesus has given us spiritual gifts with which to make ourselves ready for Him at His coming. We commit ourselves wholly and completely to Him. We are not our own because we have been bought with a price. Like the young woman waiting for her beloved to return for her, we keep ourselves pure and holy until He comes for us.

While Jesus has been gone a long time preparing a place for us, we learn from Revelation 19 that our Father in Heaven has determined that it is time for His Son to come for His Bride. The place He has prepared is ready. We learn later that the New Jerusalem is the place He has prepared for us. John even calls it *"the bride, the Lamb's wife"* (Rev. 21:9). The New Jerusalem is our wedding chamber or divine *chuppah*, the place where we will ultimately live forever with our heavenly Bridegroom.

Our heavenly Bridegroom has finished preparing a place for us and the Bride has made herself ready. In Bible times, when people were invited to a wedding, they wore white garments provided for them by the host. Here the Bride is clothed in fine linen, clean and bright, which John says is the righteous acts of the saints. This is wedding talk that means God's people are now spiritually mature enough for the actual wedding with Jesus, our divine Bridegroom, to take place.

Jesus used several wedding illustrations to explain how important it is for His Bride and the invited guests to be ready for His coming. In one of His parables, Jesus told about a king who had arranged a marriage for his son and sent out special invitations to many. But the invited guests were too busy to come and even persecuted and killed the servants who called them to the feast.

The king destroyed these ungrateful ones and invited others to the wedding. When the king arrived for the celebration, he noticed that one person was not wearing his wedding garment. The king removed the man from the celebration. (See Matthew 22:1-13.)

On another occasion, Jesus told a parable about ten virgins, who were friends of the bride. They took their lamps and went out to meet the bridegroom when he came for his betrothed. Five were wise virgins who took oil for their lamps. Five were foolish. They had no oil for their lamps. When the bridegroom was delayed, they all fell asleep. Finally, at midnight the cry was heard that the bridegroom was coming. But the foolish virgins' lamps went out, they had no oil to light them, and they were unable to attend the wedding. (See Matthew 25:1-13.)

Jesus used this parable to warn us to be ready for His coming. He said, *"Watch therefore, for you know neither the day nor the hour in which the Son of Man is coming"* (Matt. 25:13).

As the approaching bridegroom gave a shout and blew the shofar to alert his bride, so Jesus will come for us in like manner. This is the wedding phase in our relationship with the Lord. It is the time that we will be caught up to meet Him in the air, according to the teaching of Jesus in Matthew 24:29-31. He says clearly that this will take place at the last trumpet (or *shofar*) sound.

Paul confirms this with his comments:

> *For the Lord Himself will descend from heaven with a shout, with the voice of an archangel, and with the trumpet* [shofar] *of God. And the dead in Christ* [Messiah]

will rise first. Then we who are alive and remain shall be caught up together with them in the clouds to meet the Lord in the air. And thus we shall always be with the Lord. Therefore comfort one another with these words (1 Thessalonians 4:16-18).

Writing about this same event, Paul adds the following:

Behold, I tell you a mystery: we shall not all sleep, but we shall all be changed—in a moment, in the twinkling of an eye, at the last trumpet [shofar]. *For the trumpet* [shofar] *will sound, and the dead will be raised incorruptible, and we shall be changed* (1 Corinthians 15:51-52).

We will return with the Lord and experience the third phase of our relationship with Him. We will have the marriage feast or supper of the Lamb. When Jesus had His last meal with His disciples, He said, *"I say to you, I will not drink of this fruit of the vine from now on until that day when I drink it new with you in My Father's kingdom"* (Matt. 26:29).

This was the Passover or covenant meal—what believers call communion, the marriage feast or supper. Jesus said He would not partake of it again until He did so with His followers in His Father's Kingdom. His Father's Kingdom is now coming to the earth. Hallelujah!

Jesus spoke of this again and said:

I say to you that many will come from east and west, and sit down with Abraham, Isaac, and Jacob in the kingdom of heaven. But the sons of the kingdom will be cast out into outer darkness. There will be weeping and gnashing of teeth (Matthew 8:11-12).

This celebration is not in Heaven; it is on the earth.

To conclude this part of our study, John makes it clear that while the host (Jesus) has provided the wedding garment of salvation, the believers have made themselves ready through their righteous acts. Western believers must understand that, while we are not saved by works, we are saved to works of covenantal love.

Paul explains:

> By grace you have been saved through faith, and that not of yourselves; it is the gift of God, not of works, lest anyone should boast. For we are His workmanship, created in Christ Jesus [Messiah Yeshua] for good works, which God prepared beforehand that we should walk in them (Ephesians 2:8-10).

People who profess to be believers but do not live godly lives will not be invited to the marriage supper. People who have "churchianity" but do not have a relationship with Jesus as evidenced by their lives will not be properly dressed for the occasion. These are not my words but the words of Jesus: "The Son of Man will come in the glory of His Father with His angels, and then He will reward each according to his works" (Matt. 16:27).

The works are the fruit of covenantal love produced in us, through us, and out of us by the Holy Spirit. They are the true test of a genuine believer, not meaningless confessions from our lips that do not produce the fruit of the Spirit.

Jesus said, "Every tree that does not bear good fruit is cut down and thrown into the fire. Therefore, by their fruits you will know them" (Matt. 7:19-20). The Bible is clear—if there is no fruit; there is no root.

John becomes so overwhelmed that he falls at the feet of the angel to worship him. The angel rebukes John with the comment that he is a fellow servant who is giving testimony of Jesus, which is the heart of all prophecy.

We are to worship God and not His heavenly messengers, no matter how glorious their appearance.

The Messiah Returns (verses 11-16)

Jesus prophesied the great event of His return when He explained the endtimes saying:

> *Immediately after the tribulation of those days the sun will be darkened, and the moon will not give its light; the stars will fall from heaven, and the powers of the heavens will be shaken. Then the sign of the Son of Man will appear in heaven, and then all the tribes of the earth will mourn, and they will see the Son of Man coming on the clouds of heaven with power and great glory. And He will send His angels with a great sound of a trumpet* [shofar], *and they will gather together His elect from the four winds, from one end of heaven to the other* (Matthew 24:29-31).

When the High Priest Caiaphas interrogated Jesus, he made Jesus swear by God to reveal His true identity. He asked Jesus to answer plainly if He was the Messiah, the Son of God. Because Jesus was a Torah-observant Jew, He had to answer the question according to Leviticus 5:1.

Matthew records Jesus' response:

> *Jesus said to him, "It is as you said. Nevertheless, I say to you, hereafter you will see the Son of Man sitting at the right hand of the Power* [God] *and coming on the clouds of heaven"* (Matthew 26:64).

When Jesus gave this answer, the High Priest accused Jesus of speaking blasphemy. This is because Jesus was referring to Daniel 7:13 and applying it to Himself.

When Jesus ascended to Heaven, two angels appeared as men and spoke to His followers:

Men of Galilee, why do you stand gazing up into heaven? This same Jesus, who was taken up from you into heaven, will so come in like manner as you saw Him go into heaven (Acts 1:11).

Zechariah makes one of the most remarkable statements about the time of the return of Jesus. Speaking through the prophet, God says:

I will pour on the house of David and on the inhabitants of Jerusalem the Spirit of grace and supplication; then they will look on Me whom they pierced. Yes, they will mourn for Him as one mourns for his only son, and grieve for him as one grieves for a firstborn (Zechariah 12:10).

What is so remarkable about this prophecy is that God says the people will look upon Me whom they have pierced. God is talking about Himself but refers to Himself both as "Me" and "Him." They will mourn when they realize that the Messiah is God Himself, who came into the world to redeem us. But the world pierced Him when He was crucified (see John 19:34).

John was an eyewitness to this and wrote in the Book of Revelation:

Behold, He is coming with clouds, and every eye will see Him, even they who pierced Him. And all the tribes of the earth will mourn because of Him. Even so, Amen (Revelation 1:7).

The fulfillment of Jesus coming again in these and many other Scriptures is described in Revelation 19:11-16. John writes 13 statements about Jesus in these verses. We could write a whole book just on his comments. It is challenging to write so few words about our glorious Lord. My heart feels like it will explode just contemplating all that the Scripture says about the "Coming One." If you really want to be blessed, spend some quality time looking up some of the many places in the

Bible that describe this exalted Righteous Judge of the whole earth. The following is just a brief summary.

1. Jesus is riding a white horse.

In Revelation 4:1, John saw a prophetic door open into Heaven where he was able to see his spiritual vision. Now for the second time, he sees Heaven open to him so he can see the coming of the Lord. He sees Jesus sitting on a white horse. John did not mean that Jesus would literally be returning on a white horse. We have previously noted that in John's time, a rider on a white horse was the symbol of a conquering victor. This is why John described the first seal in Revelation 6:7 as a rider on a white horse. That rider was the anti-Messiah, who went forth to conquer and establish satan's kingdom on the earth. This rider is the real Messiah who is coming to establish the Kingdom of God on the earth.

2. Jesus is called "Faithful and True."

Throughout history, there have been many false prophets who claimed to speak for God. There are many false prophets today and many more are yet to come. Jesus was not one of them. He is not the false prophet beast described in the Book of Revelation. He was and is the faithful and true witness. This is because He is the only One who perfectly knows the mind and character of God.

Jesus claimed to speak and do only what was faithful and true to His Father in Heaven (see John 8:26-29; 12:44-50, etc.). In Revelation 1:5 and 3:14, Jesus is called *"the faithful witness"* and *"the Faithful and True Witness,"* respectively. We can trust our souls and our eternal destiny to Him.

3. Jesus is righteous in His judgments and war.

In His first coming, Jesus was the Lamb of God, who came to take away our sins. In His second coming, He is the Lion of the Tribe of Judah, who comes to administer God's righteous judgments and just war against those who oppose God. Jesus said: *"I can of Myself do nothing. As I hear, I judge; and My judgment is righteous, because I do not seek My own will but the will of the Father who sent Me"* (John 5:30).

As Jeremiah explained, Jesus is the righteous Branch of David, who will execute judgment and righteousness on the earth (see Jer. 23:5-6). True and righteous are His judgments. Earlier in this chapter, the great multitude in Heaven gave glory and honor to the Lord because His judgments are true and righteous. (See Revelation 19:2.)

Paul wrote, *"...it is a righteous thing with God to repay with tribulation those who trouble you"* (2 Thess. 1:6).

4. Jesus has eyes like a flame of fire.

When John first saw the vision of the exalted Son of Man, he said that the Lord's eyes were *"like a flame of fire"* (Rev. 1:14). Jesus greeted the congregation at Thyatira as *"the Son of God who has eyes like a flame of fire"* (Rev. 2:18). The Hebrew Bible Book of First Chronicles tells us that *"the LORD searches all hearts and understands all the intent of the thoughts"* (1 Chron. 28:9).

Jesus warned the congregation at Thyatira, *"...I am He who searches the minds and hearts. And I will give to each one of you according to your works"* (Rev. 2:23). Like modern machines that are able to look past people's clothes, Jesus is able to look past our outward pretense right into our hearts. Paul wrote to the believers at Thessalonica that when Jesus is revealed from Heaven with His mighty angels, He will come in flaming fire taking vengeance on those who do not know God (see 2 Thess. 1:7-10).

5. Jesus has many crowns on His head.

Whereas the dragon, satan, had seven crowns on his head (see Rev. 12:3), and the Beast, anti-Messiah, had ten crowns (see Rev. 13:1), Jesus has many crowns on His head. Babylon and Rome and modern empires such as Great Britain have ruled over much of the earth. Yet, eventually their empires came to an end. The anti-Messiah will seek to enforce his satanic power over the nations. But it will be short-lived. When Jesus comes He is going to rule over all the nations of the world forever. And God's people will rule and reign with Him. Hallelujah!

When Daniel prophesied about the coming Son of Man, this is what he said of Him:

> *To Him was given dominion and glory and a kingdom, that all peoples, nations, and languages should serve Him. His dominion is an everlasting dominion, which shall not pass away, and His kingdom the one which shall not be destroyed* (Daniel 7:14).

Isaiah proclaimed:

> *Of the increase of His government and peace there will be no end, upon the throne of David and over His kingdom, to order it and establish it with judgment and justice for that time forward, even forever. The zeal of the Lord of hosts will perform this* (Isaiah 9:7).

Jesus is not returning as the "baby in the manger." He is coming as the "King of the nations." King David prophesied this glorious time on the earth with these words:

> *All the ends of the world shall remember and turn to the* LORD, *and all the families of the nations shall worship before You. For the kingdom is the* LORD's, *and He rules over the nations* (Psalms 22:27-28).

6. Jesus has a name that no one knows "except Himself."

The next statement John makes about Jesus is that He has a name only He knows. What does this mean? In Bible times, names carried much greater meaning than just a person's identity. A person's name revealed his or her nature and character. To do something in someone's name was to act like that person.

The Bible says that God has given Jesus *"the name which is above every name"* (Phil. 2:9). This means that the person of Jesus, and who He is in all of His glory and splendor, is far beyond our human ability to understand. We will only have full knowledge of Him when we see Him face to face in His fullness. We will be able to see our Lord this way when He returns. Only then will we truly know Him when we see Him in His blazing glory and dazzling beauty. John saw Jesus high and lifted up, but that was in a vision. He did not see Jesus as we will see Him when He returns. As believers, this is what we are looking forward to. We will see the full revelation of His name.

Jesus made a reference to this and said:

> *All things have been delivered to Me by My Father, and no one knows the Son except the Father. Nor does anyone know the Father except the Son, and the one to whom the Son wills to reveal Him* (Matthew 11:27).

In Bible times, mirrors were made of metal and did not give a clear reflection of the person. Paul used this as an illustration and said, *"Now we see in a mirror, dimly, but then face to face. Now I know in part, but then I shall know just as I also am known"* (1 Corinthians 13:12).

7. Jesus is clothed in a robe dipped in blood.

Since Jesus is coming to judge and make war, John sees Him wearing a garment that is covered with blood. When Jesus was beaten and crucified, His garment was covered with His own blood. Isaiah wrote that Jesus was beaten so horribly He could barely be recognized:

> *Behold, My Servant shall deal prudently* [prosper]; *He shall be exalted and extolled* [lifted up] *and be very high. Just as many were astonished at you, so His visage*

[appearance] *was marred more than any man, and His form more than the sons of men...* (Isaiah 52:13-14).

When Jesus returns, His garment will be covered with the blood of His enemies. He will do to them as they did to Him. Obadiah explains: *"The day of the* LORD *upon all the nations is near; as you have done, it shall be done to you; your reprisal shall return upon your own head"* (Obad. 15).

8. Jesus is called the Word of God.

In Bible times and Hebraic thinking, people thought of words as being the expression of a person. Words not only communicated ideas; they also carried in them the life and personality of the person speaking. Words were personified and active in that they represented and accomplished the will of the person connected with them.

God spoke the world into existence by the creative power of His Word. Jesus was and is the personification of God. He is the active agent through whom God brought the world into existence. This is why John refers to Jesus as the "Word of God." He is the eternal expression and personal representative of the will and person of God. In other words, He is God in human flesh, who came to reveal Himself fully and completely to us.

This is the background and meaning of John's statements in his Gospel message:

> *In the beginning was the Word, and the Word was with God, and the Word was God. He was in the beginning with God. All things were made through Him, and without Him nothing was made that was made....And the Word became flesh and dwelt among us, and we beheld His glory, the glory as of the only begotten of the Father, full of grace and truth* (John 1:1-3,14).

In the first of his three letters, John wrote:

That which was from the beginning, which we have heard, which we have seen with our eyes, which we have looked upon, and our hands have handled, concerning the Word of life—the life was manifested, and we have seen, and bear witness, and declare to you that eternal life which was with the Father and was manifested to us... (1 John 1:1-2).

9. Jesus leads the armies in Heaven.

The emperors of Rome and leaders of the great empires of history led their forces into battle. Likewise, when Jesus returns, He will lead His great army of Heaven to victory over His enemies. John explains that the Lord's army follows Him on white horses, and they are clothed in fine linen, white and clean.

When God's people are caught up to meet Jesus in the air, they return with Him as His conquering army. They have overcome their enemies by the blood of the Lamb and the word of their testimony (see Rev. 12:11). They have washed their robes and made them white in the blood of the Lamb. Furthermore, their military uniforms represent their righteous acts as proof of their faith. (See Revelation 12:11; 7:14; 19:8.) These are not lukewarm, carnal professors of Christianity who talk about God but don't know Him. These are the overcomers who lived their lives to please God and gave their lives in service and witness to Him.

Jude quotes the Book of Enoch and writes:

Now Enoch, the seventh from Adam, prophesied about these men [apostates and false believers] *also, saying, "Behold, the Lord comes with ten thousands of His saints, to execute judgment on all, to convict all who are ungodly among them of all their ungodly deeds which they have committed in an ungodly way, and of all the harsh things which ungodly sinners have spoken against*

Him" (Jude 14-15; see also Zechariah 14:5; Matthew 24:29-31; 1 Thessalonians 3:13).

It is interesting that the armies of God do not actually participate in the fight. They simply return with the Lord who destroys the anti-God forces with His spoken Word. In addition to God's holy people, the angels of God also accompany Jesus at His return. (See also Mark 8:38; Luke 9:26; Second Thessalonians 1:7.)

10. Jesus strikes the nations with His spoken Word.

We have previously discussed the concept of the spoken Word of God. Just like our own spoken words have our life in them when they come out of us, so does the spoken Word of God. The difference is that when God speaks, His words contain creative power.

When John had his initial vision of Jesus, he observed that a two-edged sword came out of His mouth (see Rev. 1:16). Jesus warned the believers at Pergamos that He would fight against them with the sword of His mouth (see Rev. 2:16).

Isaiah wrote of this time when the Lord would destroy His enemies with His spoken Word: *"...He shall strike the earth with the rod of His mouth, and with the breath of His lips He shall slay the wicked"* (Isa. 11:4).

Paul makes the same comment: *"Then the lawless one will be revealed, whom the Lord will consume with the breath of His mouth and destroy with the brightness of His coming"* (2 Thess. 2:8).

Jesus will not fight His enemies with physical weapons but with the spiritual weapon of His spoken Word. John later says: *"The rest were killed with the sword which proceeded from the mouth of Him who sat on the horse..."* (Rev. 19:21).

11. Jesus rules the nations with a rod of iron.

In the Lord's letter to the believers at Thyatira, He encouraged them to be faithful because He will rule over the nations with a rod of iron.

He further said that those who overcome will rule with Him. John also mentioned that the male Child born of the woman will rule all nations with a rod of iron. (See Revelation 2:26-27; 12:5.)

John's description of Jesus coming to rule with a rod of iron is the fulfillment of the prophecy in Psalms 2: *"You shall break them with a rod of iron; You shall dash them to pieces like a potter's vessel"* (Ps. 2:9).

In view of this total victory over His enemies, the writer of this powerful psalm encourages the leaders of the nations to submit their will to God:

> *Therefore, be wise, O kings; be instructed, you judges of the earth. Serve the LORD with fear, and rejoice with trembling. Kiss the Son, lest He be angry, and you perish in the way, when His wrath is kindled but a little. Blessed are those who put their trust in Him* (Psalms 2:10-12).

12. Jesus treads the winepress of Almighty God.

We explained the winepress earlier in our discussion of Revelation 14:17-20. The winepress was both a symbol of joy and judgment. It is a symbol of joy in anticipation of the wine and oil that will come from crushing the grapes and olives. It also symbolizes judgment, as the life of the grapes and olives is being crushed.

Like the winepress or olive press, the life of Jesus was crushed beginning at the Garden of Gethsemane. Gethsemane means "oil press." Anyone who has been to the Garden of Gethsemane has seen the ancient olive trees still standing in the garden. The olive trees are probably the descendants of the olive trees that were there when Jesus prayed. This was also where Jesus was betrayed and where the Romans took Him to be interrogated. Since this was an olive orchard, there was most likely an olive press for crushing the olives.

Isaiah makes the connection between Jesus treading the winepress for us at His first coming and His treading down His enemies at His second coming. Isaiah asks the question and receives the answer:

> *Why is your apparel red, and your garments like one who treads in the winepress? I have trodden the winepress alone, and from the peoples no one was with Me. For I have trodden them in My anger, and trampled them in My fury; their blood is sprinkled upon My garments, and I have stained all My robes. For the day of vengeance is in My heart, and the year of my redeemed has come* (Isaiah 63:2-4).

13. Jesus has a name written on His robe.

John's last statement about Jesus is that He is *"KING OF KINGS AND LORD OF LORDS"* (Rev. 19:16). The emperors of Babylon, Persia, Greece, Rome, and modern empires such as Great Britain ruled over much of the known world. While their empires were vast, they were not universal, and they were short-lived.

Jesus, however, will rule over all the nations forever. This is the final fulfillment of Psalms 2, where God promised His Son universal rule over all the nations: *"Ask of Me, and I will give You the nations for Your inheritance, and the ends of the earth for Your possession"* (Ps. 2:8).

This is the event proclaimed by loud voices in Heaven when the seventh angel sounded the seventh trumpet-shofar:

> *The seventh angel sounded: and there were loud voices in heaven saying, "The kingdoms of this world have become the kingdoms of our Lord and of His Christ [Messiah], and He shall reign forever and ever"* (Revelation 11:15).

As we all know, kingdoms don't normally relinquish their rule and power without a fight. In the next chapter, we will study the futile efforts of the nations to stop the Son of Man from establishing God's Kingdom on the earth.

Let's join John in the next chapter as he describes the great Battle of Armageddon.

REVIEW QUESTIONS

1. Write a summary of what you have learned in this lesson. Write the summary in clear, concise words as if you were going to present it to another person.

2. Describe how you can apply what you have learned in this lesson to your life.

3. Share what you have learned with your family, friends, and members of your study group.

NOTES

1. Biblesoft's New Exhaustive Strong's Numbers and Concordance with Expanded Greek-Hebrew Dictionary. CD-ROM. Biblesoft, Inc. and International Bible Translators, Inc. (© 1994, 2003, 2006) s.v. "halal," (OT 1984) and s.v. "Yahh," (OT 3068).

2. Dr. Richard Booker, *Here Comes the Bride* (Sounds of the Trumpet, 1995). You can order this book directly from my online bookstore at www.rbooker.com.

Chapter 9

The Battle of Armageddon

When God created Adam and Eve, He gave them dominion over the earth, and instructed them to rule over His creation on His behalf. God also instructed them to be fruitful and multiply so their descendants would spread His Kingdom life and rule throughout the earth. (See Genesis 1:26-28.)

But Adam and Eve were not alone in the Garden of Eden. A fallen angel named satan was there to tempt them into disobeying God. Tragically for them and for the world, they yielded to the temptation. From that time until now, satan has done everything possible to usurp God's Kingdom on the earth.

In an effort to institute his own rule, satan has set up a counterfeit kingdom called "the world system." This counterfeit kingdom is expressed through the philosophies, attitudes, attractions, pleasures, ways, and means of the world. The Bible says that satan is the god of this world system (see 2 Cor. 4:4; Eph. 2:2; John 12:31; 14:30; 16:11; 1 John 5:18-19). People unwittingly serve satan when they give themselves to this world system, through which he desires to live out his god-image.

This is why the Bible says the following:

> *Do not love the world or the things in the world. If anyone loves the world, the love of the Father is not in him. For all that is in the world—the lust of the flesh, the lust of the eyes, and the pride of life—is not of the Father but is of the world. And the world is passing away, and the lust of it; but he who does the will of God abides forever* (1 John 2:15-17).

Satan seeks to deceive people into worshiping him rather than God. This clash of kingdoms will climax in the endtimes when the unbelieving world will fall for the ultimate deception of the false prophet and the anti-Messiah. They will take the Mark of the Beast as their "pledge of allegiance" to this kingdom of darkness. This kingdom will be short-lived, however, because Jesus will return to Earth to establish the fullness of God's Kingdom of Light.

When Jesus returns, He will destroy the kingdom of darkness at the great Battle of Armageddon. He will then set up a righteous Kingdom and rule over a regathered Israel as King of the Jews and over all the nations as King of kings and Lord of lords.

Let's join John once again as he shares his vision of our Lord defeating satan, the anti-Messiah, the false prophet, the nations who oppose God, and those who have taken the Mark of the Beast.

THE BATTLE OF ARMAGEDDON
(REVELATION 19:17-21)

In this encouraging chapter, John hears all of Heaven praising God for His righteous judgment on the anti-God Beast system. This demonic system has committed spiritual fornication against God and persecuted His people. Now God is answering their prayers to avenge their blood.

John also hears the announcement of the blessed event of the marriage supper of the Lamb. When Jesus celebrated the Passover covenant meal with His disciples, He said, *"But I say to you, I will not drink of this fruit of the vine from now on until that day when I drink it new with you in My Father's kingdom"* (Matt. 26:29).

The Passover covenant meal is the same as the marriage supper of the Lamb. When Jesus comes for His Bride in Revelation 19, the spiritual marriage preparations with His people will be complete. At the marriage supper, Jesus and His holy Bride will celebrate the fullness of their relationship. Jesus said He will celebrate this marriage supper in His Father's Kingdom. His Father's Kingdom will be on the earth when Jesus returns.

John has an incredible vision of the coming of the Lord in power and glory to destroy the anti-God Beast system and nations of the world. It is the final fulfillment of the proclamation in Revelation 11:15 declaring that the kingdoms of this world have become the Kingdom of our Lord and of His Messiah. Since kings don't voluntarily give up their kingdoms, Jesus must use force to destroy the Beast system. John sees this happening and writes it down for us in the last few verses of Revelation 19. Let's read about this last great battle.

The Great Clash of the Kingdoms (verses 17-21)

Throughout history, rulers of nations and empires have fought each other. Jesus prophesied this to His disciples: *"You will hear of wars and rumors of wars. See that you are not troubled; for all these things must come to pass, but the end is not yet"* (Matt. 24:6).

Note that Jesus said, "The end is not yet." Because the leaders of nations reject the rule of God, they continue to fight one another. As Jesus said, wars and rumors of wars have been the norm between nations. The only time the world has been at peace is during the time between wars. And that is only because the victor is powerful enough to impose the terms of peace on its conquered enemy. Then as soon as the victor is weakened, it is attacked. This cycle of war has continued down through the ages. Peace on Earth has been the exception, not the norm. Yet, this old world keeps going. Now with nuclear weapons, people fear that we will destroy ourselves. But this is not going to happen.

John sees this cycle of war and the world as we know it coming to an end. Peace is coming to the earth. But it won't be due to the futile efforts of the New World Order. It will be because the Prince of Peace is coming to rule over the nations. The end of wars and the world as we know it is at hand. Jesus is returning to judge and make war (see Rev. 19:11).

Jesus is going to destroy the anti-God, one-world system and establish the Kingdom of God on the earth. This is a Kingdom of righteousness and peace. Only then shall nations beat their swords into plowshares and study war no more (see Isa. 2:4). This last great battle will usher in the golden age about which the prophets spoke. We have never achieved this utopian world because we have tried to establish it without God.

The war that John sees in Revelation 19 is different from all previous wars. This is not a war of nations against nations. It is a war between the anti-God, one-world system and the righteous forces of God. It should be obvious that humankind cannot win a war against God. But satan's demonic influence has blinded and deceived the leaders of the nations into thinking they can actually defeat God in battle. This is the height of insanity and shows us that humans cannot think logically when they are possessed by sin and satanic delusions.

John previously introduced us to this battle but did not give much in the way of details. In Revelation 14:17-20, he gave us a preview and referred to it as *"the great winepress of the wrath of God."* In those verses, John saw an angel with a sharp sickle reaping the grapes of wrath:

> *The angel thrust his sickle into the earth and gathered the vine of the earth, and threw it into the great winepress of the wrath of God. And the winepress was trampled outside*

the city [Jerusalem], *and blood came out of the winepress, up to the horses' bridles, for one thousand six hundred furlongs* [180 miles] (Revelation 14:19-20).

John shows us an instant replay of the same battle in Revelation 16:12-16. This is his description of the sixth bowl judgment, which is the drying up of the Euphrates River and the demonic gathering of the armies of the world to destroy Israel. Instead, they will end up fighting God. Here John refers to this battle as the *"battle of that great day of God Almighty"* (Rev. 16:14). John adds an important detail: *"They* [demonic spirits] *gathered them together to the place called in Hebrew, Armageddon"* (Rev. 16:16).

Before describing the battle itself, let's "connect the Revelation dots" to help us see that John is talking about the same event in each of these instances, but with differing levels of detail. Remember that the Book of Revelation actually ends with the close of chapter 11. The rest of the book is an instant replay giving the details of the final destruction of the anti-God, one-world system and the coming of the Lord.

Recall that in the last verses of Revelation 11, John hears the seventh angel sounding the seventh trumpet-shofar and proclaiming, *"The kingdoms of this world have become the kingdoms of our Lord and of His Christ* [Messiah]..." (Rev. 11:15).

This is the third woe. It announces the coming of the Lord but provides no details other than the statement that God's Kingdom is now coming to reign on the earth. (We covered this earlier in our discussion of Revelation 11:15-19.) This third woe is the same as *"the great winepress of the wrath of God"* described in Revelation 14:17-20, which, in turn, is the same as *"the battle of that great day of God Almighty"* described in Revelation 16:12-16.

Then the seventh bowl judgment in Revelation 16:17-21 describes a loud voice from the throne of God proclaiming, *"It is done!"* (verse 17).

John is describing the same event with an increasing amount of detail. Finally, he gives us the final instant replay in Revelation 19:17-21.

In our previous study of the sixth bowl judgment, I explained the geographic significance of the Hill or Mount Megiddo as the staging ground for this last great battle. It would be good to review that discussion at this time. While John gives us more detail concerning this battle in Revelation 19:17-21, he does not actually describe the battle in these verses. The description of the battle is found in other places in the Hebrew Bible.

To this point, we have learned that satan, working through the anti-Messiah and the false prophet, seeks to destroy Israel as well as all of God's people. In one final effort to defeat God, satan gathers the armies of the world to attack Israel at Jerusalem.

Why would satan want to do this?

The answer is clearly revealed in the Bible. God chose the Jewish people to be His representative witnesses on the earth. God calls the Jews the apple or pupil of His eye (see Deut. 32:10), meaning that the world can know there is a God by looking at the Jews. God made an everlasting covenant with Abraham, Isaac, Jacob, and their descendants to give them a land of their own and make them a great nation. In fact God promised that one day they would be the head of the nations under the rule of Messiah (see Deut. 28:1). Israel is the only nation with a promise from God to be an everlasting nation.

God's covenant promise to Abraham has a provision to include the Gentiles. In a most remarkable verse all the way back in Deuteronomy, the Lord said:

> *Rejoice, O Gentiles, with His people; for He will avenge the blood of His servants, and render vengeance to His adversaries; He will provide atonement for His land and His people* (Deuteronomy 32:43).

The coming of the Lord in Revelation 19 is the ultimate fulfillment of this Scripture.

Although this thinking is foolishness, satan believes that if he can destroy Israel and the Jewish people, he can defeat God. He can prove that he is greater than God and that God's holy Word is a lie. When we hear the leaders of the nations of our world speaking lies to weaken and destroy Israel, we can know for sure that satan has deceived them. He is preparing them to lead their nations in a collective effort to destroy Israel and defeat God.

Albert Einstein said that there is nothing more foolish than to keep repeating the same thing over and over while expecting different results. If you wonder why government officials keep repeating the same failed policies regarding Israel, it is because they are so deceived by satan that they cannot think reasonably and logically. They are mentally and spiritually foolish; yet their policies and actions will bring the wrath of God on them and the people.

Let's be honest. The nations of the world do not want God ruling over them and will do anything within their power to remove Him from their policies and actions. The Jews and Bible-believing Christians are a human "thorn in their flesh." This is why satan seeks to kill God's people. He knows he cannot kill God, so he attacks God by attacking His people. Satan does this through world leaders who do not want to be reminded that one day they will have to account to God for their lives. Despite their hatred and evil schemes against us, God will always protect a remnant of His people.

The Battle of Armageddon in the Hebrew Scriptures

There are numerous Scriptures in the Hebrew Bible that clearly say God will gather all the nations of the earth to fight against Israel. They also say that, instead of the nations destroying Israel, God will destroy the nations.

Notice what the Lord says through the prophet Zephaniah:

...My determination is to gather the nations to My assembly of kingdoms, to pour on them My indignation, all My fierce anger; all the earth shall be devoured with the fire of My jealousy (Zephaniah 3:8).

Zephaniah goes on to say that the result of this great battle is that the King of Israel will come and dwell in the midst of Jerusalem (see Zeph. 3:8-20).

The prophet Joel also writes about this great end-time battle:

...in those days and at that time, when I bring back the captives of Judah and Jerusalem, I will also gather all nations, and bring them down to the Valley of Jehoshaphat [Kidron Valley outside Jerusalem]; and I will enter into judgment with them there on account of My people, My heritage Israel, whom they have scattered among the nations; they have also divided up My land (Joel 3:1-2).

In Joel 3:9-21, the prophet writes further about this battle. Speaking as God's mouthpiece, Joel calls the nations to prepare for war and come to the Valley of Jehoshaphat, where God will judge them. Joel describes the outcome of the battle:

The LORD will also roar from Zion, and utter His voice from Jerusalem; the heavens and earth will shake; but the LORD will be a shelter for His people, and the strength of the children of Israel (Joel 3:16).

In Scriptures we have already noted, God makes the following declaration through the prophet Zechariah:

Behold, I will make Jerusalem a cup of drunkenness to all the surrounding peoples, when they lay siege against Judah and Jerusalem. And it shall happen in that day that

*I will make Jerusalem a very heavy stone for all peoples;
all who would heave it away will surely be cut in pieces,
though all nations of the earth are gathered against it*
(Zechariah 12:2-3).

Zechariah goes on to say that God will fight on behalf of His people:

*In that day the LORD will defend the inhabitants of Jeru-
salem; the one who is feeble among them in that day shall
be like David, and the house of David shall be like God,
like the Angel of the LORD before them. It shall be in that
day that I will seek to destroy all the nations that come
against Jerusalem* (Zechariah 12:8-9).

Since Megiddo is the staging area for these armies as they make
their way toward Jerusalem, this final battle between God and the anti-
God, one-world system is called the Battle of Armageddon. The climax
of the battle will take place in Jerusalem at which time Jesus will return
and save Israel from her enemies.

Zechariah said that the inhabitants of Jerusalem will mourn when
they realize it is Jesus, the "pierced One" they have rejected:

*I will pour on the house of David and on the inhabitants
of Jerusalem the Spirit of grace and supplication; then
they will look on Me whom they have pierced. Yes, they
will mourn for Him as one mourns for His only son, and
grieve for Him as one grieves for a firstborn* (Zechariah
12:10).

Zechariah adds: "*In that day a fountain shall be opened for the house
of David and for the inhabitants of Jerusalem, for sin and for unclean-
ness*" (Zech.13:1).

Israel alone cannot defeat all the nations of the world. In Zechariah 13–14, we read about this great battle for Jerusalem. In order to

save Israel and Jerusalem, Jesus returns as the Son of Man-Son of God and greater Son of David to save Israel. He will rule over Israel as King of the Jews, and over the nations as King of kings and Lord of lords. Hallelujah!

It is at this time that "all Israel will be saved." Paul explains:

> *And so all Israel* [refers to Israel as a nation] *will be saved, as it is written, "The Deliverer will come out of Zion, and He will turn away ungodliness from Jacob; for this is My covenant with them, when I take away their sins"* (Romans 11:26-27).

Zechariah explains:

> *The LORD will go forth and fight against those nations, as He fights in the day of battle. And in that day His feet will stand on the Mount of Olives, which faces Jerusalem on the east. And the Mount of Olives shall be split in two, from east to west, making a very large valley; half of the mountain shall move toward the north and half of it toward the south. Then you shall flee through My mountain valley, for the mountain valley shall reach to Azal. Yes, you shall flee as you fled from the earthquake in the days of Uzziah king of Judah. Thus the LORD My God will come, and all the saints with You* [Him] (Zechariah 14:3-5).

Once again, we read from Zechariah:

> *The LORD shall be King over all the earth. In that day it shall be—"The LORD is one," and His name one....The people shall dwell in it* [Jerusalem]; *and no longer shall there be utter destruction, but Jerusalem shall be safely inhabited* (Zechariah 14:9,11).

The Supper of the Great God

Because no one can fight successfully against God, the battle will only last long enough for God to destroy His enemies through His spoken Word and the brightness of His coming.

Paul writes:

> *Then the lawless one will be revealed, whom the Lord will consume with the breath of His mouth and destroy with the brightness of His coming. The coming of the lawless one is according to the working of Satan, with all power, signs, and lying wonders, and with all unrighteous deception among those who perish, because they did not receive the love of the truth, that they might be saved. And for this reason God will send them strong delusion, that they should believe the lie, that they all may be condemned who did not believe the truth but had pleasure in unrighteousness* (2 Thessalonians 2:8-12).

In addition to God raining down hailstones and shaking the earth, Zechariah tells us that when God's enemies see the Lord, the armies of the Beast will be blinded, go mad, panic, and kill each other; their flesh will also melt off their bodies (see Zech. 12:4; 14:12-15).

So great is the carnage that John sees an angel as bright as the sun calling with a loud voice to all the unclean birds to clean the land of the carcasses. His invitation is clear: *"Come and gather together for the supper of the great God"* (Rev. 19:17). This is in stark contrast to the marriage feast of the Lamb. Jesus spoke of this supper of the great God:

> *As the lightning comes from the east and flashes to the west, so also will the coming of the Son of Man be. For wherever the carcass is, there the eagles* [vultures] *will be gathered together* (Matthew 24:27-28).

A preview of this final gruesome scene is recorded in Ezekiel. Ezekiel 38–39 records the war of Gog and Magog against Israel. It is similar to the battle described in Revelation 19, but appears to be a different battle that takes place at some other time. The result is the same, however. God supernaturally intervenes for Israel and destroys her enemies. In that battle, it took Israel seven months to bury the dead.

To help cleanse the earth, God calls the vultures and every predator to eat the flesh and drink the blood of the dead. God instructs Ezekiel with these words:

> As for you, son of man, thus says the Lord God, "Speak to every sort of bird and to every beast of the field: 'Assemble yourselves and come; gather together from all sides to My sacrificial meal which I am sacrificing for you, a great sacrificial meal on the mountains of Israel, that you may eat flesh and drink blood'" (Ezekiel 39:17).

As in Revelation 19:17, we learn this is God's meal and His table (see Ezek. 39:20).

This scene is certainly difficult for good people to contemplate. War should always be the last resort when trying to resolve conflicts. However, war is sometimes the only way to stop evil. In this case, it is the holy and just war of God to save His people on the earth and avenge their deaths. God provided one opportunity after another for the people of the world to repent. Instead, they hardened their hearts and cursed Him. When they made their final rejection of His mercy, God had no alternative but to destroy them.

The Beast and the False Prophet Are Taken Alive

"Take him alive." This is the instruction often given to warriors when hunting down their leaders' chief enemies. They want to capture the enemy's leader so they can have the satisfaction of seeing justice done. This is the situation at the Battle of Armageddon. John explains that the Beast and false prophet have been captured. While John does not say who captures them, obviously it is the Lord who takes them captive.

It is important to note that the Beast is a person and not just the anti-God system. This is the anti-Messiah John described in Revelation 13:1-10. He is the political leader whom John calls the Beast From the Sea. He is the one who was empowered by satan to lead the anti-God, one-world system. He is the one whom the people worshiped. He is the one who blasphemed God and made war against God's people.

The false prophet is also a person and not just the anti-God harlot religious system. He is the Beast From the Earth described by John in Revelation 13:11-18. He is the one who was empowered by satan to perform signs and wonders in order to deceive the people. He is the one who instructed the people to make an image of the Beast. He is the one who deceived the people by making it seem that the image of the Beast was speaking. And he is the one who promoted the worship of the Beast person and system by requiring people to take the Beast's mark.

Since God took His two witnesses alive to Heaven, it is appropriate that He take these two false witnesses and send them alive to hell. John says they are cast alive into the lake of fire burning with brimstone. The lake of fire is the biblical *Gehenna*, or hell. (See also Daniel 7:11-12.)

Apparently the anti-Messiah and the false prophet are the first people consigned to hell. It is the final place of judgment for those whose names are not found written in the Book of Life (see Rev. 20:15).

It is interesting to note that when satan is finally cast into hell 1,000 years later, the anti-Messiah and false prophet are still there alive being continually tormented day and night forever (see Rev. 20:10). This means that hell is not a place of annihilation or purification (purgatory) but a place of eternal separation from God.

Sheol, Hades and Gehenna

In Revelation 1:18, Jesus said that He has the *"keys of Hades and of Death."* There are three words used in the Bible to speak of the place of the dead. The first word is *Sheol,* found 65 times in the Hebrew Bible. Depending on which English version you use, *Sheol* is translated into English as "pit," "grave," and "hell." This can certainly be confusing since the word "hell" is not found in the Hebrew Bible. Since pit, grave, and hell are all translated from *Sheol,* all three English words are referring to the same place—the abode of the dead.

When we study the references to Sheol in the Hebrew Bible, we learn that it is a real place where the souls of the dead reside while awaiting the resurrection of their bodies at the end of time. This will either be a resurrection to life or a resurrection to condemnation, according to Daniel 12:2 and John 5:29. Therefore, in the Hebrew Bible, Sheol is not hell but a temporary place of conscious existence for the souls of the departed.

The New Testament word for "Sheol" is the Greek word *Hades.* Therefore, *Hades* and *Sheol* are the same place. In Greek mythology, *Hades* was the god of the underworld. The word *Hades* is found ten times in the Greek text of the New Testament (see Matt. 11:23; 16:18; Luke 10:15; 16:23; Acts 2:27,31; 1 Cor. 15:55; Rev. 1:18; 6:8; 20:13-14). Depending on what version of the Bible you use, *Hades* is translated as "Hades," "hell," or "the grave."

Before the resurrection of Jesus, the souls of the departed—both righteous and unrighteous—went to Sheol/Hades. We learn in the New Testament that Hades was divided into two compartments. The top compartment was a place of blessing called Abraham's Bosom (see Luke 16:23-31), or Paradise (see Luke 23:43). When the righteous died, their souls were carried to this top compartment of Hades, rather than directly to Heaven. This is because the final sacrifice for their sins had not yet been made. The blood of bulls and goats could only *cover* their sins; it could not take them away completely.

When the unrighteous died, they went to the bottom compartment of Hades, called the Place of Torment (see Luke 16:28). It was a place of suffering and fire separated from Paradise by a great gulf. No one could cross from one compartment to the other.

Jesus told a story about a poor man named Lazarus who died and was carried by the angels to Abraham's Bosom/Paradise. A rich man died and went to the Place of Torment. The rich man could see Lazarus with Abraham and begged Abraham to send Lazarus to place water on his tongue to cool him. Abraham could also see the rich man and talk to him. Abraham responded that both Lazarus and the rich man had determined their own destinies before they died. He also mentioned the great gulf separating them. Both Lazarus and the rich man were in a real place and fully conscious of themselves and their situations (see Luke 16:19-31).

After Jesus was resurrected, He took everyone in the top compartment of Hades with Him to Heaven. He was able to do this because His blood was the final sacrifice for sin. His blood did what the blood of bulls and goats could never do. His blood not only covers our sins, it takes them away to be remembered no more. Hallelujah! Paul seems to be writing about this in his letter to the believers at Ephesus (see Eph. 4:8-10). Paul also says that he was caught up to the third Heaven which he called Paradise (see 2 Cor. 12:1-4). Although Jesus emptied Abraham's Bosom, the unrighteous remain in the Place of Torment.

There are three spheres of Heaven: the immediate atmosphere of our earth, the celestial heaven of our universe, and the third Heaven which is the abode of God. Today, when believers die their souls are transported by angels to the third Heaven. This is why Paul could write with such assurance: *"We are confident, yes, well pleased rather to be absent from the body and to be present with the Lord"* (2 Cor. 5:8).

The third word that refers to the place of the departed souls is the word *Gehenna*. This word is found 12 times in the New Testament where it is properly translated as "hell." (See Matthew 5:22,29-30; 10:28; 18:9;

23:15,33; Mark 9:43,45,47; Luke 12:5; James 3:6.) Whereas Sheol/Hades is a temporary location, Gehenna is the final destination of the unrighteous after they have been judged at the Great White Throne Judgment mentioned in Revelation 20:11-15.

Gehenna gets its name from the Valley of Hinnom, which is located just outside the wall of the Old City of Jerusalem on the south side between the Zion Gate and the Dung Gate. Kings Ahaz and Manasseh built altars of sacrifice to the Ammonite god Molech in this valley and sacrificed Hebrew children on them (see 2 Chron. 28:3; 33:6; Jer. 32:35). Jeremiah referred to the Valley of Hinnom as the place of slaughter (see Jer. 7:31-32).

Good King Josiah tore down these altars (see 2 Kings 23:12-15). After this, the Valley of Hinnom became the dump for all the refuse of Jerusalem. The bodies of executed criminals were tossed into this valley (see Matt. 5:29-30). There a fire burned continuously to consume all the waste. The smoke ascended day and night, and the valley became known as the place of burning. To the Hebrews, the Valley of Hinnom became the symbol of hell—the place of unending torment by fire.

Isaiah spoke of the place of continuous burning as the symbol of hell:

> *They shall go forth and look upon the corpses of the men who have transgressed against Me. For their worm [soul] does not die, and their fire is not quenched. They shall be an abhorrence to all flesh* (See Isaiah 66:24).

Jesus later referred to Isaiah's words in Mark 9:42-48.

Because they are no longer needed after the Great White Throne Judgment, death and Hades are thrown into the lake of fire, or *hell* (see Rev. 20:14). This means the souls of those who remained in the bottom compartment of Hades have been resurrected to their bodies, judged, and sent to their eternal abode.

People often ask how a loving God could send people to a place like hell. God does not send people to hell. People *choose* hell. Those who choose separation from God while living in this life also choose hell as their eternal destiny. Think about it. If a person doesn't want to fellowship with God in this life, why would he or she want to be with Him in the next?

God did not prepare hell for people. Jesus said hell was prepared for the devil and his angels (see Matt. 25:41). However if people choose a life apart from God, He will honor their free will to live forever separate from Him. John describes their final outcome: *"Then Death and Hades were cast into the lake of fire. This is the second death. And anyone not found written in the Book of Life was cast into the lake of fire"* (Rev. 20:14-15).

Review Questions

1. Write a summary of what you have learned in this lesson. Write the summary in clear, concise words as if you were going to present it to another person.

2. Describe how you can apply what you have learned in this lesson to your life.

3. Share what you have learned with your family, friends, and members of your study group.

Chapter 10

The Messianic Kingdom

REVELATION REVIEW

The long journey of God with humankind began in the Garden of Eden, where God gave Adam and Eve authority to rule over creation on His behalf (see Gen. 1:28). As we all know, Adam and Eve failed in their high calling. The tragic consequences of their disobedience were passed down to all of us.

When Adam and Eve sinned, they hid from God and covered themselves with fig leaves. They did this not because they were ashamed of their nakedness, but because they had lost the glory of God. Until they sinned, God's glory was on them like an aura. His glory was their covering and they had no need of other clothing. When His glory left, Adam and Eve were embarrassed and humiliated as they now saw each other in their sinful state.

This also happened to Moses. When he came down from being in God's presence at Mount Sinai, the skin on his face shone with the glory of God. When that glory began to fade, Moses covered his face with a veil, for the same reason Adam and Eve covered themselves with fig leaves (see Exod. 34:29-35; 2 Cor. 3:13). He didn't want the people to see the glory of God fading from his face.

From the time Adam and Eve sinned until our own times, humankind has been running from God and covering up with the fig leaves of an anti-God world system. As the Bible says, *"all have sinned and fall short of the glory of God"* (Rom. 3:23). Since we have all sinned, none of us can fulfill God's desire that we rule for Him with perfect righteousness. Yet, from the beginning, God has had a plan to restore His glory and rule to humankind.

In view of our sinful fallen condition, God prepared a body for Himself and entered into the human race. He became the second or last Adam through whom God would restore His glory and rule over the earth. He would be God in human flesh, coming to do for us what we could not do for ourselves. Since He would be perfect and without sin, He would be able to rule with perfect righteousness. The Bible tells us that this last Adam is Jesus of Nazareth. (See First Corinthians 15:21-49.) While it is difficult for some to accept the thought that God could become man, there was simply no other way for Him to redeem us.

The Bible is the story of God working out His eternal plan in time and history. God chose Abraham and his descendants through Isaac and Jacob as the human vessels through whom He would reveal Himself to the world. When God called Abraham, He made him the following promise:

> *Get out of your country, from your family and from your father's house, to a land that I will show you. I will make you a great nation; I will bless you and make your name great; and you shall be a blessing* (Genesis 12:1-2).

Because God chose Abraham and his descendants for this great purpose, He promised to bless everyone who blessed Abraham, but curse those who cursed him: *"I will bless those who bless you, and I will curse him who curses you; and in you all the families of the earth shall be blessed"* (Gen. 12:3).

Notice that God promised Abraham a land, a nation, and a blessing. God further said that through Abraham all the families of the earth would be blessed and that one day Israel would be the head of the nations (see Deut. 28:1,13; Zech. 8:23).

God confirmed this promise to Abraham through a sacred blood covenant that would stand forever in time and could not be broken. Regardless of how Abraham's descendants might fail Him, God is a faithful, covenant-keeping God. The fulfillment of God's covenant promise is entirely dependent on Him and His faithfulness to His own covenant Word.

After satan successfully tempted Adam and Eve to sin, he established an anti-God world system through which he seeks to deceive people into following him. His intention is to rule over their souls in the place of God. The Bible says that satan is the god of this world system (see 2 Cor. 4:4; Eph. 2:2; John 12:31; 14:30; 16:11; 1 John 5:18-19). Satan deceives people and blinds them to truth through the philosophies, attitudes, attractions, ways, and means of his world system. Using modern words, we could say that satan's mantra is *misery loves company.* Since he lost his place of honor with God, he wants all of humankind to do the same. So he uses his deceptive ways to lead us away from God and convince us to worship him instead.

Because God chose to do His redemptive work through the Jewish people, satan has a special hatred for them. The Bible and history tell of his many attempts to destroy the Jews, because he believes that if he can kill God's people, he can defeat God. He is the one behind the history of anti-Semitism. He is the one who stirs up hatred in the hearts of Gentiles toward the Jewish people.

Yet, God has not forgotten His covenant with Abraham and his descendants. He has preserved a remnant throughout history and brought them back to their promised land just as He promised so many times in the Hebrew Bible. While the rulers of the nations seek to destroy Israel, God will destroy these rulers instead. Then He will turn the hearts of the Jewish people to Himself, and the Messiah will come as King of the Jews and King of kings over all nations.

While satan has caused so much sorrow and misery in our world, God will judge him at the return of Jesus. Revelation 20 tells us that when Jesus returns, He will set up a literal Kingdom on the earth that will last for 1,000 years. Jesus will rule over the nations as the Son of God and over Israel as the greater Son of David. Through His perfect rule, Jesus—the last Adam and the perfect Son of Man—will restore God's glory to humankind and administer God's Kingdom on the earth with perfect righteousness. Jesus is the One to whom and through whom God will restore dominion and authority and rule over the nations. Through Him, God will fulfill His promise to Abraham that Israel will be the head of all nations.

God's people will rule with Jesus. During this time, satan will be bound and all the families of the earth will be blessed. This is the fulfillment of God's decree to Adam and His ancient covenant promise to Abraham.

Let's join John as he tells us about this period of time when God's Messianic Kingdom will rule on the earth.

THE MESSIANIC KINGDOM (REVELATION 20)

The 15 verses in Revelation 20 are packed with information. John describes four separate, but related, events. These are: 1) satan is bound for 1,000 years, 2) the Messianic Kingdom is established on the earth, 3) satan is loosed and judged forever, and 4) the Great White Throne Judgment occurs.

An entire chapter of this book could easily be written on each subject, but I have chosen to emphasize the Messianic Kingdom on the earth, because that is the destiny of God's people.

Satan Is Bound for 1,000 Years (verses 1-3)

In Revelation 9, John described the fifth trumpet-shofar judgment. He saw a star (angel) with the key to the bottomless pit. The angel released a great and terrifying swarm of demonic spirits on the earth. So that his readers could understand what John wanted to communicate, he referred to this demonic army as locusts.

The bottomless pit, also called the abyss, is the abode of these demons that God kept chained or bound until releasing them as part of His end-time judgments. John explains that satan rules over these demons—the (fallen) angel of the bottomless pit. He further mentions that the Beast, possessed by satan, comes from the bottomless pit. (See Revelation 11:7; 17:8.) This might be a good time to review the information on the bottomless pit that appears in the discussion of Revelation 9:1-12.

Once again John sees an angel coming down from Heaven with the key to the bottomless pit. This may be the same angel that John saw in Revelation 9. Using apocalyptic language, John says that this angel has a great chain in his hand symbolizing a strong and secure restraint. The angel binds satan with the chain, casts him into the bottomless pit, shuts [locks] him inside, and sets a seal on him so that he cannot escape.

God confines satan to the bottomless pit for 1,000 years so that satan cannot deceive the nations during this time when Messiah will establish His Kingdom on the earth. There would be no peace if satan were free. We learned earlier that when God cast satan out of Heaven to earth, satan deceived the people of the world through the signs and wonders performed by the false prophet. (See Revelation 12:9.) During this time, God will keep satan under wraps and unable to do his evil work.

Apparently, satan's demonic spirits are bound along with him. In this way, people living during the Messianic Kingdom will have no evil spiritual influence to deceive them or lead them astray. They will be living under the rule of a perfectly righteous King. As we will see later,

God will loose satan when the 1,000 years are over for one last battle against God and His people.

The Messianic Kingdom on the Earth (verses 4-6)

In addition to those who take the Mark of the Beast and those who are sealed as God's people, there is a third group of people living on the earth when Jesus returns. The Bible refers to them as "the nations." Apparently, some had escaped the Beast. They did not take his mark, but had not committed their lives to the Lord. Others committed their lives to the Lord but were not transformed at His coming at the first resurrection of the righteous dead. Perhaps their decision was a matter of God's timing of events. Since the promises in the Book of Revelation are to the overcomers, some believe that only they will reign with the Messiah in His Kingdom while the less victorious believers will live in the Kingdom but not reign. The Bible does not clarify this enough for us to fully understand it. Therefore, we should be gracious to those with differing opinions. Whatever the circumstances, some among the nations survived the Battle of Armageddon and are alive when the Lord returns.

John says he saw thrones, and those who sat on them were given the right to judge the nations. He specifically mentions the tribulation martyrs. When Jesus establishes His rule, there will be certain divine judgments on those who have survived the tribulation period. (See Ezekiel 20:34-38; Matthew 25:31-46.) The Ezekiel verses picture Jesus as the good shepherd who counts and separates His flock according to those who have personally joined themselves to Him in covenant. The Matthew verses comprise what is known as the "sheep and goat" judgments. Jesus says that He will judge the nations (people groups) based on their treatment of the Jewish people. These judgments are essentially the same and for the purpose of identifying those who are in covenant with God.

The exalted Son of Man is clearly the Judge (see Matt. 25:31-46; John 5:24-30; Rev. 19:11). God has also promised His people that they will rule and judge the nations along with their King (see Matt. 19:28; 1 Cor. 6:2-3; Rev. 2:26; 3:21).

This judgment is to determine who will be allowed to enter into the Messianic Kingdom in their earthly bodies. Only those who love God will enter the Kingdom. The rest will be cut off and banished from God's presence until the Great White Throne Judgment takes place at the end of the Messianic Kingdom.

John says that God's people included in the first resurrection when Jesus returns are blessed and holy. They have power, or victory, over the second death, which John later defines as the lake of fire (see Rev. 20:14). Then he adds that they will serve as priests of God and of His Christ (Messiah) and shall reign with Him for 1,000 years. This is the fulfillment of the promises in the Hebrew Bible and in the New Testament that God's people (including the overcomers of Revelation 1:6 and 5:10) will live and rule with the Messiah in God's Kingdom on the earth.

John says that God's people will reign with the Messiah for 1,000 years. This period of time is known as the Millennium, from the Latin words *milli* (one thousand) and *annum* (year). John doesn't tell us what life will be like in the Messianic Kingdom. We have to look elsewhere in the Bible for that. We do know that it is the utopia for which man has so desperately strived, but never achieved, because he has tried to achieve it without God.

Now with God ruling through the Messiah, righteousness and peace bring the fullest blessing of God on the earth. Let's look at some Scriptures that describe this glorious time with God and His people.

The Messianic Government

The government in the Messianic Kingdom will be a theocracy. This means God Himself will rule over all the earth through Messiah

Jesus. This theocracy will unite the Kingdom of God and the kingdom of David through the Messiah Jesus.

As the divine Son of God, Jesus will administer the Kingdom of God through the resurrected believers of all ages. This will involve the heavenly aspects of the Kingdom on Earth. Jesus, as the human Son of David, will administer the kingdom of David through the remnant of believing Jews who are alive at His coming and enter into the Messianic Kingdom. This will involve the earthly aspects of the Kingdom. (See Daniel 7:18,22,27; Romans 8:17.)

The blessings of the Kingdom of God will come to the Gentiles through the nation of Israel as they live under the righteous rule of Messiah Jesus who will sit on the throne of David (see Isa. 49:6; 62:2; 11:10; Jer. 3:17; 16:19-21).

Psalms 2 gives us a clear statement concerning the rule of Jesus in the Messianic Kingdom:

> Yet I have set My King on My holy hill of Zion. I will declare the decree: The LORD has said to Me, "You are My Son, today I have begotten You. Ask of Me, and I will give You the nations for Your inheritance, and the ends of the earth for Your possession. You shall break them with a rod of iron; You shall dash them to pieces like a potter's vessel" (Psalms 2:6-9).

Daniel was privileged to have a vision of the coming of Messiah Jesus in all His glory and power. Again, we revisit Daniel's apocalyptic vision:

> In the days of these kings the God of heaven will set up a kingdom which shall never be destroyed; and the kingdom shall not be left to other people; it shall break in pieces and consume all these kingdoms, and it shall stand forever (Daniel 2:44).

I was watching in the night visions, and behold, One like the Son of Man, coming with the clouds of heaven! He came to the Ancient of Days, and they brought Him near before Him. Then to Him was given dominion and glory and a kingdom, that all peoples, nations, and languages should serve Him. His dominion is an everlasting dominion, which shall not pass away, and His kingdom the one which shall not be destroyed (Daniel 7:13-14).

The prophet Isaiah often spoke about the Kingdom of God. In one of his more well-known statements, Isaiah wrote:

Unto us a Child is born, unto us a Son is given; and the government will be upon His shoulder. And His name will be called Wonderful, Counselor, Mighty God, Everlasting Father, Prince of Peace. Of the increase of His government and peace there will be no end, upon the throne of David and over His kingdom, to order it and establish it with judgment and justice from that time forward, even forever. The zeal of the Lord of hosts will perform this (Isaiah 9:6-7).

These are just a few of the many prophecies about the Kingdom of God being fully manifested on the earth at the coming of Messiah Jesus. He will rule over the nations as a descendant of Abraham and the greater Son of David.

Jerusalem—the World Capital

Jesus will rule from Jerusalem, which will be the capital of the world. The news media and wire services will dateline their stories from Jerusalem, not Washington, Moscow, Paris, or London. The nations of the world will submit to the policies that the Messiah decrees from the holy city of God. The ancient prophets spoke of this time when Jerusalem would be the center of the world government.

Isaiah prophesied the following:

> It shall come to pass in the latter days that the mountain of the LORD's house shall be established on the top of the mountains, and shall be exalted above the hills; and all nations shall flow to it. Many people shall come and say, "Come and let us go up to the mountain of the LORD, to the house of the God of Jacob; He will teach us His ways, and we shall walk in His paths." For out of Zion shall go forth the law, and the word of the Lord from Jerusalem (Isaiah 2:2-3).

Isaiah also declared:

> In that day there shall be a Root of Jesse, who shall stand as a banner to the people; for the Gentiles shall seek Him, and His resting place shall be glorious (Isaiah 11:10).

Jeremiah said:

> At that time Jerusalem shall be called The Throne of the LORD, and all the nations shall be gathered to it, to the name of the LORD, to Jerusalem. No more shall they follow the dictates of their evil hearts (Jeremiah 3:17).

Micah wrote:

> It shall come to pass in the latter days that the mountain of the LORD's house shall be established on the top of the mountains, and shall be exalted above the hills; and peoples shall flow to it. Many nations shall come and say, "Come, and let us go up to the mountain of the LORD, to the house of the God of Jacob; He will teach us His ways,

and we shall walk in His paths." For out of Zion the law shall go forth, and the word of the LORD *from Jerusalem* (Micah 4:1-2).

Zechariah predicted:

And it shall come to pass that everyone who is left of all the nations which came against Jerusalem shall go up from year to year to worship the King, the LORD *of hosts, and to keep the Feast of Tabernacles* (Zechariah 14:16).

Jesus warned people not to swear by Jerusalem because *"it is the city of the great King"* (Matt. 5:35).

A Unified Government

The Messianic Kingdom will be the true and lasting one-world government. This is what the nations are now trying to establish, but without God. There will be no need for a United Nations, because Jesus will rule with absolute authority and power. There will be no political parties and special interest groups, because all nations will submit to Him, and no open rebellion will be tolerated.

In addition to the Scriptures just noted, the following often-quoted references give us further insight:

Ask of Me, and I will give You the nations for Your inheritance, and the ends of the earth for Your possession. You shall break them with a rod of iron; You shall dash them to pieces like a potter's vessel (Psalms 2:8-9).

The LORD *said to my Lord, "Sit at My right hand, till I make Your enemies Your footstool." The* LORD *shall send the rod of Your strength out of Zion. Rule in the midst of Your enemies!* (Psalms 110:1-2).

...He shall strike the earth with the rod of His mouth, and with the breath of His lips He shall slay the wicked (Isaiah 11:4).

The Lord shall be King over all the earth. In that day it shall be—"The Lord is one," and His name one (Zechariah 14:9).

The kingdoms of this world have become the kingdoms of our Lord and of His Christ [Messiah], *and He shall reign forever and ever!* (Revelation 11:15).

Out of His mouth goes a sharp sword, that with it He should strike the nations. And He Himself will rule them with a rod of iron. He Himself treads the winepress of the fierceness and wrath of Almighty God. And He has on His robe and on His thigh a name written: KING OF KINGS AND LORD OF LORDS (Revelation 19:15-16).

A Righteous Rule

Jesus will rule with righteousness and justice for all. All social problems will be solved. No one will be oppressed, taken advantage of, or cheated in any way. There will be no social workers, discrimination, inequities, or inequalities of any kind.

The Hebrew Scriptures declare:

The LORD shall endure forever; He has prepared His throne for judgment. He shall judge the world in righteousness, and He shall administer judgment for the peoples in uprightness. The LORD also will be a refuge for the oppressed, a refuge in times of trouble (Psalms 9:7-9).

His delight is in the fear of the LORD, *and He shall not judge by the sight of His eyes, nor decide by the hearing of His ears; but with righteousness He shall judge the poor, and decide with equity for the meek of the earth; He shall strike the earth with the rod of His mouth, and with the breath of His lips He shall slay the wicked. Righteousness shall be the belt of His loins, and faithfulness the belt of His waist* (Isaiah 11:3-5).

The throne will be established; and One will sit on it in truth, in the tabernacle of David, judging and seeking justice and hastening righteousness (Isaiah 16:5).

Behold, the days are coming, says the LORD, *that I will raise to David a Branch of righteousness; a King shall reign and prosper, and execute judgment and righteousness in the earth. In His days Judah will be saved, and Israel will dwell safely; now this is His name by which He will be called: THE LORD OUR RIGHTEOUSNESS* (Jeremiah 23:5-6).

A Kingdom of Peace

Because Jesus will be able to rule absolutely with perfect justice and righteousness, peace will finally come to the earth. There will no longer be border disputes between neighboring countries. One nation will not seek to dominate another. The military academies will be closed and the war machines dismantled.

We learn from the prophets:

He shall judge between the nations, and rebuke many people; they shall beat their swords into plowshares, and their spears into pruning hooks; nation shall not lift up

*sword against nation, neither shall they learn war any-
more* (Isaiah 2:4).

*He shall judge between many peoples, and rebuke strong
nations afar off; they shall beat their swords into plowshares, and their spears into pruning hooks; nation shall
not lift up sword against nation, neither shall they learn
war anymore* (Micah 4:3).

The Kingdom Religion

The Messianic Kingdom will also have a one-world religion. But it
won't be the World Council of Churches. Both the political and spiritual aspects of the Messianic Kingdom will center in the Messiah. Jesus
will rule as the King-Priest, uniting both functions in Himself.

Zechariah prophesied:

*Yes, He shall build the temple of the LORD. He shall bear
the glory, and shall sit and rule on His throne; so He shall
be a priest on His throne, and the counsel of peace shall be
between them both* (Zechariah 6:13).

Because of man's sinful nature, it is not wise for the political and religious affairs of a nation to be under one authority. An ungodly leader
who controls both of these could become a ruthless dictator destroying
and corrupting lives in the worst of ways. This is exactly what the false
messiah will do during the Great Tribulation.

But Jesus will be able to function in both capacities because He is
the perfect God-man. He will exercise His political authority with perfect righteousness, while keeping the spiritual worship pure and free
from perversion. Jerusalem will not only be the world's capital, it will
also be the religious center of the world.

*At that time Jerusalem shall be called The Throne of the
LORD, and all the nations shall be gathered to it, to the
name of the LORD, to Jerusalem. No more shall they follow
the dictates of their evil hearts* (Jeremiah 3:17).

*All the ends of the world shall remember and turn to the
LORD, and all the families of the nations shall worship
before You. For the kingdom is the LORD's, and He rules
over the nations* (Psalms 22:27-28).

*...He will reduce to nothing all the gods of the earth; peo-
ple shall worship Him, each one from his place, indeed all
the shores of the nations* (Zephaniah 2:11).

Because Jesus *(Yeshua)* is a Jewish Lord and King, the worship
expressions during this time will be Jewish, not Greco-Roman. This
is why the prophets describe worship in Jewish terms. Without want-
ing to cause offense, Western Greco-Roman Christianity, as we know it
today, is not taken from the Bible. It was established by Constantine in
the fourth century of our era. All the prophets in the Bible are Jewish.
Jesus and His first followers in the New Testament were all Jewish. They
spoke of a Jewish King and High Priest who would rule and minister
in a Jewish way. They would not have had a concept of Western Greco-
Roman Christianity. It is not in the Bible and it will not exist in the
Messianic Kingdom of God.

When Jesus was here the first time, He came as a Jew. When He
returns He will come as a Jew, not a Christian. If this is a new thought
for you, don't get upset. The Bible is very clear. In Revelation 5:5, Jesus
is called *"the Lion of the tribe of Judah, the Root of David."* In Revelation
22:16, Jesus calls Himself *"the Root and the Offspring of David...."*

Non-Jewish Christian believers need to be prepared for worship
when Messiah comes. Those who are not prepared will be shocked

when they realize Jesus is not going to "have church." He will be a Jewish King ruling over His Kingdom led by the Jewish state of Israel and biblical Jewish expressions of worship. Those who are prepared will be ready to fully enter into the experience of worshiping the Lord in a biblical way. Furthermore, Messianic believing Jews will be shocked when they discover that Jesus is not going to preside over modern rabbinic services disguised as New Testament worship.

Let me make it very clear. There will be no anti-Semitic, replacement-theology Christians living in the Messianic Kingdom of God. If you are anti-Israel, there will be no place for you there. And if you are resisting God's sovereign work of restoring Christianity to its biblical Hebraic roots, you will be miserable in God's Messianic Kingdom.

With a Jewish King and Messiah, Isaiah tells us that the world will function on the biblical Jewish calendar rather than the Greco-Roman calendar. The biblical Jewish calendar is a lunar calendar for keeping the Feasts. The Greco-Roman calendar is a solar calendar based on sun worship. Furthermore, Shabbat (Saturday) will be universally recognized as the special Day of the Lord for worship and rest. (See Isaiah 56:1-8; 58:13-14.)

Isaiah explains: *"It shall come to pass that from one New Moon to another, and from one Sabbath to another, all flesh shall come to worship before Me,' says the LORD"* (Isa. 66:23).

We also learn that people will celebrate the Feasts of the Lord not the feasts of Constantine. We will regulate our worship on the sacred biblical calendar and celebrate God's holy days rather than Greco-Roman holidays.[1]

Zechariah explains:

> *It shall come to pass that everyone who is left of all the nations which came against Jerusalem shall go up from year to year to worship the King, the LORD of hosts, and to keep the Feast of Tabernacles* (Zechariah 14:16).

The prophet Ezekiel provides information concerning worship activities during the Messianic Kingdom (see Ezek. 40–48). In these chapters, Ezekiel describes a religious system that includes a temple, priesthood, and sacrifices. None of this is in any way meant to diminish the completed work of Jesus as the perfect human Temple of God and His perfect High Priest. Nor will it diminish His work as the once-and-for-all perfect sacrifice for our sins. The sacrifices at the Temple will not be for sin. Instead, they will be offerings of praise and worship to the Lord. They are memorial offerings.

Although the Messiah will be the center of worship, He will use the religious expressions as physical object teaching lessons to show in a tangible way who He is and what He has done. The religious teachers will use these object lessons to point people who are born during the millennium to the Messiah and their need for Him to become their personal Redeemer, Lord, and Savior.

Isaiah tells us that God's house (Temple) will be called *"a house of prayer for all nations"* (Isa. 56:7).

Zechariah explains:

> *Peoples shall yet come, inhabitants of many cities; the inhabitants of one city shall go to another, saying, "Let us continue to go and pray before the LORD, and seek the LORD of hosts. I myself will go also." Yes, many peoples and strong nations shall come to seek the LORD of hosts in Jerusalem, and to pray before the LORD. Thus says the LORD of hosts: "In those days ten men from every language of the nations shall grasp the sleeve [tzitzit] of a Jewish man saying 'Let us go with you, for we have heard that God is with you'"* (Zechariah 8:20-23).

Because Israel will be the head nation, Hebrew, not English, will be the universal language. Zephaniah 3:9 reads: *"I will restore to the peoples*

a pure language that they all may call on the name of the LORD, to serve
Him with one accord."

Jeremiah 31:23 explains:

> *Thus says the LORD of hosts, the God of Israel: "They shall*
> *again use this speech in the land of Judah and in its cities,*
> *when I bring back their captivity..."*

The presence of the Messiah will ensure great spiritual blessings
for everyone. All citizens will be able to have full knowledge of God
through the Messiah and will enjoy the New Covenant blessings to the
fullest (see Isa. 11:9-10).

Kingdom Living Conditions

Living conditions in the Messianic Kingdom will be blessed beyond
our present abilities to imagine. As just noted, there will be no more
wars. (See Isaiah 2:4; Micah 4:1-4.) In view of this, we won't need to
dispatch peace-keeping forces to different trouble spots on the globe.
There will be no Iron Curtain, Bamboo Curtain, Berlin Wall, demili-
tarized zones, revolutions, or terrorist groups. The vast sums of money
now spent on the arms race will be used for the benefit of humankind.

Because Jesus will rule with perfect justice and righteousness, social
problems will no longer burden society. Each person will have equal
opportunity to work and provide for his or her family with dignity and
honor. There will be a fair day's wage for a fair day's work. The rich
will not be allowed to exploit the poor. There will be no special interest groups in Jerusalem seeking to gain favor at the expense of others.
Kingdom justice will be administered to all citizens without partiality.

There will be great economic prosperity and full employment (see
Isa. 65:21-23; Joel 2:24-26). Government housing, welfare, and ghet-
tos will be a thing of the past. There will be no need for food-relief

programs. Everyone will have plenty to eat for the earth will be greatly productive (see Amos 9:13-14).

Management and labor will work together for the common good. There will be no need for collective bargaining or crippling strikes that cut off needed services and goods. Plants will operate at full capacity. The world's economy will stabilize without the ups and downs of inflation and depression. Goods and services will be freely exchanged for the benefit of all.

Moral conditions will conform to the biblical standard (see Isa. 2:3). We won't need prophets to raise our moral consciousness, nor the Coalition for Better Television to rate the networks. No smut peddlers, drug pushers, drunk drivers, pimps, prostitutes, gambling halls, crime, or violence of any kind will be allowed.

The curse of sin will be partially removed. The result is that life expectancy will be lengthened so that a 100-year-old person will be considered a child. Hospitals, health care, and insurance programs will not be needed for there will be little or no sickness and death. The world will experience a great population explosion to replenish the earth. (See Romans 8:19-23; Isaiah 65:20; 33:24; Jeremiah 30:17,19-20). Since everyone will speak the same language, we will be able to communicate with one another no matter what our language or country of origin might be.

Light will be enjoyed around the clock so that more can be accomplished. The land will be fruitful. Even the animals will live together in peace. (See Zechariah 14:6-7; Isaiah 35:1-2; Zechariah 8:12; Isaiah 11:6-9; 65:25.)

In every way, life will be better than we can possibly imagine because God Himself will rule the nations through a perfect human King, who is the exalted Son of God-Son of Man, the Lamb of God, the Lion of the Tribe of Judah, the King of kings and Lord of lords. But this wonderful period of blessing is not yet the end. More trouble is to come as we learn in the next few verses.

Satan's Final Rebellion (verses 7-10)

With such a perfect world, why would God spoil it by releasing satan from his prison? Living conditions during the Messianic Kingdom will enable people to live long, productive, and fruitful lives. There will be a great population explosion. Over time, human nature tends to lose sight of the fact that all their blessings are a direct result of the goodness of God, even when they are living in a perfect environment with the Lord Himself.

Because Jesus is ruling with a rod of iron, people must obey His teachings but this does not mean that their hearts are in submission to Him. Obedience is an outward act while submission is an attitude of the heart. So it seems that over the long duration of the Kingdom on Earth, many of the Lord's subjects serve Him out of duty rather than love. The Hebrews did the same thing even when God was in their midst, even when He led them out of Egypt and through the wilderness. They complained and sought a leader other than Moses, someone who would take them back to Egypt. That was just during a 40-year period of time.

God releases satan from his prison to reveal to the people the true motives of their hearts toward their worship and service to King Messiah.

Even after living in a perfect world under the rule of the righteous King, people still need to have their hearts made right toward God. They still need the Holy Spirit to impart the life of God in them. Without this spiritual heart transplant, people are still vulnerable to satan's temptations. We are just too easily deceived and led astray.

So we see that when satan is released from the bottomless pit, he makes one last desperate effort to draw people away from God and destroy God's people. John explains that satan once again deceives the nations and convinces them to join him in throwing off the yoke of God's Kingdom rule. According to John's vision, so many join in the rebellion that they are compared to the sand of the sea.

Wow! This is a sad revelation of the human heart as Jeremiah observed: *"The heart is deceitful above all things, and desperately wicked; who can know it?"* (Jer. 17:9).

John refers to this army of the nations as "Gog and Magog." These are generic terms that refer to the nations who are the enemies of God and God's people. Bible students know that Ezekiel predicted a war against Israel led by a coalition also called Gog and Magog. It too is to take place in the latter years. (See Ezekiel 38–39.)

While the battle Ezekiel describes is certainly similar to the one satan leads, it seems to be at a different time (before the coming of Messiah) and with a different coalition of nations (Russia and her allies) than the one John is describing.

As he did during the Great Tribulation, satan gathers his rebellious army and readies them to attack God's people at Jerusalem. What is the result of satan's last stand against God? There is no description of the battle because it never happens. God sends fire down from Heaven and immediately destroys His enemies. Way to go, God!

This is the end for satan. Finally! God casts the devil into *Gehenna* or hell, the lake of fire and brimstone where the Beast and false prophet have been for the past 1,000 years. Because they hate God and refuse to repent, they receive their just judgment and will be tormented day and night forever.

Those who rejected God in their lives will soon join them after they are judged at the last great judgment. Then time comes to a close and eternity begins.

Let's join John in his vision of this last judgment.

The Great White Throne Judgment (verses 11-15)

The Great White Throne Judgment is the last act of God that announces the fate of those being judged before eternity begins. As human beings created in God's image, we must accept the fact that we are all accountable to God for the way we have lived our lives. While we seek to avoid being accountable to others, we cannot avoid being ultimately accountable to God. We will all stand before Him and be judged for the stewardship of the lives He has given us. While we all know this instinctively, we seek to avoid thinking about it. That does not change the reality.

King Solomon wrote about the foolishness of living life without the fear of God and reminded his readers of the consequences:

> *Let us hear the conclusion of the whole matter: Fear God and keep His commandments, for this is man's all. For God will bring every work into judgment, including every secret thing, whether good or evil* (Ecclesiastes 12:13-14).

In the New Testament we read: *"As it is appointed for men to die once, but after this the judgment..."* (Heb. 9:27). This means there is no ongoing process of reincarnation until we evolve into perfection, as some claim.

Daniel saw the Great White Throne Judgment in his apocalyptic vision (see Dan. 7:9-22; 12:1-3). Daniel says that he saw the Ancient of Days seated on His throne when the books were opened. He also saw the Son of Man participating in this judgment.

The Scriptures tell us that both God the Father and Jesus His Son are involved in the judgment (see Matt. 16:27; John 5:22,27-29; Rom. 2:5-6,16; Rom. 14:12; 1 Cor. 3:12-15; 2 Cor. 5:10; 2 Tim. 4:1; 2 Pet. 2:9; Jude 14-15). In my mind God is the presiding Judge with Jesus confirming the judgment based on His sacrificial atonement for our sins.

John makes a puzzling statement that Heaven and Earth fled from the face of God at the time of this judgment. Since the earth is cursed due to humankind's sin (see Rom. 8:19-22), God cannot come to Earth with His people until He first purifies it from its corrupt elements. This seems to relate to God beginning the transition of creating the new

Heaven and new Earth where only righteousness will dwell. (See Isaiah 51:6; Matthew 24:3-5; Second Peter 3:10-13.)

John sees two books opened. One is the "Book of Works" while the other is the "Book of Life." While scholars have differing views on exactly who is being judged (believers and unbelievers or only unbelievers), the important matter is how the people are judged and the result of the judgment.

Jesus promised the overcomers at Sardis that He would not blot their names out of the Book of Life but would confess them before His Father and the angels. (To review the information on the Book of Life, see the discussion of Revelation 3:5.)

The purpose of the Book of Life is to confirm who will spend eternity with God. In Revelation 13:8 and 21:27, the Book of Life is further identified as the Lamb's Book of Life. This is Heaven's registry book of believers—those who have personally accepted God's provision of salvation and redemption through the innocent, substitutionary blood covenant sacrifice for their sins.

In the Hebrew Bible, beginning with Adam and Eve, God provided animals as the means for the people to draw near to Him. They were saved by grace through faith in the blood of the sacrifice that took their place (see Lev. 17:11). In the New Covenant, believers accept Jesus as the Lamb of God who has taken away our sins (see John 1:29). All true believers, both in the Hebrew Bible and in the New Covenant era, have their names written in the Lamb's Book of Life.

Our eternal life with God is based on our acceptance and identification with His own righteousness made available to us through Jesus. He is the righteous Branch of David who will execute judgment and righteousness in the earth (see Jer. 23:5-6). This is a matter of faith as proclaimed throughout the Bible.

Habakkuk wrote that the just shall live by faith (see Hab. 2:4). Paul quoted Habakkuk and wrote:

I am not ashamed of the gospel of Christ [Messiah], *for it is the power of God to salvation for everyone who believes, for the Jew first and also for the Greek. For in it the righteousness of God is revealed from faith to faith; as it is written, "The just shall live by faith"* (Romans 1:16-17).

The purpose of the Book of Works is twofold. For the believers, it is to determine our rewards based on the stewardship and obedience of our lives as believers. The Bible is very clear that "faith without works is dead" (see James 2:20-26).

Jesus said, *"Let your light so shine before men, that they may see your good works and glorify your Father in heaven"* (Matt. 5:16).

God will reward believers based on their works of covenantal love that were prompted by the Holy Spirit. These Holy Spirit inspired works of godly love are the only righteous deeds that God will accept because they come from God Himself. Religious activities and other good deeds tainted by our own selfish motives will not be acceptable.

The other purpose of the Book of Works is to judge the unbelievers. Sadly, their good works cannot save them. This is also the clear teaching throughout the Bible.

When Daniel prayed for his people, he based his appeal on God's righteousness, not the good deeds of the people:

O my God incline Your ear and hear; open Your eyes and see our desolations, and the city which is called by Your name; for we do not present our supplications before You because of our righteous deeds, but because of Your great mercies (Daniel 9:18).

Isaiah confessed to God the complete unworthiness of his people: *"We are all like an unclean thing, and all our righteousnesses are like filthy rags..."* (Isa. 64:6). Isaiah clearly did not appeal to God based on the moral or religious merits of the people.

Paul added that salvation and favor with God are *"not by works of righteousness which we have done, but according to His mercy He saved us..."* (Titus 3:5). Yet he wrote that our works bear witness to our faith (see Titus 1:16; 2:7,14; 3:8,14).

In Revelation 1:18, Jesus said that He has the keys of Hades and death. The One who has conquered Hades and death cast them both into the lake of fire as they have served their purpose. From this moment on, there will be no more death and those in Hades will have gone to the lake of fire.

Because God made a way for salvation, those who have rejected it do so of their own free will. If their names are not in the Lamb's Book of Life, they are cast into the lake of fire. (To review the information on hell and the lake of fire, see the discussion in the previous chapter of Sheol, Hades, and Gehenna.)

REVIEW QUESTIONS

1. Write a summary of what you have learned in this lesson. Write the summary in clear, concise words as if you were going to present it to another person.

2. Describe how you can apply what you have learned in this lesson to your life.

3. Share what you have learned with your family, friends, and members of your study group.

NOTE

1. If you would like an in-depth understanding of the Feasts of the Lord and how they apply to Christians, please order my book, *Celebrating Jesus in the Biblical Feasts* (Shippensburg, PA: Destiny Image, 2009), from my online bookstore at www.rbooker.com.

Chapter 11

A New Heaven and New Earth

The Bible tells us that God created humankind in His image and after His likeness (see Gen. 1:26). Since God is totally and completely sufficient within Himself, why would He create us? And why would God create us in His image and after His likeness? What does that mean?

We can understand the answer to these questions when we realize why a husband and wife would want to have a child.

Married couples are certainly sufficient within themselves. They don't need children to become a family. Yet, out of pure love, they desire to share their lives with another human being. In cases where it is difficult for the wife to conceive, it's not uncommon for a couple to spend much time and money trying various medical procedures in hopes of having a baby. This is an expression of their intense desire to share their lives and love with someone made in their own image. The child born to them is bone of their bone and flesh of their flesh. He or she carries their DNA. In a very literal way, they have passed their lives on to another human being.

Long before making this momentous decision, would-be parents realize that bringing a child into the world will not only bring them great joy, but great heartaches and challenges as well. They know that the child will have a free will to be a blessing or a source of sorrow. They know that there is an adversary who wants to lead children astray. Yet, the power of love is so great that they are willing to endure the hardships and disappointments they know they will have in bearing and raising children. This is the way of life.

Although human examples always fall short in explaining God, they are all we have. While the Creator of the universe is in need of nothing and no one, He too desired to share His life with someone other than Himself. Since God is all-knowing, He knew that creating us would not only bring Him great joy but also great sorrow and heartache. Yet, the power of His love was so great that He created us. God did not create us in the image of something different from Himself. He created us in His image and after His likeness so that He could fellowship with us, and we with Him. He gave us a free will so we could choose to love Him or rebel against Him.

As it is with human parents and their children, so it has been with us and God. We have not always been loving and obedient children to our Father in Heaven. More times than not, we have been rebellious and disobedient. Yet, like human parents, God loves us simply because we are His. We carry His DNA, and He longs for us to be in right relationship with Him.

Because God loves us so much, He took the initiative to bring us back into right relationship with Him. He came to us in the person of Jesus of Nazareth for the purpose of forgiving our sins and reconciling us to Himself—all so that we could have fellowship with Him. God chose Abraham and his descendants through Isaac and Jacob as the ethnic people through whom He would be born.

Yet, there has been an adversary, satan, who has sought to stop this reconciliation process. Like our own children, satan has deceived and tempted God's people in an effort to lead them astray. In his hatred and rage against God, he has worked throughout history to hinder God's plan of redemption and reconciliation by destroying the Jewish people. But God made an everlasting covenant that He swore to uphold. He would make Israel the head of nations under the greater Son of David.

When Jesus came the first time, satan provoked political and religious leaders to crucify Jesus. But this had been God's plan from eternity past. Just like human parents make plans in advance to overcome situations with their children, so God had made plans in advance for Jesus to bear our sins. He is the Lamb slain from the foundations of the world (see 1 Pet. 1:20-21).

Because Jesus never sinned, death could not hold Him. After 2,000 years, there is still an empty tomb in Jerusalem. Jesus was resurrected to Heaven until the time when He would return to rule over all the nations of the earth on behalf of His Father in Heaven.

Peter explained that Jesus was received into Heaven until the times of restoration of all things (see Acts 3:21). Until that time in God's sovereign plan, He has given us the right to choose to return to Him or follow the adversary. Now that time has come to an end.

In our last chapter, we saw this incredible drama of redemption that has lasted throughout history coming to a close. Jesus has returned to establish the fullness of the Kingdom of God on the earth. He is the perfect divine-human who came as the Lion of the Tribe of Judah to administer God's righteous rule on the earth. Through Jesus, the last Adam, God has restored dominion and rule over the earth to humankind. As King David prophesied:

> *All the ends of the world shall remember and turn to the LORD, and all the families of the nations shall worship before You. For the kingdom is the LORD's, and He rules over the nations* (Psalms 22:27-28).

Jesus has ruled with His people over a Kingdom of righteousness and peace for 1,000 years. He has banished satan forever to the lake of fire. Along with His Father, Jesus has sat as the Son of Man at the Great White Throne Judgment. The dead of all the ages are judged. Those whose names are found in the Lamb's Book of Life live forever in the glorious presence of God.

Tragically, those who rejected God's gift of love will be banished forever to the lake of fire that was prepared for the devil and his angels. This was not God's will for His human creation. He had no choice, because He refused to violate the free will of His children to return to Him or follow the adversary. As difficult as this is to contemplate, human parents should be able to understand this in relationship to their own children.

A New Heaven and New Earth (Revelation 21)

God began time and history in a garden with Adam and Eve in the Book of Genesis. Now He ends time and history in another garden with His people in the Book of Revelation. Eternity begins with God's people living forever with Him in a new Heaven and a new Earth and a New Jerusalem.

This is the final destiny for God's people. It is the promise that the Son of Man made to the faithful believers at Philadelphia. It is His promise to all the overcomers throughout history. (See Revelation 3:12.) All that we as God's faithful people have endured will certainly be worth the suffering and heartache when we see Him face to face.

Let's join John in this and the next chapter for his final apocalyptic vision of what lies ahead for the people of God. He sees a new Heaven, a new Earth, and a New Jerusalem where God dwells among His people. May our hope be renewed, our hearts refreshed, and our burdens lightened as we contemplate the glorious future God has for us.

A New Heaven and New Earth (verse 1)

Once again, John sees in the spiritual realm what he cannot comprehend with his physical senses. He sees a new Heaven and a new Earth replacing the first Heaven and the first earth. He adds that there is no more sea. Since the Bible tells the same story from Genesis to Revelation, we would expect to find the Hebrew prophets writing about what John now sees. We are not disappointed.

The Lord gave Isaiah several prophetic previews about our physical universe wearing out and needing to be replaced. Isaiah recorded what the Lord told him:

> *Lift up your eyes to the heavens, and look on the earth beneath. For the heavens will vanish away like smoke, the earth will grow old like a garment, and those who dwell in it will die in like manner; but My salvation will be forever, and My righteousness will not be abolished* (Isaiah 51:6).

In this word, Isaiah compares this old planet of ours to a garment that is wearing out due to the curse of sin. Science calls this the Second Law of Thermodynamics. This law simply means that the world and everything in it is wearing out. That's why we need WD-40.

Paul stated the same truth when he said that all of creation is groaning like a woman in labor waiting to be delivered from the curse of sin into a new Heaven and new Earth (see Rom. 8:18-22). Heaven and Earth will be reborn when God makes all things new.

The psalmist used similar words:

> *Of old You laid the foundation of the earth, and the heavens are the work of Your hands. They will perish, but You will endure; yes, they will grow old like a garment; like a cloak You will change them, and they will be changed.*

But you are the same, and Your years will have no end
(Psalms 102:25-27).

The writer of Hebrews refers to this psalm in Hebrews 1:10-12. Isaiah further describes a new Heaven and new Earth and a New Jerusalem:

Behold, I create new heavens and a new earth; and the former shall not be remembered or come to mind. But be glad and rejoice forever in what I create; for behold, I create Jerusalem as a rejoicing, and her people a joy. I will rejoice in Jerusalem, and joy in My people; the voice of weeping shall no longer be heard in her, nor the voice of crying (Isaiah 65:17-19; see also Isaiah 66:22).

Jesus also spoke about the passing away of our physical universe as we know it. He said, *"Heaven and earth will pass away, but My words will by no means pass away"* (Matt. 24:35).

Peter explains that God will purge the curse of sin from our physical universe with fire. As we all know, fire is destructive; but it also cleanses and purifies. Forest fires burn up the old but bring rejuvenation and new growth.

Peter explains:

But the day of the Lord will come as a thief in the night, in which the heavens will pass away with a great noise, and the elements will melt with fervent heat; both the earth and the works that are in it will be burned up. Therefore, since all these things will be dissolved, what manner of persons ought you to be in holy conduct and godliness, looking for and hastening the coming of the day of God, because of which the heavens will be dissolved, being on fire, and the elements will melt with fervent heat? Nevertheless we, according to His promise, look for new heavens and a new earth in which righteousness dwells (2 Peter 3:10-13).

As noted, John said there would be no more sea. Since the sea was the place of upheaval, terror, and dread to his first-century readers, we don't know if John means this literally or is speaking in figurative terms. He may be comforting his readers with the understanding that they won't have to fear sinking forever into the abyss, which to them was the abode of the Beast and every frightening creature imaginable.

The New Jerusalem Revealed (verses 2-8)

The new Heaven and the new Earth are now ready for God to dwell with His people on the earth. Then the dramatic moment happens. John sees the holy city, the New Jerusalem coming down out of Heaven from God.

This is the city Abraham saw by faith. While Abraham journeyed in the Promised Land, and made his way to Jerusalem, he saw far beyond the earthly Jerusalem to a more glorious Jerusalem where God would dwell among His people forever.

The writer of Hebrews explains:

> *By faith Abraham obeyed when he was called to go out to the place which he would receive as an inheritance. And he went out, not knowing where he was going. By faith he dwelt in the land of promise as in a foreign country, dwelling in tents with Isaac and Jacob, the heirs with him of the same promise; for he waited for the city which has foundations, whose builder and maker is God* (Hebrews 11:8-10).

Hebrews further explains:

You have come to Mount Zion and to the city of the living God, the heavenly Jerusalem, to an innumerable company of angels, to the general assembly and church [congregation] of the firstborn who are registered in heaven, to God the Judge of all, to the spirits of just men made perfect, to Jesus the Mediator of the new covenant, and to the blood of sprinkling that speaks better things than that of Abel (Hebrews 12:22-24).

While millions of believers love the present Old City of Jerusalem, the New Jerusalem is the one we are waiting to enter. It is the ultimate destination of all of God's people as well as those angels that stayed true to God when satan rebelled. From the beginning of creation, the New Jerusalem has been the heavenly home of God and the angels. But now it can come to the earth. What this means is that God's people will not spend eternity in Heaven floating on clouds in some kind of heavenly mist. No, they will live with Him forever in this grand, eternal city on a new Earth. Hallelujah!

John says that the city is prepared as a bride adorned for her husband. Comparing a city to a bride is not part of our way of thinking and speaking. However, in times past, rulers and citizens expressed their love for and bonding to their land and city in marriage terms. At their coronation, emperors and kings pledged their fidelity to the land and the city. They and their subjects were one with the land and the city as a husband and wife are bonded to one another. The land, the city, and the people were one.

This is why God used marriage talk when He spoke about the people of Israel and the land of Israel. Ancient people understood His meaning. He said that He would not leave Zion and Jerusalem like a forsaken wife but that He would restore the land and the people to one another. The land and the people would be married to each other.

God speaks tenderly to the land through the prophet Isaiah:

*You shall no longer be termed Forsaken, nor shall your
land any more be termed Desolate; but you shall be called
Hephzibah* [My delight],*[1] and your land Beulah* [mar-
ried],*[2] for the* LORD *delights in you, and your land shall
be married. For as a young man marries a virgin, so shall
your sons marry you; and as the bridegroom rejoices
over the bride, so shall your God rejoice over you* (Isaiah
62:4-5).

Next John hears a loud voice proclaiming what God's people have
longed to hear throughout the ages—our Father in Heaven is now personally going to live with us. Wow! This is breathtaking. We can hardly
grasp it; it is almost too much for our physical beings to handle. The
fullness of the majesty and glory of God will be with us, and we will be
able to live with Him in that fullness—forever!

The voice John hears makes five statements saying what *will be* and
six statements saying what *will not be* when God comes to live with
His people.

The tabernacle of God is with men.

The tabernacle of God is the phrase that defines God's dwelling
place. It is the *Sh'khinah* (manifested presence of God). Our Father in
Heaven has always desired to "tabernacle" among His people. He has
said this many times in the Scriptures. God's Word in Leviticus connects to all of these positive statements: *"I will set My tabernacle among
you, and My soul shall not abhor you. I will walk among you and be your
God, and you shall be My people"* (Lev. 26:11-12).

He will dwell with them.

The voice explains that for God to tabernacle among us means that
He will dwell among us in His manifested presence. Because of sin, God

could only dwell among His people indirectly. But He gave previews of what it would be like when He could come in the fullness of His glory.

This is what happened when God appeared at the Tabernacle of Moses:

> *The cloud covered the tabernacle of meeting, and the glory of the LORD filled the tabernacle. And Moses was not able to enter the tabernacle of meeting, because the cloud rested above it, and the glory of the LORD filled the tabernacle* (Exodus 40:34-35).

God manifested His presence again when Solomon dedicated the Temple. This is what happened while the people were praising Him:

> *It came to pass, when the priests came out of the holy place, that the cloud filled the house of the LORD, so that the priests could not continue ministering because of the cloud; for the glory of the LORD filled the house of the LORD* (1 Kings 8:10-11).

As wonderful as this was, God had something better in mind. He would come in bodily form, as one of us, to live among us. Certainly the Creator can stay in Heaven and at the same time prepare a body for Himself in order to live among us. Isaiah saw this in the future and wrote: *"The Lord Himself will give you a sign: Behold the virgin shall conceive and bear a Son, and shall call His name Immanuel"* (Isa. 7:14).

Immanuel means "God with us." While there was an immediate, historical understanding of this word, prophetically it pointed to the coming of the Lord to live in our midst as one of us and to be the perfect revelation of His glory. We are talking about Jesus of Nazareth.

This same John wrote of Jesus:

> *The Word* [full expression of God] *became flesh and dwelt* [tabernacled] *among us, and we beheld His glory,*

the glory as of the only begotten of the Father, full of grace and truth. No one has seen God at any time. The only begotten [uniquely born] *Son, who is in the bosom of the Father, He has declared Him* (John 1:14, 18).

Now that God has removed the evidence of humankind's sins and created a new Heaven and new Earth, He can dwell among us in the fullness of His blazing glory and dazzling beauty. We will be able to behold Him as He is because we will be like Him—without sin.

Beloved, now we are children of God; and it has not yet been revealed what we shall be, but we know that when He is revealed, we shall be like Him, for we shall see Him as He is (1 John 3:2).

They shall be His people.

Out of His own sovereign desire to reveal Himself to us, the Creator of the universe needed a people through whom He could make Himself known. He could not reveal Himself to us in the fullness of His glory without destroying us with His manifested presence. He needed a people. God could have chosen any people group. As we learn in the Bible, He chose Abraham, Isaac, Jacob, and their descendants as the ethnic people through whom He would reveal His redemptive plans and purposes on the earth.

God did not choose the Jewish people because they were better than any other group. He chose them because He found in Abraham a man who believed in the One True God and followed Him. Abraham's descendants, later known as the Jews, were not special because of some inherit superiority but because of their high calling:

You are a holy people to the Lord *your God; the* Lord *your God has chosen you to be a people for Himself, a special treasure above all the peoples on the face of the earth* (Deuteronomy 7:6).

The Jewish people were called to be a holy people who would bring the knowledge of God to the world. They gave us the revelation of the One True God, the Holy Scriptures, and the Messiah. It is their calling that makes them special, and they have paid a high price for that calling. They have been the primary target of satan's hatred against God.

While the Jews were the first of God's people, the Creator made it clear that He would also call a people to Himself from among the Gentiles. In all three divisions of the Hebrew Bible, the Law (*Torah*), the Prophets (*Nevi'im*) and the Psalms (*K'tivim*), the Lord revealed that He would include Gentiles as part of "My people."

From the moment God called Abraham, He told Abraham that he would be a blessing to all the families of the earth (see Gen. 12:3). God's covenant people would include "whosoever will" as they responded to the revelation He gave through Abraham.

Before God even brought the Hebrews into the Promised Land, He reached out to the Gentiles and said, *"Rejoice, O Gentiles, with His people..."* (Deut. 32:43). The psalmist calls the Gentiles to worship the Lord: *"Praise the LORD, all you Gentiles! Laud Him, all you peoples!"* (Ps. 117:1).

Isaiah spoke of the Messiah who would come from the seed of Jesse, the father of King David. He prophesied that the Gentiles would seek Him: *"In that day there shall be a Root of Jesse, who shall stand as a banner to the people; for the Gentiles shall seek Him, and His resting place shall be glorious"* (Isa. 11:10).

Luke tells the story of Simeon, a devout Jewish man, who was waiting for the Messiah to appear. The Lord told him that he would not die until he saw the Messiah. When Jesus was presented at the Temple, Simeon prophesied:

Lord, now You are letting Your servant depart in peace, according to Your word; for my eyes have seen Your salvation which You have prepared before the face of all peoples, a light to bring revelation to the Gentiles, and the glory of Your people Israel (Luke 2:29-32).

Simeon was referring to Isaiah's prophecy where the Lord said of the Messiah: *"...I will also give You as a light to the Gentiles, that You should be My salvation to the ends of the earth"* (Isa. 49:6).

Through Messiah, God has made a way for all people to be His people, regardless of ethnic or national background, skin color, gender, economic status, social position, education, life achievements, age, language, customs, or traditions.

There are no human barriers to keep us from being in God's Kingdom family. All of His people will be forever in His glorious presence. As Paul writes:

There is neither Jew nor Greek, there is neither slave nor free, there is neither male nor female; for you are all one in Christ [Messiah] *Jesus. And if you are Christ's* [Messiah's], *then you are Abraham's seed* [natural and spiritually adopted], *and heirs according to the promise* (Galatians 3:28-29).

God will be with them.

Because of the curse of sin, and our own rebellious ways, God our Father has not personally been with us. He walked in The Garden with Adam and Eve (see Gen. 3:8). But sin separated us from Him. Ever since then, He has desired to be with us.

He manifested His presence from time to time in His cloud of glory. He sent His angels with messages. He reached out to us through creation, our human conscience, His written Word and His Living Word,

Jesus of Nazareth. When His disciple asked Jesus to show him the Father, Jesus answered, *"...He who has seen Me has seen the Father..."* (John 14:9).

Furthermore, our Father in Heaven sent His Spirit to live in us so that we could have fellowship with Him until that time when He could be with us in His fullness. Jesus explained:

> *I will pray the Father, and He will give you another Helper* [Comforter], *that He may abide with you forever—the Spirit of truth, whom the world cannot receive, because it neither sees Him nor knows Him; but you know Him, for He dwells with you and will be in you* (John 14:16-17).

Any good father wants to be with his children. Likewise, our Father in Heaven wants to be with us. Now that He has made us like Him, He can once again walk in the garden with us. Jesus promised: *"If anyone loves Me, he will keep My word; and My Father will love him, and We will come to him and make Our home with him"* (John 14:23).

God has made His home with us and in us through the Holy Spirit. But in the New Jerusalem, our entire beings will be filled with Him. We will be able to live in the fullness of His manifested presence. We will be fully with Him and fully like Him. His blazing glory and dazzling beauty will no longer overwhelm us because it will be in us as well as with us.

He will be their God.

God will not only tabernacle with us, dwell with us, and be with us as His people, He will also be our God. When God created us in His image and likeness, He put within us the need to know Him and worship Him. Human beings have an innate need to worship. If we do not worship God, we will worship something or someone else.

Tragically, when our ancient ancestors rebelled against God, they lost the knowledge of Him. And yet, that innate need within them to worship something or someone greater than themselves would not be ignored. Finally, they responded by worshiping demonic spirits and images and idols made with their own hands. This led them to live self-destructive lives of wickedness and immorality, poverty, disease, superstition, fear, despair, hopelessness, and bondage to every unclean thought and practice. Their minds became so deceived and darkened that they could not see the reality of their wretched and shameful lives. Paul described this terrible depravity of life without God in Romans 1:18-32.

This was certainly not God's intention for His human offspring. He entered into an everlasting blood covenant with Abraham promising that he and his descendants would be His people and He would be their God:

> *I will establish My covenant between Me and you and your descendants after you in their generations, for an everlasting covenant, to be God to you and your descendants after you* (Genesis 17:7).

From that moment forward, God consistently stated that He wanted to be their God (see Exod. 6:7; Jer. 31:33-34; Ezek. 37:27; Zech. 8:8, etc.).

While God became God to the Hebrews, the Gentiles were still far from Him. As Paul wrote:

> *At that time you were without Christ* [Messiah], *being aliens from the commonwealth of Israel and strangers from the covenants of promise, having no hope and without God in the world* (Ephesians 2:12).

In His mercy, God made a way for the Gentiles. He renewed His ancient covenant through the person of Jesus. Paul adds:

In Christ [Messiah] *Jesus you who once were far off have been brought near by the blood of Christ* [Messiah].... *For through Him we both have access by one Spirit to the Father* (Ephesians 2:13,18).

God is now the God of all who come to Him through the blood of the everlasting covenant fully realized in the Lamb of God slain from the foundations of the world. He is God to us. Hallelujah!

These five declarations tell us that we will forever be in the presence of our glorious Father in Heaven. We will have unbroken fellowship with joy unspeakable and full of glory. Jude was looking to this time when he wrote:

Now to Him who is able to keep you from stumbling [falling], *and to present you faultless before the presence of His glory with exceeding joy, to God our Savior, who alone is wise, be glory and majesty, dominion and power, both now and forever. Amen* (Jude 24-25).

The next six statements tell us what will *not* be in the New Jerusalem. In a negative sense, these are just as encouraging as the positive statements we just contemplated. Although John wrote these words of comfort and encouragement to the believers in the seven congregations, his words are certainly for all of God's people throughout history who have suffered for their faith. May we also find the strength and courage to be faithful knowing that there will be "no more" of the following when our Father in Heaven is with us.

There will be no more tears.

When God created Adam and Eve, they were without sin. This means they were also without tears, death, sorrow, crying, and pain. All of these human liabilities came about because of sin. God told Adam and Eve that the day they sinned, they would die (see Gen. 2:17; 3:3).

When they disobeyed, they lost the glory of God (began to die) and covered themselves with fig leaves. When God came to fellowship with them, they ran and hid from Him (see Gen. 3:8). Thus began the process of death and sorrow that to this day characterizes human existence on the earth.

Throughout history, God has kept a record of the tears His people have shed in their struggles to live righteous lives and stand strong when persecuted for their faith. In fact, ancient people had tear bottles in which they preserved their tears during times of great sorrow and grief. King David had such a tear bottle and figured that God also had one for each of His children. When David had to fight the Philistines, he literally cried to God, saying, *"You number my wanderings; put my tears into Your bottle; are they not in Your book?"* (Ps. 56:8).

First-century Romans kept tear bottles and placed them in the tombs of their deceased family members as a way of showing respect. In more modern times, the American Civil War for example, women wept in tear bottles for their husbands and sons who had gone to fight. Some companies today specialize in selling tear bottles. From cradle to grave, life is accompanied by tears.

With the curse of sin removed, there will be no more tears. God will wipe every tear from our eyes. Isaiah looked to this time and wrote: *"He will swallow up death forever, and the Lord God will wipe tears from all faces; the rebuke of His people He will take away from all the earth..."* (Isa. 25:8).

When God makes all things new, He will open our heavenly tear bottles and empty them. They will no longer be needed. So here is the good news for all of God's people: there will be no tear bottles in the New Jerusalem.

There will be no more death.

The Bible tells us (see Rom. 6:23), all of history bears witness, and our own personal experiences do as well: the judgment for sin is death.

From the moment we are born, we begin to die. Our time on this earth is limited. As Job wrote: *"Man who is born of woman is of few days and full of trouble"* (Job 14:1). We all have to live with the reality of death and the grave. When the curse of sin is removed, there will be no more death. We will live forever in a new body that is free from the corrupting influence of sin.

Paul quoted Isaiah when he wrote these words of assurance:

> *For this corruptible must put on incorruption, and this mortal must put on immortality. So when this corruptible has put on incorruption, and this mortal has put on immortality, then shall be brought to pass the saying that is written: "Death is swallowed up in victory." "O Death, where is your sting? O Hades, where is your victory?" The sting of death is sin, and the strength of sin is the law. But thanks be to God, who gives us the victory through our Lord Jesus Christ. Therefore, my beloved brethren, be steadfast, immovable, always abounding in the work of the Lord, knowing that your labor is not in vain in the Lord* (1 Corinthians 15:53-58).

There will be no more sorrow.

Before Adam and Eve sinned, they knew only joy. They did not know sorrow, which is the death process of the soul. Unfortunately, they passed on their anguish of soul to all of us. The history of the human race and our own life experiences tell us that we have inherited their mental and emotional distress. There is no other sensible explanation for the condition of humankind. While we might not want to face this truth and acknowledge it, we should be able to understand it knowing that we pass on both the good and the bad to our own children. We do to our children just what Adam and Eve did to us.

Human life is characterized by joy and sorrow, happiness and heart-ache, triumph and trials, delight and despair. Millions of people suffer from anxiety attacks, and depression is a plague of the soul as real as plagues that attack the body. Some of our fellow human beings have such troubled and tortured souls that they take their own lives.

While God's Spirit produces joy in the souls of His people, believers are certainly not immune to the sorrow and heartaches that are part of living in this world. We sometimes have more than our share because of deep-rooted concerns for our troubled world and compassion for hurting people.

All of this will change when we are in the full presence of our Father in Heaven. With sin no longer present to afflict our souls, there will be nothing to trouble us. There will be no anguish, no grief, no heartache, no disappointments, no regrets, no despair, no sadness, no mourning, no anxieties, and no sleepless nights fretting over loved ones and the issues of life.

During the Messianic Kingdom, we will have a preview of life without sorrow (see Isa. 35:10). King David experienced a foretaste of this in his own life with God. David wrote: *"In Your presence is fullness of joy; at Your right hand are pleasures* [spiritual bliss] *forevermore"* (Ps. 16:11). Lord, let it be soon!

There will be no more crying.

Whereas tears refer to a quiet expression of grief, crying is a vocal manifestation of our inward heartaches. Crying expresses in an outward way the inner anguish of our souls and physical afflictions. Sometimes we suffer to the point where we can "no longer hold it in." For the sake of our own inner healing, we have to "let it out."

Humans cry out to God. We cry out in physical pain. We cry out in times of extreme soul affliction. We cry when we lose something of great value. We cry when our world falls apart. We cry in times of great distress. We cry when people fail to live up to our expectations. We cry when people we love are suffering. We cry at funerals.

Humans cry. It is part of living in a world so full of death and sorrow, injustice, poverty, disease, and inevitable disappointment.

But we won't cry when we live in the New Jerusalem. With no tears, no death, and no sorrow, crying will be a thing of the past. There won't be anything to cry about. In Isaiah's words which we read earlier, when God makes all things new the voice of weeping and the voice of crying will be heard no more (see Isa. 65:19).

There will be no more pain.

Ever since Adam and Eve sinned, the human race has known pain as a normal part of life. Life begins with birth pains, and ends with the pain of death. Genesis tells us that God proclaimed the following judgment on Eve: *"To the woman He said: 'I will greatly multiply your sorrow and your conception; in pain you shall bring forth children'"* (Gen. 3:16).

Every woman who has brought a child into the world is a living testimony to the reality of this pronouncement. While the mom-to-be looks forward to the joy of bringing a new life into the world, she certainly doesn't look forward to the labor pains. This was particularly stressful for women in Bible times who considered having lots of children a blessing from God in spite of the pain of childbirth. I suppose we could say of childbirth that women have the blessed joy of labor pains.

To Adam, God said:

> *Cursed is the ground for your sake; in toil you shall eat of it all the days of your life. Both thorns and thistles it shall bring forth for you, and you shall eat the herb of the field. In the sweat of your face you shall eat bread till you return to the ground, for out of it you were taken; for dust you are, and to dust you shall return* (Genesis 3:17-19).

People who live off the land can certainly bear witness to the reality of this statement. Oh, the life of a farmer—so rewarding and so many aches and pains. Every farmer and tiller of the soil knows how challenging it is to make the land productive. It is hard and difficult work from sunup to sunset. And after it's all said and done, there is no guarantee of a good crop.

We don't have to live on the farm to appreciate this difficulty. Anyone who wants to grow a garden or beautify a yard knows the difficulty of planting just the right vegetables or flowers in the right place at the right time with the right amount of sun, shade, and drainage. We have to prepare the soil, pull the weeds, cut down the thornbushes, spray the bugs, keep out the critters, plant, fertilize and water the plantings—just to enjoy a few tomatoes or flowers in the yard.

The pain our bodies feel in birthing and working is only a part of our human experience with pain. We have to cope with pain caused by health issues. We suffer from dreaded diseases, broken bones, allergies, infections, bodily injuries, organic disorders, and accidents that can maim and cripple us. The list is endless.

In addition to these physical challenges, we struggle with mental and emotional pain that can hurt just as much as physical pain. We must deal with the pain of broken relationships, lost love, separation from loved ones, unkind words, persecution, hate and prejudice, poverty, injustice, and ultimately the pain of death.

Here is some more good news. With no more curse of sin, no more tears, no more death, no more sorrow, and no more crying, there will also be no more pain in the New Jerusalem.

The former things will have passed away.

The reason we will no longer have to deal with tears, death, sorrow, crying, and pain is because the former things will have passed away. There is no place for suffering in God's newly established Kingdom. No matter what we are enduring as believers, it will not last. We will live in eternity free of all the human liabilities caused by sin. Just as this old world will pass away, so will our old heartaches, our failures, our frustrations, our disappointments, the pain, agony, and grief of body, soul, and spirit.

Jesus spoke these words of reassurance to His followers:

> *Let not your heart be troubled; you believe in God, believe also in Me. In My Father's house are many mansions* [dwellings]; *if it were not so, I would have told you. I go to prepare a place for you. And if I go and prepare a place for you, I will come again and receive you to Myself; that where I am there you may be also* (John 14:1-3).

> *These things I have spoken to you, that in Me you may have peace. In the world you will have tribulation; but be of good cheer, I have overcome the world* (John 16:33).

Once the loud voice clarifies our place with God in the New Jerusalem, God Himself declares that Heaven and Earth as we know them are gone. The creation of the new Heaven and new Earth is done. We can have faith and confidence of a better world to come because God's words are true and He is faithful to perform them.

The truth and faithfulness of God is emphasized again in Revelation 22:6. When we look back in time and see that God has done everything just as it was written in the Bible, we can look to the future and know that He will also keep His promise to make all things new. As Jesus said: *"Heaven and earth will pass away, but My words will by no means pass away"* (Matt. 24:35).

The Creator of the universe is outside of time. He was before time, He is after time, and when time is no more. All of time and space are contained within Him. This is why God can declare the end from the beginning (see Isa. 46:10). Like a book is contained within the author, all of creation history is contained within God.

Writing to a Greek-speaking audience, John uses the Greek alphabet to communicate the eternal nature of God. He is the Alpha and the Omega, the Beginning and the End. The Alpha and the Omega are the first and last letters of the Greek alphabet. If John had written this to Hebrew speakers, he would say that God is the Aleph and the Tav, the first and last letters of the Hebrew alphabet. Since Jesus has the divine DNA of His Father, He speaks of Himself in the same way in His letters to the seven congregations (see Rev. 1:8,11,17; 2:8; 22:13).

God gives a further word of encouragement to the overcomers. He promises the faithful that: they will drink freely of the waters of life; they will inherit all things; He will be their God and they will be His children. These grand sweeping statements simply mean that God has made full provision for His people to live with Him forever without need or want.

God has made this same promise to us in this life (see Phil. 4:19), but the curse of sin often hinders us from experiencing the fullness of this promise. In the new Heaven and new Earth, as well as in the New Jerusalem, there will be no hindrances keeping us from enjoying the overflowing presence of God and His provision throughout eternity.

Unfortunately, this is not the fate of those who reject God. Because they did not have faith and courage when faced with persecution, they "fixed their sandals" in front of the statue of the emperor. Similarly, many people living in the last days will take the Mark of the Beast, choosing temporary physical safety with the Beast rather than life with God. As a result, they are banished from God's presence and doomed to spend eternity with the Beast in the lake of fire.

The New Jerusalem Described (verses 9-21)

With God's word of promise to the overcomers now confirmed, it is time for John to see the New Jerusalem. One of the angels who poured out the seven bowl judgments calls John to come with him for one last apocalyptic vision. Once again, we remember that John was not literally carried away to a high mountain. He is still on Patmos. He is "in the Spirit," meaning God enables him to see with his spiritual eyes what he cannot see with his natural eyes.

We just learned that ancient people considered themselves married to their land. They pledged their fidelity to defend and protect the land, just as a husband would pledge to defend and protect his bride-wife. Since John is writing to an audience that understood this, the angel mentions that the Lamb's wife, the people, and the city are one. A city is more than a place. It is also the people who live in the city. Just as the New Jerusalem reflects the glory of God, so do the people who live there. They are one with their God and King and with their city.

While the New Jerusalem is a literal city, John describes it using symbolic language that his readers would understand to represent perfection in every way. To the ancient mind, a structure that was as high as it was deep and wide and made with rare gems was something people could only imagine. It was certainly not attainable by human efforts. The New Jerusalem is what Babylon and Rome are not. It is the ultimate *"perfection of beauty, the joy of the whole earth"* (Lam. 2:15). It is pure and holy and radiates the spectacular splendor and glory of God and His people.

It is also good to be reminded that the Hebraic way of thinking is to emphasize function rather than form. In other words, John would expect his readers to understand why he describes the New Jerusalem as he does (function) and not just the physical description (form). The ancient mind would be more interested in what a structure is for than what the structure actually looks like.

While the New Jerusalem is presently in Heaven, John is told that it will come down from Heaven to Earth as the eternal home of all God's people and the angels of God.

This is how John describes the city: *"The construction of its wall was of jasper; and the city was pure gold, like clear glass"* (Rev. 21:18). Even the street of the city is pure gold, like transparent glass (see Rev. 21:21).

John gives this description to explain that the function of the city is to reflect the glory of God everywhere.

Our eternal hometown seems to be in the shape of a cube, which John's readers would have considered the perfect shape. It is approximately 1500 miles high, 1500 miles wide, and 1500 miles long (see Rev. 21:15-16). While not necessarily to be understood literally, John's description of the shape, the height, the width, and the length was his way of saying the city is perfect in every way. While Babylon and Rome were built for the glory of man, the New Jerusalem is built for the glory of God. It is perfect, just as He is perfect.

The wall around the city is 216 feet high. A cubit is approximately 18 inches, or 1.5 feet, and the wall is 144 cubits high (see Rev. 21:17). It is made of transparent gold jasper (see Rev. 21:18). The wall has 12 gates, each attended by an angel. The names of the 12 tribes of Israel are written on the gates. (See Revelation 21:12-13.) Each gate is made of a single pearl (see Rev. 21:21).

In Bible times, the function of a wall was to protect the people inside by keeping the enemy outside. John describes a wall so high that his readers would immediately understand his point—no enemy of God or His people could ever hurt them again. They were protected and safe forever. Furthermore, God posted angels at each gate as His ultimate "watchmen on the wall"—even though no watchmen were needed.

John says that the names of the 12 tribes of Israel are written on the gates. He mentions this to remind us that God's covenant with Abraham, Isaac, and Jacob is eternal. Furthermore, the tribes have never been lost. They did not become Gentiles living in far-off lands. Nor were they replaced by Christians.

The wall of the city has 12 foundations made of precious stones. Each foundation is named after one of the 12 apostles of Jesus who brought the Gospel of the Kingdom to the Gentiles. (See Revelation 21:14.) While we cannot be certain of some of the exact colors of these stones, John is making the point that the foundations are designed to reflect the glory of God in a dazzling spectrum of brilliant colors. (See Revelation 21:19-20.) That is their function.

Here is a brief description of the foundations:

- The first foundation is a jasper gold, clear as crystal.

- The second foundation is a sapphire blue.

- The third foundation is a chalcedony (agate) thought to be sky blue with other colors running through it.

- The fourth foundation is a bright green emerald.

- The fifth foundation is sardonyx, which is red with white stripes.

- The sixth foundation is sardius, a beautiful red.

- The seventh foundation is chrysolite, a transparent stone golden green in color.

- The eighth foundation is a sea-green beryl.

- The ninth foundation is a transparent yellow topaz.

- The tenth foundation is chrysoprase, a shade of green.

- The eleventh foundation is jacinth, a violet color.

- The twelfth foundation is a beautiful purple amethyst.

The Glory of the New Jerusalem (verses 22-27)

When King Solomon built the Temple to God, he realized that no earthly structure could contain the fullness of the glory of God (see 2 Chron. 2:6). It was simply a place where God could meet with His people and they could draw near to Him through their sacrifices.

Solomon was right, which is why there is no temple in the New Jerusalem. The fullness of God's presence *is* the temple. Every citizen of the New Jerusalem will be in His presence wherever they are, because His glory fills the city.

Isaiah saw this city and wrote:

> *Arise, shine; for your light has come! And the glory of the* LORD *has risen upon you....The sun shall no longer be your light by day, nor for brightness shall the moon give light to you; but the* LORD *will be to you an everlasting light, and your God your glory. Your sun shall no longer go down, nor shall your moon withdraw itself; for the* LORD *will be your everlasting light, and the days of your mourning shall be ended* (Isaiah 60:1,19-20).

While this prophecy will certainly be fulfilled in part during the Messianic Kingdom, its fullness awaits the coming of the New Jerusalem to the earth. John connects his vision to Isaiah's prophecy. He says there will be no sun or moon in the new Heaven and Earth or in the New Jerusalem. The glory of God is the light of the city (see Rev. 21:23).

Today, believers are the temple of God because His Spirit lives in them. Paul writes:

> *Do you not know that your body is the temple of the Holy Spirit who is in you, whom you have from God, and you are not your own? For you were bought at a price; there-fore glorify God in your body and in your spirit, which are God's* (1 Corinthians 6:19-20).

Because we sometimes yield to the lusts of our flesh, we can grieve and quench the Holy Spirit in us (see Eph. 4:30; 1 Thess. 5:19). Sometimes we do not glorify God. We will not have this challenge in the New Jerusalem. The city is designed to transmit the light of God's glory without hindrance so that all the inhabitants will see His glory and be in His glory wherever they are. Because the glory of the Lord is the light of the city, there is no need for the sun and moon, for there will be no nighttime in eternity (see Rev. 21:23).

Ancient people closed the gates of their cities at night for security reasons. They needed to keep out invaders. Because evil and sin have been completely purged from the earth, the gates of the city will always remain open (see Rev. 21:25). We won't need to lock our doors or set our alarm systems. Nor will we need to close the gates because there will be no invaders to keep out.

Isaiah also said of the future Jerusalem: *"The Gentiles shall come to your light, and the kings to the brightness of your rising"* (Isa. 60:3). John sees the final fulfillment of Isaiah's prophecy and says that the nations (the redeemed Gentiles from the Messianic Kingdom) shall walk in the light of God's brightness and bring their glory and honor to Him. This is the New Jerusalem—the eternal destiny of those whose names are written in the Lamb's Book of Life. (See Revelation 21:24-27.)

May God comfort us with these words as we face a world that hates God and His people with an ever-increasing fervor. The near future is uncertain, but our eternal destiny is sure. Regardless of what difficulties are to come, God has a glorious home for His people, a place where we will live with Him forever. His Word is true and He is faithful to His Word.

Paul encouraged the believers at Thessalonica with the following words. May they speak to our hearts as well:

> *May the God of peace Himself sanctify you completely; and may your whole spirit, soul and body be preserved blameless at the coming of our Lord Jesus Christ [Messiah]. He who calls you is faithful, who also will do it* (1 Thessalonians 5:23-24).

REVIEW QUESTIONS

1. Write a summary of what you have learned in this lesson. Write the summary in clear, concise words as if you were going to present it to another person.

2. Describe how you can apply what you have learned in this lesson to your life.

3. Share what you have learned with your family, friends, and members of your study group.

NOTES

1. Literally, "my delight is in her," Biblesoft's New Exhaustive Strong's Numbers and Concordance with Expanded Greek-Hebrew Dictionary. CD-ROM. Biblesoft, Inc. and International Bible Translators, Inc. (© 1994, 2003, 2006) s.v. "Chephtsiy bahh," (OT 2657).

2. Literally, "to marry," Ibid., s.v. "ba`al," (OT 1166).

Chapter 12

Paradise Restored

WHEN God created our existing Heaven and Earth, they were perfect. When He created Adam and Eve, they were perfect. He put them in a perfect garden in a perfect world. He gave them everything they needed. And He gave Adam and Eve a free will, with which to choose whether they would obey or disobey Him.

Tragically, they chose to disobey. Because of their sin, they began to die physically, mentally, emotionally, and spiritually. Then they passed their curse of death to the entire human race. We have inherited their DNA, which carries the curse of sin and death within each of us. Science refers to these human flaws as "genetic disorders," and DNA research continues to unravel the mystery of life and the reality of this truth. Even the heavens and the earth God made have suffered from the curse of sin (see Rom. 8:22).

While unbelievers are not willing to accept this biblical revelation as truth, there is no other reasonable explanation for the way people behave and the inevitability of death. Those who reject this explanation of the human condition clearly live in denial. But the fact that they deny the biblical record of creation does not change the fact that from birth on, we are all dying.

God put eternity in the hearts of His human creation (see Eccles. 3:11), but without Him, cut off from Him, the future holds nothing for us but death. Furthermore, we will all answer to our Creator for the way we live our lives.

Perhaps this is why many unbelievers refuse to acknowledge the biblical story of creation. They don't want to be accountable to their Creator. It seems easier just to deny the whole thing. However, denial doesn't change the facts. Just as surely as we die, we will stand before God and account for our actions.

The writer of Hebrews explains: *"...It is appointed for men to die once, but after this the judgment"* (Heb. 9:27). Peter adds: *"They will give an account to Him who is ready to judge the living and the dead"* (1 Pet. 4:5).

When Adam and Eve sinned, God expelled them from the Garden of Eden. Because God is perfectly holy, it was necessary that He banish them from His presence just as parents must sometimes send their misbehaving children to their rooms. God then placed cherubim to guard the entrance to keep Adam and Eve from entering the Garden of Eden and eating from the tree of life. Genesis reads:

> *The LORD God said, "Behold the man has become like one of Us, to know good and evil. And now, lest he put out his hand and take also of the tree of life, and eat, and live forever"—therefore the LORD God sent him out of the garden of Eden to till the ground from which he was taken. So He drove out the man; and He placed cherubim at the east of the garden of Eden, and a flaming sword which turned every way, to guard the way to the tree of life* (Genesis 3:22-24).

While this may seem like a cruel thing for God to do, it was really an act of mercy. Consider this: if Adam and Eve had gained access to The Garden and eaten from the tree of life, they would have been doomed to live forever in their cursed bodies. Would you want to live forever in your body with all its aches and pains, ailments and diseases? Of course not! We don't want to live forever in these bodies. Believers are looking forward to getting new bodies that are free from the curse of sin. Hallelujah!

When God expelled Adam and Eve from the Garden of Eden, it was paradise lost. Now in Revelation 22, we learn that paradise has been restored. Once again, God's people are in a garden with a river of life flowing through it. God starts all over with a new Heaven, a new Earth and a New Jerusalem. While this old world and everything in it is wearing out, God's new creation is eternal. Our heavenly home, the New Jerusalem, will come to the earth, where God will once again dwell in the midst of His people.

As we learned in our previous chapter, God will walk in the garden with His people as He did with Adam and Eve (see Gen. 3:8). But this time, we won't be hiding from Him as Adam and Eve did. The Creator of the universe will *tabernacle* with us, dwell with us, we will be His people and He will be our God. We will be in His presence in the fullness of His glory because we will be like Him, without sin—forever!

With the curse of sin removed, John tells us there will be no more tears, no more death, no more sorrow, no more crying, and no more pain. All of these human liabilities caused by sin will be gone for good. We won't even remember the heartache and suffering we endured in this present world. As John says: *"...the former things have passed away"* (Rev. 21:4).

PARADISE RESTORED (REVELATION 22)

We now come to the end of the Book of Revelation, but it is just the beginning of eternity for the people of God. What an incredible revelation the Lord gave to John. It was a source of hope and comfort for first-century believers as well as believers throughout history—up to and beyond our own time here on Earth.

While believers have had different understandings of the Book of Revelation, they have all agreed on the main theme of the book—the Son of Man is exalted to the throne of God and will return for His people. He has defeated satan and will rule over the nations. God's people will be resurrected with new bodies and rule with Him in a Messianic Kingdom characterized by righteousness and peace. When that time comes to a close, the Creator of the universe will establish a new Heaven and new Earth. God's people will live with Him in eternity in a perfect world free of sin and its curse.

Let's join John one last time as he tells us what the angel revealed to him about Paradise restored.

The River of Life (verses 1-2)

We learn in Genesis that when God created the Garden of Eden, He made a river to water it: *"A river went out of Eden to water the garden..."* (Gen. 2:10).

The story in Genesis is not an allegory. Adam and Eve were real people. The Garden of Eden was a real place with a literal river flowing through it. In the restored Paradise, John also sees a river. We have every reason to believe that this is a real river just as it was in the Genesis account.

In ancient times, as well as our own times, water has always been a symbol of life. In the world of the Bible and much of our world today—including Israel and her neighbors—water is scarce. One of the biggest challenges in Israel today is determining how to preserve and distribute the water in the Jordan River. In fact, one of the main causes of the 1967 Six-Day War was Syria's effort to divert the headwaters of the Jordan River from Israel to Syria.

This scarcity of water has spawned an essential emerging industry: desalination technology designed to turn seawater into drinking water. We can live without oil, but we can't live without water.

In Israel, there is a definite rainy season that begins in late September or early October. At that time, the people of Israel pray for rain, without which there can be no harvest. This was, and still is, the time of the biblical Feast of Tabernacles.

The Hebrews had several special rituals they called upon when seeking God for rain. The first was the ritual of the pouring of water. This took place on the last day of the Feast of Tabernacles. The day was called in Hebrew *Hoshana Rabba*, which means the "Day of the Great Hosanna." (The phrase translates into English as "save now.") On the Day of the Great Hosanna, the Jews would pray for rain and for God's salvation through the Messiah.

The ritual of the pouring of the water had both a physical and spiritual significance. At the beginning of the rainy season, the Jews needed the rain to soften the ground for plowing. In view of this, they made a special thanksgiving offering to God for the rain He was going to send. The spiritual significance pointed to the coming of the Messiah, who would give them the living waters that flow from His Spirit.

As part of the ritual proceeding, a designated priest would use a golden pitcher to draw water from the Pool of Siloam and carry it to the altar at the Temple. The High Priest would then take the pitcher and pour the water into a basin at the foot of the altar. As this was taking place, the priests would blow their trumpet-shofars and the Levites and all the people would wave palm branches and sing to the Lord.

About the time the water was being poured, the people would sing and praise God with these words from Isaiah: "*With joy you will draw water from the wells of salvation*" (Isa. 12:3).

They also sought the Lord from Isaiah 44:3, which reads: "*I will pour water on him who is thirsty, and floods on the dry ground; I will pour My*

Spirit on your descendants, and My blessing on your offspring...." This was the most joyous day of the celebration and the pouring of the water was the most joyous moment of the day.

Jesus kept the Feast in obedience to the Torah. Just as the fervor of the celebration reached its peak at the pouring of water, Jesus made a bold declaration. John was an eyewitness to it and wrote:

> *On the last day, that great day of the feast, Jesus stood and cried out, saying, "If anyone thirsts, let him come to Me and drink. He who believes in Me, as the Scripture has said, out of his heart will flow rivers of living water." But this He spoke concerning the Spirit, whom those believing in Him would receive; for the Holy Spirit was not yet given, because Jesus was not yet glorified"* (John 7:37-39).

Jesus made a similar statement to the Samaritan woman at the well. John also records this conversation:

> *Jesus answered and said to her, "Whoever drinks of this water* [the physical well] *will thirst again, but whoever drinks of the water that I shall give him will never thirst. But the water that I shall give him* [the spiritual well] *will become in him a fountain of water springing up into everlasting life"* (John 4:13-14).

We understand from the Bible and history that water is not only necessary for physical life, but universally recognized as a symbol of spiritual life. The Hebrew prophets spoke of a time when a river would flow from the Temple of God to refresh the land and the people (see Ezek. 47:1-12; Zech. 14:8). Both Ezekiel and Zechariah were speaking about the time of the Messianic Kingdom, which would be a preview of life in the New Jerusalem with God.

The river of life John sees is pure and clear as crystal. It flows from the throne of God and of the Lamb. This description is meant to communicate to us that the river of life is uncontaminated and unde-filed and represents the fullness of God's life and blessings forevermore.

Although the Holy Spirit in believers today quenches our souls' thirst for God, our sins often keep us from enjoying the fullest measure of His life flowing in us, through us, and out of us. When we are fully like God without sin, there will be nothing to hinder us from drinking freely of the river of life.

The sons of Korah expressed the heart cry of God's people through-out the ages: *"As the deer pants for the water brooks, so pants my soul for You, O God. My soul thirsts for God, for the living God..."* (Ps. 42:1-2). This cry of our souls for God is fully satisfied by His eternal presence in our midst when Paradise is restored. The psalmist looked propheti-cally to this time and wrote: *"There is a river whose streams shall make glad the city of God, the holy place of the tabernacle of the Most High"* (Ps. 46:4).

In another connection to the Garden of Eden (see Gen. 2:9; Ezek. 47:12), John sees the tree of life. The Lord made this promise to the overcomers at Ephesus: *"To him who overcomes I will give to eat from the tree of life, which is in the midst of the Paradise of God"* (Rev. 2:7).

Revelation 22:2 shows God's faithfulness to His word of promise. It is possible that the tree of life is really many trees growing alongside the river of life, from which they are watered by the life of God. The tree(s) of life bear fruit every month. John explains that the leaves are for the healing (health) of the nations. The word *nations* can also be translated as "peoples."[1] We don't know if this refers to the citizens of the New Jerusalem or people groups that will make a transition from the Mes-sianic Kingdom into eternity. However God works this out, the result is that God's people will live with Him forever.

In eternity, the normal cycles of planting, sowing, and reaping no longer apply. The tree(s) of life bear fruit every month. When John says the leaves are for the healing or health of the nations, he does not mean that people will actually get sick. He has already said that the *"former things have passed away"* (Rev. 21:4). This simply means that the bodies we will have in eternity will not be subject to corruption.

Whether you believe what John sees is literal or symbolic, he means for us to understand that God's life will be fully and completely sufficient for our every need. All the "no mores" of the New Jerusalem will be no more because we will no longer live with the curse of sin. Instead, we will live in the direct, unveiled presence of the manifested glory of God.

The Throne of God and of the Lamb (verses 3-5)

John now makes seven mind-boggling comments about the eternal home of God's people. Since we are bound by time and space and limited to our experiences in this world, it takes a revelation from God's Spirit for us to grasp the enormous blessings of living in God's new world.

There shall be no more curse.

First, John gives the good news that he hinted at in Revelation 21:3-4. The curse of sin is gone. The Lord made the following promise to the overcomers at Smyrna: *"He who overcomes shall not be hurt by the second death* [which is the result of the curse of sin]" (Rev. 2:11).

When Adam and Eve sinned, their rebellion resulted in what Paul calls the law (or principle) of sin and death. Jesus took the curse of this law on Himself when He died as the innocent substitutionary sacrifice for sin. Paul explains: *"The law of the Spirit of life in Christ* [Messiah] *Jesus has made me free from the law of sin and death"* (Rom. 8:2).

When God's Spirit comes to live in us, He changes the desires of our hearts and empowers us to live in victory over the sinful thoughts and ways we entertained in the past. As Paul comments: *"It is God who works in you both to will and to do for His good pleasure"* (Phil. 2:13). In Galatians 5:16-25, Paul explains this dramatic change in our lives.

Internally, we are new creations: *"old things have passed away...*[and] *all things have become new"* (2 Cor. 5:17).

Believers are no longer under the curse of the law of sin and death. Our changed lives are a testimony to this reality. We can and should live in the victory Jesus has made possible for us. Yet we still sin and we still die. This is because, in this present world, the law or principle of sin and death is still in us, with us, and everywhere around us.

That will change in God's eternity. While we should give place to the Holy Spirit every day of our lives, in the New Jerusalem, we will no longer have to struggle to overcome the law of sin and death. The curse of sin will be gone forever. Hallelujah!

The throne of God and of the Lamb is seen.

In Revelation 4–5, John sees the throne of God and the Lamb, which he now understands is in the New Jerusalem. In ancient times, it was not unusual for an honorable king to share his throne with his firstborn son, who would one day be his heir. In the same way a father often shares responsibilities with his oldest son. Here we see our Father in Heaven sharing His throne with His firstborn Son—the heir of all things.

Not only has our Father in Heaven promised to share His throne with His Son, Jesus has promised to share His rule with us. While His rule is that of the sovereign Lord, ours is that of the overcomer. The Lord made this promise to the overcomers at Laodicea: *"To him who overcomes I will grant to sit with Me on My throne, as I also overcame and sat down with My Father on His throne"* (Rev. 3:21). In John's vision of the throne room of God, he sees the 24 elders sitting on thrones (see Rev. 4:4).

John consistently makes the point that God's glory is shared with His Son. In Revelation 21:22, John says that the Lord God Almighty and the Lamb are the Temple in the New Jerusalem. This means we will not have to go to a temple or other place to worship God because the entire City is God's Temple or dwelling place.

This is true for believers today as well. So many have been led to believe that they have to go to some building or place to worship God, when, in fact, they *are* the building of God (see 1 Cor. 3:16). In the New Jerusalem, this will be clear to everyone.

John also says that the river of life flows from the throne of God and of the Lamb. Now he adds that the manifested glory of God and the Lamb are the light of the New Jerusalem.

We should live our lives with a constant awareness of Jesus as our Lord and King. He should be on the throne of our hearts. This is a decision we must make anew every day of our lives. We should live overcoming lives today.

We will not have to struggle with this in the New Jerusalem. Neither will we have to make a pilgrimage to Jerusalem to appear before God. His throne will be *in our midst*. Our Creator and Lord will be with us forever in the fullness of His blazing glory and dazzling beauty. We will have complete access at all times to His spectacular splendor and awesome majesty. The New Jerusalem, our eternal hometown, is the ultimate "throne city of God."

His servants shall serve Him.

What will we be doing in eternity? Some of us still have the ridiculous idea that we will spend eternity floating on clouds and playing harps. Nothing could be further from the truth. John explains that we will spend eternity serving God. While he doesn't say what we will be doing, we know that before they sinned, Adam and Eve stayed busy tending God's Garden.

In addition to our unfettered worship and praise in the presence of God, our Father in Heaven will have many assignments for us that quite possibly will relate to administering and carrying out His will throughout the universe.

With no hindrances from satan and with freedom from the curse of sin, we will be able to accomplish our God-given tasks with fullness of joy and satisfaction. Our service will be pure and holy and will in no way be tainted by self-promotion or hidden agendas. There will be no need for money to finance our assignments and no need to pray for helpers to come alongside and bear the burden of the ministry. The presence of God Himself will be the eternal source of all that we will need to do His will.

They shall see His face.

When Moses met with God at Mount Sinai, he pleaded with God, saying, *"Please show me Your glory"* (Exod. 33:18). The Lord told Moses He would reveal Himself, but explained that Moses could not see His face. What God meant was that neither Moses, nor any human, could see the fullness of God's glory (and live to tell it). The Lord said to Moses, *"You cannot see My face; for no man shall see Me, and live"* (Exod. 33:20).

I explained previously that when Scripture says the Lord spoke to Moses face to face, it means that Moses was literally and physically in the presence of God as opposed to a vision or dream (see Exod. 33:11). It is a Jewish figure of speech that indicates personal fellowship with the Almighty.

This is what John means when he says we will see God's face. As we learned in the last chapter, we will be able to behold God as He is because we will be like Him—without sin. We will live in the presence of the grandeur of His glory and the awesomeness of His aura as John explains in the first of his three letters:

> *Beloved, now we are children of God; and it has not yet been revealed what we shall be, but we know that when*

He is revealed, we shall be like Him, for we shall see Him as He is (1 John 3:2).

His name shall be on their foreheads.

In the Lord's letter to the believers at Philadelphia, He promised to write His name on the overcomers, that they would be citizens of the New Jerusalem and pillars in the Temple of God. Revelation 3:12 says:

He who overcomes, I will make him a pillar in the temple of My God, and he shall go out no more. I will write on him the name of My God and the name of the city of My God, the New Jerusalem, which comes down out of heaven from My God. And I will write on Him My new name.

This Scripture is now fulfilled, as John explains in Revelation 22.

The concept of writing a deities' name on someone was an ancient custom that showed ownership and devotion. The mark on a person was a form of witnessing in that it expressed that person's devotion to a particular deity. In some cultures (India, for example) this is still done today.

When God revealed Himself to the Hebrews, He did so with words and ways that related to the customs of their day. Since they were familiar with the idea of bearing the mark of a deity, God said He would write His name on them. This is like a "P.S." to the blessing that God told Aaron to pronounce over the people.

This blessing in Hebrew is called the *Birkat Cohanim* (the priestly blessing). The blessing reads:

The LORD bless you and keep you; the LORD make His face shine upon you, and be gracious to you; the LORD lift up His countenance upon you, and give you peace (Numbers 6:24-26).

The Lord then adds the following: *"They shall put My name on the children of Israel, and I will bless them"* (Num. 6:27).

God literally instructed the Hebrews to write His name on their foreheads and on their hands as an outward sign that they were devoted to Him. Deuteronomy reads:*"You shall lay up these words of mine in your heart and in your soul, and bind them as a sign on your hand, and they shall be as frontlets between your eyes"* (Deut. 11:18).

God even told them to write His words on the doorposts of their houses (see Deut. 11:20).

God did not tell the Jewish people how to do this. Over time, the religious leaders decided to make two small leather boxes that would contain the Scriptures, commanding the people to attach them to their foreheads and hands.

The box attached to their foreheads and hands is called a *tefillin*. The *mezuzah* is a container for holding God's Word that is attached to the doorpost. The Jews write the Hebrew letter *shin* on the outside of the *tefillin* and the *mezuzah*. The *shin* stands for *Shaddai*, which means "Almighty."

We have already learned that God put a seal on the foreheads of His people to protect them from His judgments against those who oppose Him (see Rev. 7:3). Later in Revelation 14:1, we learned that this seal is God's name. Now in Revelation 22, we see that God's name will be on the foreheads of His people for eternity.

Whether you believe this is a literal name written on our foreheads or a symbolic way of saying we belong to the One True God, the point is that we will be God's people forever.

God is the light of eternity.

In Revelation 21, John repeats something he said earlier. He tells us that there is no night in eternity because God and the Lamb are the light. He previously explained:

The city had no need of the sun or of the moon to shine in it, for the glory of God illuminated it. The Lamb is its light. And the nations of those who are saved shall walk in its light, and the kings of the earth shall bring their glory and honor into it. Its gates shall not be shut at all by day (there shall be no night there)" (Revelation 21:23-25).

In the last chapter, we noted that Isaiah prophesied concerning a time when God's own glorious presence would be the light of the New Jerusalem (see Isa. 60:1,19-20).

In the Genesis account of creation, God made the sun and the moon for light:

God made two great lights: the greater light to rule the day, and the lesser light to rule the night. He made the stars also. God set them in the firmament of the heavens to give light on the earth, and to rule over the day and over the night, and to divide the light from the darkness. And God saw that it was good (Genesis 1:16-18).

The sun and the moon not only give light, they are also necessary for our agricultural seasons. Since God and the Lamb are the light of the New Jerusalem and the river of life and the tree(s) of life are perpetual, agricultural seasons will not be needed in eternity. As John noted, the tree(s) of life will bear fruit every month, not just in certain seasons. There will be no time or seasons in eternity.

In the first of his three short letters, John wrote: *"This is the message which we have heard from Him and declare to you, that God is light and in Him is no darkness at all"* (1 John 1:5). John is referring to both the manifested glory of God as well as His moral character.

When Jesus walked the earth, He said, *"I am the light of the world. He who follows Me shall not walk in darkness, but have the light of life"*

(John 8:12). When healing a blind man, Jesus said, *"As long as I am in the world, I am the light of the world"* (John 9:5).

Jesus also told His followers, *"You are the light of the world…. Let your light so shine before men, that they may see your good works and glorify your Father in heaven"* (Matt. 5:14,16). As believers, the light of God's life lives in us in the person of the Holy Spirit. Yet, sometimes our light is not very bright. It will be bright in the New Jerusalem because the glory of God will be the light of our eternal home. We will fully radiate His light throughout eternity.

They shall reign forever and ever.

The last comment John makes is that God's people will reign with Him forever and ever. Wow, think about that! When God created Adam and Eve, He gave them His delegated authority to rule and subdue all that He had created (see Gen. 1:28). When they sinned, their authority was lost to satan, who became the god of this world system (see John 14:30; 16:11).

Because we have all sinned, God was not able to restore His authority to any of us. This is one of the reasons He came to earth in the person of Jesus of Nazareth. Since He was the Worthy Redeemer, without sin, God was able to restore His delegated authority to Jesus. He is the exalted Son of Man (one like us) to whom and through whom God has restored His authority to humankind.

Paul explains:

> *Therefore God also has highly exalted Him and given Him the name which is above every name, that at the name of Jesus every knee should bow, of those in heaven, and of those on earth, and of those under the earth, and that every tongue should confess that Jesus Christ* [Yeshua the Messiah] *is Lord, to the glory of God the Father* (Philippians 2:9-11).

When we receive Jesus into our lives, His power and authority come into us through the person of the Holy Spirit. John wrote in his first letter: *"You are of God, little children, and have overcome them, because He who is in you* [the Holy Spirit] *is greater than he* [satanic forces] *who is in the world"* (1 John 4:4). We are able to exercise our God-given authority when we are under attack by satanic forces.

Even though God has placed His Spirit within us, we don't always yield to His life and power. As a result, we don't always walk in the victory God has won for us. But we will in the New Jerusalem. Paul wrote to Timothy, *"If we endure, we shall also reign with Him..."* (2 Tim. 2:12).

THE TIME IS AT HAND (VERSES 6-11)

John has now seen all that God wanted to show him. The remainder of the chapter contains some final words of encouragement given to John by the angel and Jesus, for us. As a further confirmation and confidence-builder, the angel reminds John that the words he has received are faithful and true.

In Revelation 1:5, John declares that Jesus is *"the faithful witness."* Jesus introduced Himself to the believers at Laodicea as *"the Faithful and True Witness"* (Rev. 3:14). In Revelation 19:11, Jesus is called *"Faithful and True."* In Revelation 21:5, God Himself tells John that the words he is writing are *"true and faithful."*

These words may seem repetitive, but they provide John with the assurance that his vision and the words he has heard are trustworthy. He can now have courage, knowing God's people will prevail. He has seen all true believers at the throne of God beholding Him and glorified with Him, forever.

Jesus has conquered Caesar and Zeus and satan. He is exalted in Heaven as the glorified Son of Man, and He is returning for those who are His. God's people will rule and reign with Him throughout eternity in a new Heaven, a new Earth and a New Jerusalem. Therefore, we should not fear what evil leaders and governments can do to us. We should not be the least bit tempted to "fix our sandals" before the altar of anti-God governments. In God's own time, He will judge them while glorifying His own.

For more than 35 years, I have had the privilege of studying God's Word, including the history of how God has faithfully watched over His Word to perform it. I have written 38 books on the Bible. My life experiences as well as my academic and scholarly study have proven to me that the Bible is the most reliably preserved of all ancient manuscripts. We can bet our lives on its faithfulness and truthfulness. As Jesus said: *"Heaven and earth will pass away, but My words will by no means pass away"* (Matt. 24:35).

With the exception of Jesus' letters to the seven congregations and one other instance recorded in Revelation 16:15, God used angels to reveal His words to John. Now here in the last chapter, Jesus Himself confirms that He is returning to the earth. No fewer than three times, He says that He is coming quickly (see Rev. 22:7,12,20).

Two thousand years have passed since Jesus made this promise, and He has not yet returned. Therefore, we might understand His words to mean something other than chronological time.

Peter helps clarify His meaning for us:

> *Beloved, do not forget this one thing, that with the Lord one day is as a thousand years, and a thousand years as one day. The Lord is not slack concerning His promise, as some count slackness, but is longsuffering toward us, not willing that any should perish but that all should come to repentance* (2 Peter 3:8-9).

When Jesus says that He will come quickly, I believe He means that His coming is a prophetic certainty. As the final events unfold, His coming will be eminent. Jesus is speaking about God's prophetic calendar more so than our chronological one. His admonition is that we will not have time to prepare once these events are upon us. We must prepare now if we are to be ready for the marvelous events that are ahead. When teaching about the end of days, Jesus told His followers: *"You also be ready, for the Son of Man is coming at an hour you do not expect"* (Matt. 24:44).

Jesus connects His words in Revelation 22:7 with what has already been said in Revelation 1:3. After reassuring John and his first-century readers that He is coming, Jesus pronounces a blessing on those who keep or obey the prophecies written in the Book of Revelation. Because Western Christianity emphasizes faith as a mental agreement rather than a faithful and obedient way of life, it is most important to be reminded that true faith is evidenced by obedience to the will of God.

When God called the Hebrews out of Egypt, He said to them:

> *Therefore know that the LORD your God, He is God, the faithful God who keeps covenant and mercy for a thousand generations with those who love Him and keep His commandments...* (Deuteronomy 7:9).

Many of those who read this will say these words are for the Jews in the Old Testament and they do not apply to New Testament believers. This is clearly not true. Jesus alluded to this Scripture and said to His followers: *"If you love Me, keep My commandments"* (John 14:15).

John also wrote in his first letter, *"This is the love of God, that we keep His commandments. And His commandments are not burdensome"* (1 John 5:3). We note also that the promises God gave to the believers in the Book of Revelation are to the overcomers who hear and do His will. So let us examine ourselves to see if we truly love God—not just by a confession of faith, but also by the way we live our lives (see 2 Cor. 13:5).

Now we have to forgive John for being overwhelmed by all he sees and hears because, once again, he tries to worship the angel. Remember he did this in Revelation 19:10. Again, the angel rebukes John and tells him to worship God. This is in stark contrast to lucifer, the fallen angel, who desires worship for himself.

The angel then gives his last words to John. Perhaps it is the same angel who said the following to Daniel:

> *You Daniel, shut up the words, and seal the book until the time of the end; many shall run to and fro, and knowledge shall increase* (Daniel 12:4).

The angel also said:

> *Go your way, Daniel, for the words are closed up and sealed till the time of the end..."* (Daniel 12:9).

Now that it is the time of the end, the angel tells John *not* to seal the words of the prophecy of this book for the time is at hand. God has nothing further to say, and He wants to make this revelation known to His people.

This is why the angel says what he says to the unrighteous and to the righteous. Since God has nothing further to say, the unrighteous who reject God's Revelation cannot expect any further word from Him. Unless they repent, they will continue in their unrighteous ways, while the righteous who accept this Revelation will continue to live holy lives.

Once again, the words of the angel come from the words he gave to Daniel:

> *Many shall be purified, made white, and refined, but the wicked shall do wickedly; and none of the wicked shall understand, but the wise shall understand* (Daniel 12:10).

Rewarding the Righteous

For the second time, Jesus says that He is coming quickly, or as just explained, *"in a moment, in the twinkling of an eye"* (1 Cor. 15:52; see also verses 50-58). The Lord repeats this statement in order to urge His own to be spiritually sober and alert.

Paul wrote the following to the believers at Thessalonica:

> *Let us who are of the day be sober, putting on the breast-plate of faith and love, and as a helmet the hope of salvation. For God did not appoint us to wrath, but to obtain salvation through our Lord Jesus Christ* [Messiah], *who died for us, that whether we wake or sleep, we should live together with Him. Therefore comfort each other and edify one another, just as you also are doing* (1 Thessalonians 5:8-11).

Jesus reminds the righteous that He will reward them according to their works. Once again, we realize that salvation is God's gift to us by grace through faith. However, faith without works of covenantal love produced by the Holy Spirit is not true saving faith. This is the consistent theme throughout both testaments of the Bible.

The same Paul who explained grace and faith wrote these words to Titus:

> *The grace of God that brings salvation has appeared to all men, teaching us that, denying ungodliness and worldly lusts, we should live soberly, righteously, and godly in the present age, looking for the blessed hope and glorious appearing of our great God and Savior Jesus Christ* [Yeshua the Messiah], *who gave Himself for us, that He might redeem us from every lawless deed and purify for Himself His own special people, zealous for good works* (Titus 2:11-14).

We revisit the words of Jesus in Matthew 5:16: *"Let your light so shine before men, that they may see your good works and glorify your Father in heaven."*

When the Bible talks about works it does not mean the religious activities or good deeds we do out of our own self-interests, even though they are good things. In the biblical context, the word *good* means "acceptable." The only works God considers good or acceptable to Him are those motivated by pure spiritual love that comes from the Holy Spirit who resides within the believer.

The Bible tells us that God's love is put into our hearts when we receive the Holy Spirit (see Rom. 5:5). The Holy Spirit teaches us God's ways, motivates us with God's love, and then empowers us to do that which is pleasing to Him. These Spirit-inspired works of covenantal love are the basis of every believer's rewards. They are the only actions we do on this earth that we take with us to Heaven. As a result, they have eternal consequences.

In the Hebrew Bible, God made the following declaration: *"Thus says the LORD, the King of Israel, and His Redeemer, the LORD of hosts: I am the First and I am the Last; besides Me there is no God"* (Isa. 44:6; see also 41:4).

We note in this verse that God not only speaks about Himself but also refers to His Redeemer in the sense that the Redeemer is one with God but a unique and different personality. This wording is repeated numerous times in the Book of Revelation.

In Revelation 1:8, the same God who spoke to Isaiah said this to John: *"'I am the Alpha and the Omega, the Beginning and the End,' says the Lord, 'who is and who was and who is to come, the Almighty.'"* God repeats this in Revelation 21:6.

Jesus is the Redeemer of humankind that God mentioned in the Isaiah verse. Therefore, we see Jesus making the same claims about Himself. He says in Revelation 1:11: *"I am the Alpha and the Omega, the First and the Last...."* He repeats similar wording in Revelation 1:17 and 2:8.

Now, as if to put an exclamation point to the vision given to John, Jesus provides a final affirmation of who He is. In one last sweeping statement, Jesus puts all of these references to deity into one declaration and applies them to Himself: *"I am the Alpha and the Omega, the Beginning and the End, the First and the Last"* (Rev. 22:13).

With this statement, Jesus clearly declares His oneness with the Creator of the universe. As God's uniquely born Son, He shares the divine DNA of His Father. This means that Jesus is more than just a great prophet, teacher, or role model. He is Immanuel, God with us— God in human flesh who came to redeem us from our sins.

A person might not believe this about Jesus but there is no doubting that Jesus believed this about Himself. After spending three years as His constant companions, Jesus' disciples also believed this to be true.

In the end, Jesus is either who He says He is or He is a liar and a self-delusional lunatic.

Any intelligent, thinking person must acknowledge that a liar or someone who is self-delusional could not have said and done the things that Jesus said and did when He walked the earth. Furthermore, when we read the stories about Jesus in the Bible, we know in our hearts that such a person could not be fabricated. Our minds could never imagine a "Jesus." He is far beyond what we could invent. We either accept Him for who He is or reject Him.

When Adam and Eve sinned, they were banished from the Garden of Eden and lost their access to the tree of life. That situation is now reversed. In the very last blessing promised in the Book of Revelation, John confirms that God's people have access to the tree of life, and the right to go in and out of the Holy City, the New Jerusalem. Some Bible versions translate the blessing promise to read: "those who do His commandments." Other versions read, "those who wash their robes."

We recall that the great multitude standing before the throne of God and the Lamb in Heaven are said to be those who *"washed their robes and made them white in the blood of the Lamb"* (Rev. 7:14). All true believers have washed their robes in the blood of the Lamb and will do (keep) His commandments. Even though we might often fall short in our walk with God, our desire is to please Him in word, thought, and deed. God is holy and calls His children to be holy, even while showing us mercy when we grieve Him. Human parents can certainly understand this because of the relationship they have with their own children.

Tragically, those who have not washed their clothes in the blood of the Lamb and do not strive to keep His commandments do not have access to the tree of life and the eternal city of God. When John says they are outside the gates, he does not mean this literally. He means that they are banished forever from the presence of God. They have been exiled to Gehenna, the eternal destination of those who have rejected God's love and offer of redemption. (See Revelation 21:8.)

Jesus confirms that He personally sent His angel to bear witness to John through this vision. For this reason, John can write it to the congregations for their encouragement, edification, and warning. Of course, the Book of Revelation is not exclusively for the seven congregations of the first century. It is for all of God's people from then until now.

One last time Jesus identifies Himself with the Jewish people and the family of David. As the Root and the Offspring of David, Jesus was both before David and after David. He was before David as the Son of God and after David as the greater Son of David. (To review the earlier discussion of Jesus as the Root and the Offspring of David, see the comments on Revelation 5:5, as well as Isaiah 11:1-2,10; Psalms 110:1; and Matthew 22:42-46.)

Once again, it is important for non-Jewish believers to understand that Jesus is not returning as a Western Christian. He is returning as the Jewish Messiah and Redeemer of the tribe of Judah. He is returning to Israel to rule as the King of the Jews and as King of kings and Lord of lords over the nations. His coming is not based on the Greco-Roman

Christian calendar but on the biblical Feasts of the Lord. Life and worship expressions during the Messianic Kingdom will be biblically Jewish, not modern rabbinic, with Jesus as their ultimate reality and perfect embodiment.

This is why it is strange when some Christians say they love Jesus but are anti-Semitic. They know the Western Jesus but not the biblical *Yeshua*. It simply isn't possible to love Jesus and be anti-Semitic. Jesus was and always will be a Jew! Of course, if Christians think of Jesus in Greco-Roman terms, they won't identify with Him this way. They will be shocked when the real Jesus of the Bible (*Yeshua*) returns as a Jew.

Jesus also refers to Himself as the Bright and Morning Star. In His letter to the overcomers at Thyatira, Jesus promised to give them the morning star (see Rev. 2:28). Here, in Revelation 22:16, He claims to be the Morning Star. As the morning star is the first star we see just before sunrise and the start of each new day, Jesus is the light of the world and the light of the new day of redemption. By identifying Himself in this way, Jesus encourages His readers that the darkness of the Great Tribulation is over and God's people will forevermore live in the light of the glory of God and of the Lamb. There will be no night in eternity because the Bright and Morning Star is the light. (To review the earlier discussion on the morning star, see the comments on Revelation 2:28, as well as Peter's word in Second Peter 1:19.)

Before the closing words of warning regarding this Revelation, John writes that the Holy Spirit and the believers make one last appeal, asking people to respond to God and to His offer of love and redemption made possible through Jesus. The appeal is to those who hear God's invitation, to those who are spiritually thirsty, and to whoever desires salvation and redemption. God offers to quench their spiritual thirst by giving them the water of life. Do you remember Jesus making this promise to the overcomers in Revelation 7:16?

This is the same invitation the Lord has always offered to humanity, even as he spoke through the prophet Isaiah:

*Ho! Everyone who thirsts, come to the waters... Seek the
LORD while He may be found, call upon Him while He is
near. Let the wicked forsake his way, and the unrighteous
man his thoughts; let him return to the LORD, and He will
have mercy on him; and to our God, for He will abun-
dantly pardon* (Isaiah 55:1, 6-7).

Before reading the last few words of the Book of Revelation, let us
spiritually drink the following words of Jesus. They are from his conversation with a Samaritan woman who came to draw water at the well.
He asked her for a drink from the well, and stirred up a conversation
about everlasting life:

*Whoever drinks of this water will thirst again, but who-
ever drinks of the water that I shall give him will never
thirst. But the water that I shall give him will become in
him a fountain of water springing up into everlasting life*
(John 4:13-14).

A Final Warning and Assurance

John warns everyone who hears this Revelation not to add to it nor
take anything away from it. This was a common expression in Bible
times before the days of copyright laws designed to protect the integrity
of written documents. It was a solemn warning not to edit a person's
words. The normal warning was stated in terms of blessings and curses.
I know as a fact that people have translated some of my writings into
other languages without my knowledge or permission. I have no idea of
the reliability or integrity of those translations.

We find a similar expression all the way back in Deuteronomy.
There God Himself gives the following warning regarding His words:
*"You shall not add to the word which I command you, nor take from it,
that you may keep the commandments of the LORD your God which I*

command you" (Deut. 4:2). He repeats this warning in Deuteronomy 12:32 and Proverbs 30:6.

God's people must be careful to fear (reverentially) the Lord and His holy Word. We must seek God for wisdom and understanding of His Word and not take it for granted nor have a casual attitude toward it, for out of it flow the issues of life. We must take seriously Paul's exhortation to his disciple, Timothy:

> *Be diligent to present yourself approved to God, a worker who does not need to be ashamed, rightly dividing* [making a straight row or correctly interpreting] *the word of truth* (2 Timothy 2:15).

We must do our best to understand God's Word within the historical, cultural, and Hebraic setting in which it was written. If we view God's Word with Western eyes, we will certainly misunderstand much of it. We must not take God's Word out of context nor read into it what we would like it to say. We must not prefer our own traditions over the Word of God.

We must clearly distinguish between what the Word of God actually says and what we think it means. When we say, "God said" we had better be sure it is God who is doing the saying. While I have done my best to explain the Book of Revelation as I understand it, we each must seek the Holy Spirit for guidance and truth as He is the true teacher of God's Word (see John 14:26).

In His closing words, Jesus affirms the truthfulness of the Revelation and the certainty of His coming. John voices his agreement with the words of Jesus and expresses what has been for the last 2,000 years the deepest heart desire and hope of God's people: *"Even so, come Lord Jesus!"* (Rev. 22:20).

John closes the Book of Revelation by speaking the blessing of God's grace for the people and a final amen, meaning in everyday words: "Yes, Lord, You are a faithful covenant-keeping God and King."

In Closing

Because of intense spiritual warfare, it has taken me two years to write this three-volume series on the Book of Revelation. Thank God He has enabled me to finish it. It has been a labor of love, joy, and hope of a certain glorious future in an uncertain, troubled world. I pray it has been an encouragement to you.

While there are difficult times ahead for God's people, I believe we will soon see the greatest outpouring of God's Kingdom activities in the history of humankind. In spite of the growing anti-God world and its hatred of believers, the glory of God will be manifested to us, in us, through us, and out of us with the spiritual strength and moral courage of overcomers. We will do great signs and wonders as witnesses to the God of Abraham, Isaac, Jacob and the exalted Son of God-Son of Man, Jesus the Lamb of God, and Lion of the Tribe of Judah. May His name be praised forever.

The apostle Paul experienced the anointed power of God as well as great suffering for his faith and testimony. He not only explained the truths of God's Word, he also wrote from his own personal experiences. He understood better than anyone that God's love was greater than any hardship or persecution believers might go through.

No matter what tribulation you may face now or in the future, Paul's words will encourage you:

> *Yet in all these things we are more than conquerors through Him who loved us. For I am persuaded that neither death nor life, nor angels nor principalities nor powers, nor things present nor things to come, nor height nor depth, nor any other created thing, shall be able to separate us from the love of God which is in Christ [Messiah] Jesus our Lord* (Romans 8:37-39).

Paul wrote his last letter to Timothy shortly before he was martyred in Rome at the hands of Nero. While we do not know what the Lord may require of us in the days ahead, may our lives and testimonies be such that we can say what Paul said:

> *I have fought the good fight, I have finished the race, I have kept the faith. Finally, there is laid up for me the crown of righteousness, which the Lord, the righteous Judge, will give to me on that Day, and not to me only but also to all who have loved His appearing* (2 Timothy 4:7-8).

REVIEW QUESTIONS

1. Write a summary of what you have learned in this lesson. Write the summary in clear, concise words as if you were going to present it to another person.

2. Describe how you can apply what you have learned in this lesson to your life.

3. Share what you have learned with your family, friends, and members of your study group.

NOTE

1. Biblesoft's New Exhaustive Strong's Numbers and Concordance with Expanded Greek-Hebrew Dictionary. CD-ROM. Biblesoft, Inc. and International Bible Translators, Inc. (© 1994, 2003, 2006) s.v. "ethnos," (NT 1484).

Bibliography

Booker, Richard. *The End of All Things Is at Hand: Are You Ready?* Alachua, FL: Bridge-Logos, 2008.

Booker, Richard. *The Shofar: Ancient Sound of the Messiah.* Houston, TX: Sounds of the Trumpet Inc., 1999.

Booker, Richard. *Here Comes the Bride: Ancient Jewish Wedding Customs and the Messiah.* Houston, TX: Sounds of the Trumpet Inc., 1995.

Booker, Richard. *Ancient Jewish Prayers and the Messiah.* Houston, TX: Sounds of the Trumpet Inc., 2003.

Charlesworth, James, editor. *The Old Testament Pseudepigrapha: Apocalyptic Literature & Testaments Volume 1.* New York: Doubleday, 1983.

Fleming, Jim. *Understanding the Revelation.* Bellaire, TX: Biblical Resources, 1999.

Hemer, Colin J. *The Letters to the Seven Churches of Asia in Their Local Setting.* Grand Rapids, MI: Eerdmans, 2001.

Ladd, George Eldon. *A Theology of the New Testament.* Grand Rapids, MI: Eerdmans, 1993.

Online Sources: Numerous well-researched articles on Greek mythology and the history, geography and archaeology of the seven cities in Asia Minor.

Osborne, Grant, general editor. *Life Application Bible Commentary: Revelation*. Carol Stream, IL: Tyndale House, 2000.

Tenney, Merrill. *Interpreting Revelation*. Grand Rapids, MI: Eerdmans, 1970.

Stern, David H. *Jewish New Testament Commentary*. Clarksville, MD: Jewish New Testament Publications, 1992.

Varner, William. *Jacob's Dozen: A Prophetic Look at the Tribes of Israel*. Bellmawr, NJ: The Friends of Israel Gospel Ministry, 1987.

Walters, Brent. *Ante-Nicene Christianity: The First Three Centuries*. San Jose, CA: The Ante-Nicene Archive, 1993.

Wilson, Mark, and Clinton Arnold, editor. *Zondervan Illustrated Bible Backgrounds Commentary: Revelation*. Grand Rapids, MI: Zondervan, 2002.

About the Author

Dr. Richard Booker, MBA, PhD, is an ordained Christian minister, President of Sounds of the Trumpet, Inc., and the Founder/Director of the Institute for Hebraic-Christian Studies. Prior to entering the ministry, he had a successful business career. He is the author of 38 books, numerous Bible courses and study materials used by churches and Bible schools around the world.

Dr. Booker has traveled extensively for over 30 years, teaching in churches and at conferences on various aspects of the Christian life as well as Bible prophecy, Israel, and the Hebraic roots of Christianity. He and his wife Peggy, have led yearly tour groups to Israel for more than 25 years, where for 18 years, Dr. Booker was a speaker at the Christian celebration of the Feast of Tabernacles in Jerusalem. This gathering is attended by 5,000 Christians from 100 nations.

In 1997, Dr. Booker and his wife, Peggy, founded the Institute for Hebraic-Christian Studies (IHCS) as a ministry to educate Christians in the Hebraic culture and background of the Bible, build relationships between Christians and Jews, and give comfort and support to the people of Israel. Their tireless work on behalf of Christians and Jews has been recognized around the world as well as by the Knesset Christian Allies Caucus in Jerusalem.

Dr. Booker is considered a pioneer, spiritual father, and prophetic voice in respect to teaching on Bible prophecy, radical Islam, Israel, Jewish-Christian relations, and the biblical Hebraic roots of Christianity. He has made more than 500 television programs, which can be seen worldwide on God's Learning Channel. To learn more about his ministry, Dr. Booker invites you to visit his Web site and online bookstore at www.rbooker.com. If you want to invite Dr. Booker to speak to your congregation or conference, you can contact him at www.shofarprb@aol.com.

Printed in Great Britain
by Amazon.co.uk, Ltd.,
Marston Gate.